By His Spirit and Word

Books by Cornelis P. Venema

But for the Grace of God: An Exposition of the Canons of Dort

What We Believe: An Exposition of the Apostles' Creed

Children at the Lord's Table? Assessing the Case for Paedocommunion

Christ and the Future

Getting the Gospel Right: Assessing the Reformation and the New Perspectives on Paul

Heinrich Bullinger and the Doctrine of Predestination: Author of "The Other Reformed Tradition"

The Gospel of Free Acceptance in Christ

The Promise of the Future

Cornelis P. Venema

By His
Spirit and
WORD

HOW CHRIST
Builds His Church

Reformed
Fellowship Inc.
www.reformedfellowship.net

By His Spirit and Word

Copyright © 2015 by Cornelis P. Venema

Reformed Fellowship, Inc. is a religious and strictly nonprofit organization composed of a group of Christian believers who hold to the biblical Reformed faith. Our purpose is to advocate and propagate this faith, to nurture those who seek to live in obedience to it, to give sharpened expression to it, to stimulate the doctrinal sensitivities of those who profess it, to promote the spiritual welfare and purity of the Reformed churches, and to encourage Christian action.

Requests for permission to quote from this book should be directed to:

Reformed Fellowship, Inc.
(877) 532–8510
president@reformedfellowship.net
www.reformedfellowship.net

Book design by Jeff Steenholdt

Printed in the United States of America

ISBN 978-1-935369-08-0

Contents

Preface

The title of this book, *By His Spirit and Word,* is taken from question 54 of the much-loved Heidelberg Catechism of the sixteenth-century Reformation. In this answer, the Christian believer confesses "that the Son of God, out of the whole human race, from the beginning to the end of the world, gathers, defends, and preserves for Himself, *by His Spirit and Word,* in the unity of the true faith, a Church chosen to everlasting life; and that I am, and forever shall remain, a living member thereof" (emphasis added).

As this answer attests, the church of Jesus Christ is born out of the working of the Holy Spirit through the means Christ has appointed to gather his people—namely, the preaching of the gospel Word and the administration of the sacraments. Though this confession may seem quaint in our day, when the church is viewed primarily as a voluntary and thoroughly human institution, it echoes accurately the teaching of Scripture and the promise of Christ himself: "And I tell you, you are Peter, and on this rock I will build my church, and the gates of hell shall not prevail against it" (Matt. 16:18). Through the ministry of the Word and sacraments, Christ is pleased to build his church, producing and confirming the faith of believers. Or, to paraphrase John Calvin's lovely affirmation: "It is not possible to have God as your father, unless you have the church as your mother."

In this study, the Reformation's high view of the ministry of Word and sacrament is illustrated through an exposition of the principal confessions and catechisms of the sixteenth- and early seventeenth-century Reformed churches. Several chapters that survey the development of the Reformation's doctrine of the church's ministry of the Word and sacraments were first written as a series of three articles in the *Mid-America Journal of Theology.* I have significantly revised these chapters and have placed the summary of the Reformation doctrine of the church within the context of contemporary challenges to its high regard for the official means of grace. An introductory chapter outlines such challenges associated with the church growth, the seeker-sensitive, and the emergent church movements in recent decades. In the concluding chapter, I offer some suggestions as to how these challenges might be met from within the framework of the confessions' doctrine of the church's ministry.

References to the confessions are drawn from a variety of sources, which are identified throughout the study. While the study appeals to the confessions as subordinate standards, I acknowledge that their authority depends upon their agreement with the teaching of Scripture.

I wish to express my gratitude to several people who contributed to the completion of the book: Glenda Mathes, who graciously edited and improved the original draft; Rachel Luttjeboer, who helped to prepare the select bibliography; Annette Gysen, who completed the editing process; and Henry Gysen, who steered the project along to publication on behalf of the Reformed Fellowship. I am especially grateful to the Board of Trustees of Mid-America Reformed Seminary, who granted me a sabbatical during which the book was completed.

Chapter 1

Contemporary Challenges to the Doctrine of the Church

Today's Christian church does not enjoy a good reputation. In polls of the public's confidence in and respect for persons and institutions in North American society, remarkably, Christian pastors and churches often rank poorly. While it is surprising how low the church ranks in many people's estimation, it is even more startling how low the church ranks among those who purport to be Christian believers. Even the most ardent evangelical believers are frequently lukewarm about the church's life and ministry. They may demonstrate an evident and strong commitment and love for Jesus Christ, but their commitment and love for Christ's body, the church, is tepid at best and nonexistent at worst. Though believers would never think of finding fault with the bridegroom of the church, Jesus Christ, it has become popular to find fault with his bride.

Because convictions have legs propelling them forward, it is not surprising that widespread disrespect for the church has led to declining participation in the local church. In a recent book with the telling title *Quitting Church,* an observer of contemporary ecclesiastical developments notes that leaders and pew-sitters alike are abandoning the local church.[1] A widely circulated newspaper in North America, *USA Today*, reported that there is a "gated community in the evangelical world" and goes on to say that many of the most prominent leaders of the evangelical church in North America are content to participate in a variety of small-group Bible studies or accountability groups, but they eschew membership and participation in a

---

1. Julia Duin, *Quitting Church: Why the Faithful Are Fleeing and What to Do about It* (Grand Rapids: Baker, 2008).

local congregation of Jesus Christ.[2]

George Barna, an influential interpreter of trends within the churches in North America, has even gone so far as to suggest that the local church should be abolished. He believes a new form of the church needs to emerge that is really no church at all, at least not in any traditional sense. This new manifestation will be an informal, ad hoc association of believers with no formal structure, place of worship, commitments, or physical presence in the community. In Barna's words, "I am not called to attend or join a church. I am called to be the church."[3] He maintains we need a revolution in our understanding of what it means to "be" the church.

Given the contemporary loss of esteem for the church, especially in anything resembling its traditional form, this book's focus may seem like an invitation to a different world. This study will focus on the doctrine of the church and its method of communicating the gospel of Jesus Christ through preaching and sacraments. In traditional theological language, these methods are called the means of grace. The Reformational understanding is that these two means are the official instruments Christ is pleased to use in calling believers to faith and nourishing them for their life in service to him.[4] Our study will consist specifically of an extended exposition on the doctrine of the church and its ministry as described in the historic confessions and catechisms of the Reformation churches.

We will discover that these confessions offer a robust affirmation of Christ's church and its ministry. Far from disparaging the role of the church or the esteem in which the church should be held, these confessions emphasize the church's indispensability to the

---

2. D. Michael Lindsay, "A Gated Community in the Evangelical World," *USA Today,* February 18, 2008.

3. George Barna, *Revolution* (Carol Stream, IL: Tyndale House, 2005), 129.

4. Louis Berkhof offers the following summary of the historic Reformed view of the means of grace: "Strictly speaking, only the Word and the sacraments can be regarded as means of grace, that is, as objective channels which Christ has instituted in the Church, and to which he ordinarily binds Himself in the communication of His grace. Of course, these may never be dissociated from Christ, nor from the powerful operation of the Holy Spirit, nor from the Church which is the appointed organ for the distribution of the blessings of divine grace." *Systematic Theology* (Grand Rapids: Eerdmans, 1941), 604–5.

salvation of believers. So far as the Reformation confessions are concerned, the triune God's redemptive mission is principally effected through the ministry of the church. In the confessions' teaching, the church is no mere human society or project, but an institution born and enervated within the purposes of the triune God—Father, Son, and Holy Spirit. The ecclesiology of the Protestant Reformation, as expressed in the historic confessions of the Reformed churches, speaks a different language from the church's contemporary critics. Nothing in the confessions stemming from the Reformation encourages the modern tendency to look askance at the church and its ministry.

Before embarking upon our study of the church and its ministry in the confessions of the Reformed churches, I will briefly overview some reasons contemporary evangelical and Reformed believers have lost their understanding of the historic Protestant doctrine of the church, which will help us explore the doctrine of the church in the Reformation confessions with an awareness of current challenges. It will also set the stage for the concluding chapter, which reflects on implications of the Reformational doctrine of the church for facing present challenges to evangelical and Reformed churches in North America.

Losing a Biblical View of the Church

The low esteem in which the church of Jesus Christ is held today, even among evangelical believers, raises an obvious question: How did we get to this point? What accounts for the absence of a robust doctrine of the church among many Christians in North America? After all, today's low view of the church stands in stark contrast with historic Christian teaching. It is scarcely imaginable that a self-respecting Roman Catholic or Eastern Orthodox theologian would disparage the church. In their communions, the church is the place where Christ dwells by his Spirit and through whose ministry, especially the ministry of the sacraments, believers enjoy saving communion with Jesus Christ. But this high view of the church and its ministry is not the exclusive property of these communions. As we shall discover in our study of the Reformed confessions' doctrine of the church, the ecclesiology of the sixteenth- and seventeenth-century Protestant Reformers emphasized the indispensable role of the church and its ministry within the redemptive plan of God. Nothing in the Reformation's teaching about Christ's church encourages a low regard for it or its ministry. Indeed, the whole point of the Reformation was to recover the church's understanding of the gospel of salvation by God's grace alone through the work of Christ alone, and to contribute to the church's faithful administration of this gospel through preaching and sacraments.

Although the current weakened ecclesiology among many evangelical believers has deep historical roots and diverse causes, three broad, successive movements in the recent history of the evangelical churches in North America have played an especially important role: the church growth movement, the seeker-sensitive model, and the emergent church development.[5] Though they are often well intentioned and desire to equip the church to face more effectively its present challenges in post-Christian and postmodern North America, these movements have contributed significantly to the loss of the historic Protestant doctrine of the church and her ministry.

The Church Growth Movement

The first and most influential of these three movements is the church growth movement, which had its formal beginnings in the 1960s and 1970s. The history of the church growth movement is an interesting and complicated story in its own right. It is even possible to distinguish between different phases of the church growth movement.[6] For the purpose of this overview, however,

---

5. These historical roots reflect the emergence of a pragmatic approach to the ministry of the church, which is especially illustrated in the revivalist and "new measures" methodology of Charles Finney, an influential figure during the Second Great Awakening in the early nineteenth century. For a summary of Finney's contribution to a pragmatic approach to the church's ministry, see the following: Charles G. Finney, *Charles G. Finney: An Autobiography* (Old Tappan, NJ: Revell, n.d.); B. B. Warfield, *Perfectionism,* ed. Samuel G. Craig (New York: Oxford, 1931), 2:166–215; Iain H. Murray, *Revival and Revivalism: The Making and Marring of American Evangelicalism 1750–1858* (Carlisle, PA: Banner of Truth, 1994), esp. 223–52; and John E. MacArthur, "Charles Finney and American Evangelical Pragmatism," in *Ashamed of the Gospel: When the Church Becomes Like the World* (Wheaton, IL: Crossway, 1993), 227–35.

6. See Os Guinness, *Dining with the Devil: The Megachurch Movement Flirts*

it is the early and most fundamental phase of the church growth movement that is of special importance.

In the early period of the church growth movement, Donald McGavran, the acknowledged dean of church growth theologians, set out to articulate a comprehensive understanding of the church's mission upon a biblical and theological foundation.[7] McGavran aimed to develop a mission strategy that would enable the church to fulfill the Great Commission of Matthew 28:16–20 in an effective and fruitful manner. In McGavran's estimation, success in the church's mission required careful reflection upon the Bible's teaching regarding the numerical growth of the church. McGavran, who had previously served as a missionary in India, was keenly interested in analyzing the most effective way in which churches could be planted and experience growth in numbers of new believers. Whereas the older approach to missions focused upon seeking the lost, regardless of whether the church grew in number, McGavran insisted that it was biblically proper to think in terms of a strategy that focused upon finding the lost. If the church was to be successful in its missionary calling, it needed to embrace a strategy that was shaped by an awareness of God's will for the numerical growth of the church.

In the course of his formulation of a missiology that stressed the importance of church growth, McGavran identified what he termed the "homogeneous unit" principle. A church growth model that emphasizes not only seeking the lost but also especially finding and adding them to the number of the church requires that special attention be given to the church's target audience. The sciences of anthropology and sociology, therefore, are particularly useful in forming an effective church growth strategy. In order for the church to enjoy success in seeking and finding the lost, it must "contextualize" the gospel

---

with Modernity (Grand Rapids: Baker, 1993), 20–21. Guinness distinguishes three phases in the development of the church growth movement: an early missionary phase, an early North American phase, and the megachurch phase.

7. Donald McGavran, *Understanding Church Growth* (Grand Rapids: Eerdmans, 1970). See also Alan R. Tippett, *Church Growth and the Word of God* (Grand Rapids: Eerdmans, 1970); and C. Peter Wagner, *Your Church Can Grow: Seven Vital Signs of a Healthy Church* (Glendale, CA: G/L Publications, 1976).

to its target audience, finding and employing methods that are most likely to work with different groups. Both the church's message and method have to be sensitive to the social, cultural, ethnic, and historical identities of different people groups among whom new churches are planted. McGavran also observed, on the basis of his analysis of the homogeneous unit principle, that some groups of people prove more receptive to the gospel than others. He reasoned that an effective missionary strategy, therefore, will accurately identify which people groups are more receptive to the gospel and then concentrate upon a strategy for finding and enfolding them into churches congenial to their particular identity. Because people "like to become Christians without crossing racial, linguistic, or class barriers," an effective strategy for the growth of the church will aim to reach people groups rather than individuals who come from widely divergent backgrounds.[8]

In contrast with the older doctrine of the church that emphasized the church's fixed identity in terms of its characteristic marks and attributes, the church growth model offered a vision of the church as a dynamic, growing organism. It additionally encouraged crafting strategies for effective and growing churches, tailoring the church's message and method to accommodate different target audiences or demographic groups. The church growth movement's original interest in a biblical and theological understanding of missiology gradually gave way to an increasingly pragmatic, accommodating approach. The proverbial end—the growth of the church primarily in numbers of converts—gave birth to a raft of different means, each of which crafted the message and method of the church to suit the tastes of the targeted audience. Once the anthropological and sociological analyses of the earlier church growth missiology were increasingly untethered from any substantial biblical moorings, a doctrine of the church emerged that was more sociological than theological, more focused upon numerical increase than biblical message, and more attuned to contemporary success strategies and methods than timeless gospel preaching and ministry.[9]

---

8. McGavran, *Understanding Church Growth*, 198.

9. For a critical assessment of the pragmatism of the church growth movement, see MacArthur, *Ashamed of the Gospel*, 67–104.

The Seeker-Sensitive, User-Friendly Church

A short road leads from the church growth movement to the seeker-sensitive model, which has contributed significantly to a loss of the historic doctrine of the church among many North American evangelicals. It might be argued that this second movement represents a stage in the unfolding of the church growth movement more than a distinct development of its own. For the purpose of our overview of these developments, however, we will identify this second movement as a distinct and important one in the demise of the older Protestant doctrine of the church.

The second movement is commonly termed the seeker-sensitive movement, or model, for the ministry and growth of the church.[10] The connection between the missiology of the church growth movement and the subsequent emergence of the seeker-sensitive model for church growth is rather transparent. If church growth requires the church to be attentive to the target audience it wishes to reach with the gospel, then crafting its message and methods for effectiveness requires sensitivity to the felt needs of that group. The seeker-sensitive model for the church's growth and ministry is, therefore, an attempt to carry through consistently one of the essential tenets of the early church growth movement: the growth of the church depends upon the sociological analysis of the people groups the church aims to reach with the gospel. Unlike the earlier church growth movement, however, the seeker-sensitive movement has demonstrated less interest in biblical and theological underpinnings for its doctrine of the church and ministry.

Though the seeker-sensitive movement embraces the ministry of megachurches, whose diverse programs accommodate a wide net of distinct people groups or targeted audiences, and boutique churches, whose ministry is geared to one group in particular, it does so upon the basis of similar assumptions about the church. According to the proponents of the seeker-

---

10. For an introduction to the main tenets and practices of the seeker-sensitive movement, see G. A. Pritchard, *Willow Creek Seeker Services: Evaluating a New Way of Doing Church* (Grand Rapids: Baker, 1996); and Lee Strobel, *Inside the Mind of Unchurched Harry: How to Reach Friends and Family Who Avoid God and the Church* (Grand Rapids: Zondervan, 1993).

sensitive movement, the reason many churches are no longer effective in reaching and enfolding the lost is that they tailor their ministry to the churched rather than the unchurched. Rather than cater to those already familiar with the church's traditional teaching and culture, the seeker-sensitive movement endeavors to get "inside the mind of unchurched Harry."[11] Careful analysis of the circumstances, desires, fears and social, cultural, and intellectual traits of the unchurched, the target of the church's ministry must shape the church's crafting of its gospel message. In the same way a retailer markets a product, the church needs to determine a profile of its target audience, decide what it believes it needs or wants, and then fashion its product accordingly. Many of the techniques and strategies of good marketing need to be harnessed to the end of gospel proclamation and church growth.

The two best-known illustrations of the seeker-sensitive movement today are the Willow Creek Community Church near Chicago, pastored by Bill Hybels, and the Saddleback Community Church south of Los Angeles, pastored by Rick Warren. The reach and influence of these churches can hardly be overstated. Nearly ten thousand churches belong to an association with Willow Creek Community Church, which has approximately ninety-five hundred members. At annual conferences of these churches, thousands of pastors and church leaders receive training and direction in developing a seeker-sensitive ministry. More than 250,000 pastors are estimated to have attended Rick Warren's Purpose Driven Church seminars, and some sixty thousand pastors are regular subscribers to his weekly e-mail newsletter.

The Willow Creek seeker-sensitive model illustrates well the way this second movement affects the church's doctrine. The problem with many traditional churches, according to Hybels, is that they are seeker-hostile. Not only do such churches fail to enlist the service of their members in the use of their spiritual gifts, but they also emphasize a form of worship that consists primarily of a didactic sermon and other elements (traditional songs, lengthy prayers, sacraments) that may be familiar to the

---

11. The language is Lee Strobel's in *Inside the Mind of Unchurched Harry.*

churched, but are unfamiliar to the unchurched. The style and nature of the church's services are foreign, unwelcoming, and unattractive to the unchurched, who are often put off by the language and culture of the traditional church. The traditional model of the church typically comforts the churched but discomforts the unchurched.

In order to reach effectively the unchurched, the traditional church needs to undergo a radical restructuring. Since unchurched Harry and Mary are uncomfortable with buildings that are transparently "churchy," with features like stained glass windows and pipe organs, the Willow Creek Community Church gathers in a facility that has the feel of a modern civic center, with an atrium suitable to a four- or five-star hotel. Sunday services are carefully planned to appeal to the unchurched: no creeds are recited; no hymnals are used; if a collection is taken, visitors are encouraged not to participate; contemporary instruments and music, professional drama, and multimedia presentations are an integral part of the service; and the message is delivered in language that is accessible to unchurched Harry and Mary. These Sunday services are not, strictly speaking, worship services. Worship services for the churched are typically held on weeknights. The services on Sunday are strictly evangelistic in nature and are governed by the seeker-sensitive model for gospel ministry and communication. Everything revolves around the goal of offering a message in a manner that fits the tastes of the unchurched seeker. If the church is to reach the unchurched, it must die to its traditional ways and come to life in a radically new form.

The Emergent Church

The third movement in the recent history of reconceiving the church and its ministry is the most difficult to describe. Though this third development has a commonly acknowledged name, the emergent church, it is more amorphous and elusive than the previous two we have considered. For this reason, some acknowledged proponents of the emergent church movement prefer to speak of it as a conversation about the church rather than a movement.[12] The broad and elastic boundaries of the emergent church movement include a wide variety of theological perspectives and practices. Consequently, any attempt to offer a brief characterization of the emergent church movement is rather risky, if not foolhardy. Due to the importance of this third movement for the doctrine of the church, however, we need to give it our attention.

While proponents of the emergent church often represent themselves as disillusioned with the slightly older church growth and seeker-sensitive models (especially in its megachurch expressions), there is an obvious connection between all three of these movements. Like the church growth and seeker-sensitive approaches, the emergent movement wants to formulate and practice a way of being church that answers to the new situation Christians face within the context of what emergent church proponents call "postmodernism."[13] Just as the earlier two movements insisted upon crafting a doctrine of the church and its ministry that would effectively address its target audience, so the emergent church movement wants to shape its view of the church in a way that accommodates the new and distinct challenges of a postmodern world. However, the emergent church movement insists that the older church growth and the more recent seeker-sensitive movements are no longer adequate. Because these earlier movements still relied heavily upon a message or methodology for the church s ministry that

12. Although the literature on the emergent church movement is considerable and as disparate as the movement itself, some of the better sources are Brian D. McClaren, *A Generous Orthodoxy* (Grand Rapids: Zondervan, 2004); Kevin Corcoran, ed., *Church in the Present Tense: A Candid Look at What's Emerging* (Grand Rapids: Brazos Press, 2011); Mike Yaconelli, ed., *Stories of Emergence: Moving from Absolute to Authentic* (Grand Rapids: Zondervan, 2003); Dan Kimball, *The Emerging Church: Vintage Christianity for New Generations* (Grand Rapids: Zondervan, 2003); D. A. Carson, *Becoming Conversant with the Emerging Church: Understanding a Movement and Its Implications* (Grand Rapids: Zondervan, 2005); and Kevin De Young and Ted Kluck, *Why We're Not Emergent: By Two Guys Who Should Be* (Chicago: Moody, 2008).

13. For a critique of modernism, which has been influential among emergent church authors, see Stanley J. Grenz and John R. Francke, *Beyond Foundationalism: Shaping Theology in a Postmodern Context* (Louisville, KY: Westminster John Knox Press, 2000). For an extensive critique of postmodern pluralism, which he views largely as a version of (late) modernism, see D. A. Carson, *The Gagging of God: Christianity Confronts Pluralism* (Grand Rapids: Zondervan, 1996).

was modern rather than postmodern, they are now passé. If the church is to relate to the next generation, which has been shaped largely by the spirit and forms of postmodernism, it must cease to be church in anything like the historical sense of the term. Three features of the emergent church movement deserve mention and are especially significant to its proposals for a new view of the church and its ministry.

First, the emergent church movement is built upon the conviction that the people to whom the contemporary church speaks and ministers are occupants of a postmodern rather than modern world. If the church is to reach those whose worldview and assumptions are shaped by postmodernism, then it must proceed on the basis of a sympathetic awareness of postmodernism's key features. For the church to win a hearing or have a beneficial impact upon the lives of people today, it must shape its ministry in a way that shows proper sensitivity to the way postmodern people think and behave. We need a postmodern church—one with a postmodern message and manner—in order to speak and act effectively in a postmodern world.

Though emergent authors stress a number of different features of postmodernism, the feature they most often emphasize has to do with the way postmoderns view how we know what we know or believe what we believe. In the older worldview of modernism, it was assumed that people could know the truth and that what is true for one person must also be true for others. Modernism had confidence in human reason or other acknowledged sources of authority (e.g., the Bible) as a surefooted basis for apprehending the truth in any legitimate area of human knowledge.[14] In the words of D. A. Carson, a careful critic of the emergent church movement, modernism "is often pictured [by emergent authors] as pursuing truth, absolutism, linear thinking, rationalism, certainty, the cerebral as opposed to the affective—which in turn breeds arrogance, inflexibility, a lust to be right, the desire to control."[15] So far as the church and its ministry are concerned, modernism encouraged the church and

14. See Grenz and Francke, *Beyond Foundationalism,* 28–54; and Carson, *Gagging of God,* 13–92.

15. Carson, *Becoming Conversant with the Emerging Church,* 27.

its theologians to emphasize right doctrine as a primary mark of the true church. What mattered to the church, especially to many evangelicals in the grip of modernism, was the church's adherence to and faithful propagation of the set of doctrines (or doctrinal propositions) taught in the Word of God.

Representatives of the emergent church movement maintain that the church can no longer afford to exhibit an overbearing confidence in its grasp of the truth. In a postmodern world that applauds the virtues of tolerance and diversity, the church may not communicate in a doctrinally inflexible and monochrome fashion. In a world where people's beliefs and practices are explained largely in terms of the influence of historical heritage, as well as various social and cultural factors, the church must recognize how much its own beliefs and practices are the fruit of similar factors. A "one-size-fits-all" approach to doctrine and practice on the part of the church may work within the framework of modernism but is woefully misguided in the world of postmodernism, which celebrates diversity. Though the church needs to maintain its continuity with the broad tradition of Christian teaching and practice, the world of postmodernism calls for a "generous orthodoxy" that includes more than it excludes.[16] A generous orthodoxy will cut across and transcend the sharp boundaries that modernism often posited between evangelical and mainline, Protestant and Roman Catholic, charismatic and noncharismatic, conservative and liberal. Rather than insisting upon one great all-embracing story, or "metanarrative," as it is often termed, the church needs to make room for the coexistence of many different stories, none of which captures the fullness of truth or declares all others to be untrue.

Second, consistent with its celebration of a postmodern diversity of viewpoints, stories, experiences, and perspectives,

---

16. McClaren, *Generous Orthodoxy,* 18: "Because generous orthodoxy is aware of the need to keep listening and learning in openness to the Spirit and to the world for the sake of the gospel, it seeks to keep conversations going and not to end them. Generous orthodoxy does not so much specify a particular point or position as it establishes a spacious territory defined by certain distinct boundaries in which there is space to live, move, and breathe while exploring the wonders and mysteries of the faith."

the emergent church can primarily be described in terms of what it opposes. The emergent church movement is in many ways a protest movement against older ways of being church that its proponents claim no longer work in a postmodern world. Accordingly, it is easier to identify what the emergent church protests than what it embraces.

We have already identified the first of these protests. The emergent church comes in a kaleidoscope-like diversity of shapes and sizes precisely because it aims to protest the one-size-fits-all pretensions of many traditional churches. Since no church may lay claim to the truth in any absolute or comprehensive fashion, all churches should be left free to embrace with modesty their particular understanding of the gospel together with its application in practice, so long as they do not thereby exclude the differing viewpoints of others. While many evangelical churches require adherence to a precise system of doctrinal teaching and practice, emergent churches cultivate a conversational style of gospel communication. A "generous orthodoxy" commends a gospel message and practice that involves a journey in which the truth is discovered or approximated but never grasped or mastered. Emergent churches are less interested in whether people believe the right doctrine than in whether they belong to a genuine community of believers. Authenticity is more important than orthodoxy.

In addition to their protest against the pretensions of many traditional evangelical churches, emergent church proponents often protest the megachurch model of the seeker-sensitive movement. Megachurches within evangelicalism commonly betray commitments to aspects of the older worldview of modernism that are objectionable from the standpoint of postmodernism. Megachurches are frequently churches with authoritarian pastors and leaders. They employ the latest media to communicate, often with large audiences, in a way that seems gimmicky and manipulative. They still insist that their members embrace a common understanding of the gospel or live as Christians in a particular way that is exclusive of alternative viewpoints. Many megachurches reflect the values of suburbia or entrepreneurial capitalism rather than the values of the kingdom of God. Rather than cultivating genuine community among believers in an intimate, nonjudgmental setting, the megachurch simultaneously encourages Christian anonymity and cultural conformity. In an ironic sort of way, the megachurch model represents a kind of cultural captivity on the part of the Christian church to worldly standards that belong more to the world of modernism than postmodernism. The captivity of the megachurch movement within evangelicalism is reflected further in its identification with a conservative social and political agenda, which identifies the values of the gospel with the values of a certain segment of North American society.

And third, the emergent church movement is committed to a radical revision of what it means to be church in a postmodern world. The older doctrine of the church requires more than a facelift or superficial modification. According to emergent church leaders, the older doctrine of the church needs to be rejected wholesale and replaced with a substantially different "missional" doctrine of the church.

Though the language of a missional church, which is regularly found in the literature of emergent church authors, may seem vague, it is primarily aimed against the allegedly nonmissional character of the traditional doctrine of the church.[17] The Reformers, in their effort to affirm the authority of the Bible and ensure sound doctrine, emphasized the need to identify the marks of the true church. The church was defined as a place where the gospel is rightly preached, the sacraments are rightly administered, and church discipline is faithfully exercised.

---

17. For a helpful evaluation of the way the term *missional* can serve a variety of sometimes vague purposes, see Kevin De Young and Greg Gilbert, *What Is the Mission of the Church? Making Sense of Social Justice, Shalom, and the Great Commission* (Wheaton, IL: Crossway, 2011), 15–28. See also Darrell L. Guder, ed., *Missional Church: A Vision for the Sending of the Church in North America* (Grand Rapids: Eerdmans, 1998); Michael Horton, *The Gospel Commission: Recovering God's Strategy for Making Disciples* (Grand Rapids: Baker, 2011), 266–93; and Tim Keller, *Center Church: Doing Balanced, Gospel-Centered Ministry in Your City* (Grand Rapids: Zondervan, 2012), 251–90. Keller offers an extensive assessment of the missional understanding of the church, affirming its sensitivity to the new context of the church in post-Christian or neo-pagan societies and to the missionary identity of the church. Though Keller affirms a more holistic view of the gospel's claim upon human life and culture than does Horton, he also rightly cautions against the loss of a gospel focus in the ministry of many mainline, liberal churches.

However, over time these marks narrowed the definition of the church to a "place where" instead of a "people who are" reality. The word church came to be defined as "a place where certain things happen," such as preaching and the celebration of Holy Communion.[18] With its emphasis upon the characteristic marks that distinguish the true church from the false and its understanding of the role of preaching and sacraments as essential to the church's ministry, the historic Protestant doctrine of the church implies that the church precedes or exists independently of its mission. In this model of the church, the creation and preservation of the church is separated from the church's participation in God's mission to redeem humanity and restore a broken world. Rather than the church's mission defining what it is, the church's existence is independent of and prior to the performance of its mission. Furthermore, the historic emphasis upon an ordained clergy who are responsible for executing the mission of the church, which involves the administration of the Word through preaching and sacrament, excludes most of the church's members from direct participation in the church's mission.

If the older doctrine of the church must be jettisoned, then what does a missional church look like? Negatively, a missional church is not primarily a place where people gather for worship, hear the Word of God taught, and receive the sacraments. Positively, a missional church is a community of authentic believers who embrace and participate in God's great mission of healing the brokenness of human life in God's creation. Emergent church proponents believe that a missional church consists of genuine Christians who share equally in the responsibility to align their stories with God's story. Just as God is a missional God who aims to restore and redeem the brokenness of human life, even

---

18. For a critical assessment and debate regarding the claim that a new missional doctrine of the church is needed to displace the older Reformational doctrine, see John Bolt and Richard A. Muller, "Does the Church Today Need a New 'Mission Paradigm?'" *Calvin Theological Journal* 31, no. 1 (1996): 196–208; Craig Van Gelder and Dirk Hart, "The Church Needs to Understand Its Missionary Nature: A Response to John Bolt and Richard Muller," *Calvin Theological Journal* 31, no. 2 (1996): 504–19; and John Bolt and Richard A. Muller, "For the Sake of the Church: A Response to Van Gelder and Hart," *Calvin Theological Journal* 31, no. 2 (1996): 520–26.

the brokenness of the creation itself, so believers are missional in so far as they participate in this great missionary endeavor. When the Christian community lives authentically within the larger story of God's mission in the world, the church does not have a mission but rather is mission.[19]

The implications of the emergent church movement for the doctrine of the church are far-reaching. The historic understanding of the church's special mission to teach the Word of the gospel and to administer the sacraments is largely displaced by an emphasis upon the authenticity of the believing community's participation in the mission of God. In the emergent church's understanding of God's mission, there is little room for a traditional emphasis upon the church's use of the means of grace in preaching and sacrament. Consistent with the emergent church's view of the missional nature of the church, authentic participation in any legitimate facet of human life in God's creation becomes a kind of means of grace, or sacramental sign, of God's presence. Brian McLaren, for example, one of the leading figures in the emergent church movement, offers an expansive view of the means of grace:

> A sacrament is an object or practice that mediates the divine to humans. It carries something of God to us; it is a means of grace, and it conveys sacredness. I care little for arguments about how many sacraments there are (although I tend to prefer longer lists than shorter ones). What I really like about the sacramental nature of Catholicism is this: through learning that a few things can carry the sacred, we become open to the fact all things (all good things, all created things) can ultimately carry the sacred: the kind smile of a Down's syndrome child, the bouncy jubilation of a puppy, the graceful arch of a dancer's back, the camera work in a fine film, good coffee, good wine, good friends, good conversation. Start with three sacraments—or seven—and pretty soon everything becomes potentially sacramental as, I believe, it should be.[20]

---

19. For an extensive biblical-theological exposition of the "mission of God" that develops some of the themes of the missional understanding of the church in the emergent church movement, see Christopher J. H. Wright, *The Mission of God: Unlocking the Bible's Grand Narrative* (Downers Grove, IL: IVP Academic, 2006).

20. McClaren, *Generous Orthodoxy*, 225–26.

In this expansive view of the means of grace, which cultivates an authentic participation in the redemptive mission of God in the world, the church's traditional institutional and ministerial identity vanish altogether. When virtually anything can become a means of grace for believers, then nothing remains to distinguish the particular means of grace administered by the church of Jesus Christ in carrying out its mission.

The Approach and Outline of the Study

Though much more could be said regarding contemporary Christianity's loss of the historic doctrine of the church, this short tour dé force through recent developments within segments of contemporary evangelicalism serves my purpose: a demonstration of the profound loss of conviction regarding the historic Reformation understanding of the nature and calling of Jesus Christ's church in the world. These developments illustrate how far many in the contemporary church have strayed from the prevalent understanding of the church's ministry during the reformation of the church in the sixteenth century.

In our study of the Reformation confessions' doctrine of the church, we will rediscover a quite different understanding of the church of Jesus Christ. In this understanding, the church is confessed as an institution that Christ himself calls into existence, preserves, and protects. As a divinely appointed institution, the church is further called to administer the Word and sacraments in the power of Christ's Spirit as the ordained means to gather and nourish the people of God in the faith. From the perspective of the historic confessions of the Reformation, the church is not a human institution that may be defined in primarily sociological, cultural, and historical terms. The church is a dwelling place of God in the Spirit (Eph. 2:22) and the divinely authorized administrant of the means of grace that Christ has appointed and is pleased to use to redeem his people. Viewed from the standpoint of contemporary developments in the doctrine of the church, the world of the Reformed confessions will seem like a strange new world indeed.

Though there are several different approaches that I could take to the doctrine of the church, especially the topic of the means of grace, the approach of my study will be to examine the confessional symbols of the Reformation era. While many evangelical churches and traditions tend to neglect their inheritance in the faith, expressed as it is in the confessional documents of the churches, the Reformed churches have always had a high regard for the authority and place of the confessions in the life of the church. The confessions constitute the corporate and traditional understanding of the Scriptures on a full range of doctrinal subjects. These confessions do not have the kind of infallible authority alongside the Scriptures that has characterized the Roman Catholic view of the church's *magisterium.* They are not tradition, in the sense of infallibly determined dogma. But they do represent the confessional tradition of the Reformation, a distillation of the church's common understanding of the Scriptures. The confessions are a *repetitio Sacrae Scripturae,* a "repetition of Sacred Scripture," whose teaching has real, albeit subordinate, authority in the churches.[21]

In the following chapters, I will use a wide representation of the great confessions of the Reformed churches, commenting on their understanding of the principal means of grace: the preaching of the gospel and the administration of the sacraments. Rather than taking a synthetic approach to these confessions, treating them systematically under a number of distinct heads or topics, I will take a more analytic and diachronic approach, tracing the confessions in their historical order and considering the teaching of each on the subject of the church's ministry. Needless to say, my interest in what follows will not be primarily historical. There are good studies of the historical background and occasion as well as the distinctive contributions of these confessions, some of which will be noted along the way. My interest is primarily to summarize the doctrine of preaching and sacraments set forth in these confessional documents. Furthermore, I will not be discussing all of the important confessions (including catechisms) produced during the sixteenth and seventeenth centuries by the various Reformed churches. With the exception of the Scots Confession of 1560, my principle of selection will be to cite only

---

21. For a fine recent defense, or apology, for the church's use of creeds and confessions, see Carl Trueman, *The Creedal Imperative* (Wheaton, IL: Crossway, 2012).

those confessional documents that have become ecclesiastical standards among the Reformed churches since the time of the Reformation. Those confessions or symbols that have served the Reformed churches as ecclesiastically acknowledged and official forms of unity will be the focus of our attention.

Due to the extensiveness of the confessional material on the topics of preaching and the sacraments, I will divide my summary into six chapters. I will begin with two chapters on the subject of preaching, which is the foremost medium for the communication of Christ to his people according to the Reformation confessions. I will devote chapter 4 to the doctrine of the sacraments in general, before treating distinctly the sacraments of baptism (chapter 5) and the Lord's Supper (chapters 6 and 7). Because of the considerable debate and controversy regarding the sacraments in the sixteenth-century Reformation, the confessions offer a rather extensive and detailed exposition of the role of the sacraments as means of grace. For this reason, my treatment of the confessional doctrine of the sacraments will require multiple chapters.

Though my exposition of the confessions' teaching regarding the ministry of the church will not be explicitly governed or directed to the contemporary challenges the church faces, I will return to them in this study's concluding chapter. This is the question I wish to address in the conclusion: Can the doctrine of the means of grace, as it is affirmed in the historical confessional symbols of the Reformation, address meaningfully the challenges facing the evangelical and Reformed church in our day? Or, to put the question a little differently: How can the church's ministry reflect a high view of the means of grace, preaching and sacraments, and yet simultaneously meet the challenge to fulfill its evangelistic and missionary calling to disciple the nations? Rather than simply dismissing the challenges of the church growth, seeker-sensitive, and emergent church movements, it is necessary to answer them with a defense of the church's ministry of Word and sacrament that addresses the legitimate concerns these movements express.

Chapter 2

Faith Comes by Hearing: Preaching in the Reformed Confessions (1)

During a teaching stint in the ancient Baltic city of Riga, Latvia, I had the opportunity to visit Rigas Dom, the largest, most prestigious church in the city. Originally built in the thirteenth century as a Roman Catholic cathedral, it is a Lutheran church today. Walking through this massive edifice, I was struck by the large, ornate pulpit that was centrally located, dominating the sanctuary. The placement of this pulpit spoke eloquently of the centrality and indispensability of the preaching of the Word to communicate Christ and his saving work to his people. The Reformation's restoration of preaching to the center of Christian worship and life could not have been more dramatically illustrated. The worship of the medieval Roman Catholic Church focused upon the altar and the sacrament of the Mass, while the worship of the Reformation churches focused upon the pulpit. Christ's dwelling in the midst of his people was understood to be primarily mediated through the proclamation of the gospel, and only secondarily through the administration of the sacraments.[1]

Restoring preaching to a central place in worship was a feature of the Reformation embraced by Lutheran and Reformed

---

1. In his classic study *The Spirit of Catholicism,* Karl Adam expresses well the historic Catholic view of Christ's presence in the church: "Thus we see that in the sacraments, and especially in the Sacrament of the Altar, the fundamental idea of the Church is most plainly represented, the idea, that is, of the incorporation of the faithful into Christ"(Garden City, NY: Image Books, 1954), 19. In the new *Catechism of the Catholic Church* (Liguori, MO: United States Catholic Conference Inc., 1994), the exposition of "the sacramental economy" (para. 1076ff.) makes clear that this feature of Catholicism remains unchanged: Christ's presence is essentially mediated through the sacraments. The preaching of the Word merits hardly any attention at all in this catechism.

churches alike, but it was especially distinctive of the Reformed churches. Though the Reformed churches did not abandon the historic Christian view of Christ's real presence in the sacraments, they insisted that Christ preeminently communes with his people through the preaching of the gospel Word. The sacraments are an indispensable accompaniment of the Word, but for their use and efficacy they depend upon the Word and its promises. Without the Word, the sacraments would be empty and useless.

The historic, uniform conviction of the Reformation churches of the centrality of preaching as a means of grace does not enjoy a lively reception among many evangelical churches today. The Reformation's view of preaching has been seriously challenged in recent years, even in churches and communions that fall within the Protestant tradition. On the one hand, there is a spirit of democratization and egalitarianism that chafes at the notion of an ordained ministry whose administration of the Word of God in preaching has a place of preeminence in the church. When this spirit captivates the churches, all of the members alike become equally "ministers" of the Word of God, the minister of the Word and sacraments being only a specialized expression of a more general calling. And on the other hand, there is a growing sentiment that preaching no longer serves as an effective means of communicating the gospel. This sentiment can give birth to an almost endless proliferation of new systems or strategies for communicating the gospel—from a kind of neosacramentalism among some evangelicals to drama, music, and other, sometimes more exotic, worship practices. The only common thread tying these methods together is that they represent alternatives to the traditional means of preaching the gospel. The sorry reputation of preaching in the contemporary church is illustrated by the negative connotation of the expression "to preach to or at someone."[2]

---

2. I mention this only for the purpose of illustrating the contrast between the historic Reformed conviction about preaching and what is often the case today. I do not intend to explore the variety of reasons—philosophical (in the development of postmodernism); theological (in the demise of scriptural authority); cultural (individualism and relativism); and communicational (the triumph of image over word)—that may explain the demise of respect for preaching. See Carson, *Gagging of God*, for an extensive analysis of the philosophical and conceptual environment that characterized Western culture at the end of the twentieth century. The

In this and a subsequent chapter's treatment of the doctrine of preaching in the Reformed confessions, we will see that the language of the Reformed confessions is quite different from that of many contemporary evangelical churches. While preaching the gospel has lost its primacy in many evangelical circles, these confessions breathe a confident spirit regarding the proclamation of the gospel as the principal means that Christ has appointed for the gathering and equipping of his people for their faith and practice.

As noted in the previous chapter, the approach to the confessions throughout this chapter and our study as a whole will not be synthetic or topical. Our approach will trace the confessions in their historical order and consider the distinctive contribution of each to the topic under consideration. This approach helps illustrate the progress of Reformed doctrine during the sixteenth-century Reformation and its aftermath. It allows us to more clearly discern the distinctive accents of the various confessions. Our primary interest will not be to trace the historical development of confessional teaching but to offer a summary of the doctrinal content of their understanding regarding the means of grace, the preaching of the Word and the administration of the sacraments.

The Gallican (French) Confession of 1559[3]

The first great confession of the Reformed churches that we consider is the Gallican (French) Confession of 1559. Studies of the origin and development of the Reformed confessions

---

implications of that environment for preaching are aptly suggested by Carson's evocative title.

3. The English translation of the Gallican Confession, cited here and throughout, is from Philip Schaff, *The Creeds of Christendom: The Evangelical Protestant Creeds with Translations* (1931; repr., Grand Rapids: Baker, 1985), 356–82. The French quotations are taken from a standard collection of the Reformed confessions: Wilhelm Niesel, *Bekenntnisschriften und Kirchenordnungen der nach Gottes Wort reformierten Kirche* (A. G. Zollikon-Zürich, 1938), 65–79. Quotations from Niesel's collection throughout this book will be referenced by page number and line number (e.g., 65.17 refers to page 65, line 17). In addition to these sources, important collections of the Reformed confessions, either in the original languages or in English translation, include E. F. K. Müller, *Die Bekenntnisschriften der reformierten Kirche* (Leipzig, 1903); Paul Jacobs, *Reformierte Bekenntnisschriften und Kirchenordnungen in deutscher*

generally acknowledge that this confession belongs to the early period of consolidation and more mature articulation of the Reformed faith in distinction from the Roman Catholic Church and, to a lesser extent, the Lutheran and other Reformational churches.[4] This confession was the first, in conjunction with the preparation and acceptance of a church order, to bind the churches of a nation together on a Reformed basis.

After a dispute had arisen among the Reformed churches regarding the doctrine of predestination, Antoine de la Roche-Chandieu, a student of Calvin, had proposed that a confession and church order be produced for the Reformed churches of France. This proposal met with favor, and at a constituting synod held in Paris in 1559, a draft confession originally written by Calvin and revised by Chandieu was adopted as the Gallican Confession.[5] Subsequently, Beza presented this confession to

---

Ubersetzung (Neukirchen, 1949); Arthur C. Cochrane, *Reformed Confessions of the 16th Century* (Philadelphia: Westminster Press, 1966); John H. Leith, ed., *Creeds of the Churches* (Garden City, NY: Doubleday, 1963); Mark A. Noll, *Confessions and Catechisms of the Reformation* (Grand Rapids: Baker, 1991); *The Book of Confessions,* 2nd ed. (Office of the General Assembly of the United Presbyterian Church in the United States of America, 1966, 1967); Thomas F. Torrance, *The School of Faith: The Catechisms of the Reformed Church* (London: James Clarke, 1959); John Calvin, *Calvin: Theological Treatises*, ed. J. K. S. Reid (Philadelphia: Westminster Press, 1954); and I. John Hesselink, ed., *Calvin's First Catechism* (Louisville, KY: Westminster John Knox Press, 1997). I should also mention a collection of the Reformed confessions in English or English translation that has been produced by Mid-America Reformed Seminary: *Ecumenical and Reformed Creeds and Confessions,* classroom ed. (Orange City, IA: Mid-America Reformed Seminary, 1991). In the following, I will indicate which source and translation I am using for each respective confession. In many instances, I will cite the original text in a footnote for the benefit of those who wish to compare the English translation with the original.

4. Benno Gassmann, *Ecclesia Reformata: Die Kirche in den reformierten Bekenntnisschriften* (Freiburg: Herder, 1968), divides the history and development of the Reformed confessions into five periods: first reflection and consolidation (e.g., Zwingli's Sixty-Seven Articles of 1523); new orientation (e.g., Calvin's Geneva Confession of 1536); national confessions of Reformed churches "under the cross" (e.g., the Gallican Confession of 1559); the second reformation (e.g., the Heidelberg Catechism of 1563); and confessions of Reformed "posterity" (e.g., the Canons of Dort and the Westminster Standards). This is a useful, albeit rather rough periodization of the development of Reformed confessionalism in the sixteenth and seventeenth centuries.

5. See Jan Rohls, *Reformed Confessions: Theology from Zurich to Barmen* (Louisville, KY: Westminster John Knox Press, 1997), 16–17. Rohls points out that Calvin had some reservations about this synod's decision to revise his draft

Charles IX at Poissy in 1561; the Synod of La Rochelle adopted it in 1571 (hence, it is sometimes called the Confession of Rochelle); and Henry IV sanctioned it. It stands, therefore, as one of the first binding statements of faith to be produced by the Reformed churches in the sixteenth century.

The Gallican Confession considers the subject of preaching within the sequence of articles that address the doctrine of the church and its ministry. Like the Belgic Confession, for which the Gallican Confession was a model and archetype, the Gallican Confession has the following outline: article 1 confesses who God is; articles 2–6 deal with the subjects of revelation and Scripture; articles 7–8 speak of God's works of creation and providence, respectively; articles 9–11 articulate the doctrine of sin; articles 12–17 explain God's purpose of election and provision for the redemption of his people through Christ; articles 18–24 consider the application of this redemption by the Holy Spirit through the gospel; articles 25–38 set forth the doctrine of the church, its ministry and sacraments; and articles 39–40 conclude with a brief statement regarding the ordinance of and limits upon the authority of the state.

The preaching of the gospel surfaces in this confession in the first article addressing the doctrine of the church.[6] Since "we enjoy Christ only through the gospel,"[7] the pressing questions become these: Where is the gospel to be found, and how is Christ communicated to believers? According to the Gallican Confession, Christ has entrusted the gospel to the church and its ministry. Christ is pleased to communicate himself through the gospel as it is ministered through pastoral instruction or teaching. Pastors who have been "properly called and exercise

---

confession and adopt it as a unifying confession of faith for the French Reformed churches.

6.   Article 25: "Now as we enjoy Christ only through the gospel, we believe that the order of the Church, established by his authority, ought to be sacred and inviolable, and that, therefore, the Church can not exist without pastors for instruction, whom we should respect and reverently listen to, when they are properly called and exercise their office faithfully. Not that God is bound to such aid and subordinate means, but because it pleaseth him to govern us by such restraints. In this we detest all visionaries who would like, so far as lies in their power, to destroy the ministry and preaching of the Word and sacraments."

7.   Article 25: "Pource que nous ne iouissons de Jésus Christ que par l'Evangile. . ." Niesel, *Bekenntnisschriften*, 72.8–9.

their office faithfully"[8] deserve to be respected and reverently obeyed. Through their ministry of the Word, Christ's saving presence is mediated to the faithful. Though the confession is careful to note that God is not "bound to such aid and subordinate means," he is nonetheless pleased to be governed by such restraints.[9] The indispensable place of the preaching ministry to enjoying Christ is contrasted with the false teaching of the "visionaries" (*fantastiques*) who would destroy the ministry and preaching of the Word and sacraments. Because Christ has appointed preaching as the means by which he dwells among his people, it would be ungrateful and disobedient to despise or neglect the preaching of the Word.

In addition to its principal claim that the preaching of the gospel is the indispensable means for obtaining fellowship with Christ, the Gallican Confession affirms two corollary points regarding the preaching of the gospel. First, no person is free to be solitary, refusing to keep the unity of the church by failing to submit to "the public preaching" of the gospel.[10] Second, the faithful reception of the preaching of God's Word is the foremost distinguishing mark of the true church. With these points, the Gallican Confession confirms the central role of preaching in the ministry of the church, though without adding anything further to its previous emphasis upon preaching as means of grace.

---

8. Article 25: ". . . quand ils sont deuement appelés et exercent fidèlement leur office." Niesel, *Bekenntnisschriften*, 72.12–13.

9. Article 25: ". . . attaché à telles aides, ou moyens inférieurs. . ." Niesel, *Bekenntnisschriften* 72.14.

10. Article 26: "We believe that no one ought to seclude himself and be contented to be alone; but that all jointly should keep and maintain the union of the Church, and submit to the public preaching ('se soumettans à l'instruction commune' [Niesel, *Bekenntnisschriften,* 72.28–29]), and to the yoke of Jesus Christ, wherever God shall have established a true order of the Church, even if magistrates and their edicts are contrary to it. For if they do not take part in it, or if they separate themselves from it, they do contrary to the Word of God." Article 27: "Nevertheless we believe that it is important to discern with care and prudence which is the true Church, for this title has been much abused. We say, then, according to the Word of God, that it is the company of the faithful who agree to follow his Word, and the pure religion which it teaches; who advance in it all their lives, growing and becoming more confirmed in the fear of God according as they feel the want of growing and pressing onward."

The Scots Confession of 1560[11]

The Scots Confession of 1560 does not elaborate extensively upon the doctrine of preaching. Originally drafted by John Knox while he was serving English refugee congregations in Frankfurt and Geneva, this confession was adopted by an act of Parliament in 1560. Shortly thereafter, the first General Assembly of the Scottish church prepared a church order, the First Book of Discipline. Destined to be supplanted by the Westminster Confession of Faith and Catechisms, the Scots Confession of Faith represents the first and original expression of the Reformed faith on the British Isles. The structure of the Scots Confession resembles that of the Gallican Confession of 1559, but it does not consider in any substantial way the doctrines of revelation and Scripture, the Trinity, creation, and providence. The one significant reference to the preaching of the gospel is found in an extensive section devoted to the doctrine of the church. This section is noteworthy for its treatment of the power and authority of general councils and the sacraments.

The one important statement about preaching in the Scots Confession occurs in chapter 18, "The Notes by Which the True Kirk Shall Be Determined from the False, and Who Shall Be Judge of Doctrine."[12] Though sixteenth-century Reformers varied on the number of the marks of the true church, the Scots Confession designates three: the "true preaching of the Word of God," the "right administration of the sacraments of Jesus Christ," and "ecclesiastical discipline uprightly ministered."[13]

---

11. The text of the Scots Confession of 1560 is from *The Book of Confessions,* 2nd ed. (Office of the General Assembly of the UPC in the USA, 1967), 3.18.

12. Chapter 18: "The notes of the true Kirk, therefore, we believe, confess, and avow to be: first, the true preaching of the Word of God, in which God has revealed himself to us, as the writings of the prophets and apostles declare; secondly, the right administration of the sacraments of Christ Jesus, with which must be associated the Word and promise of God to seal and confirm them in our hearts; and lastly, ecclesiastical discipline uprightly ministered, as God's Word prescribes, whereby vice is repressed and virtue nourished."

13. In his *Institutes of the Christian Religion*, Calvin designates only two marks of the true church: "where the preaching of the gospel is reverently heard (*ubi reverenter auditur Evangelii praedicatio*) and the sacraments are not neglected, there for the time being no deceitful or ambiguous form of the church is seen." Ed. John T. McNeill, trans. Ford Lewis Battles (Philadelphia: Westminster Press, 1960), 4.1.8. Among the Reformers, Bucer spoke of discipline as a third

Without elaborating upon the subject of preaching, this designation of it as the preeminent and first mark of the church says a great deal, even if only indirectly, about its importance. For the Reformers, the marks of the true church were those authenticating features that distinguish the true church from the false so-called church. The marks of the church were those normative features that, when applied to any company that claimed to be an expression of Christ's church, warranted a distinction between the authentic and inauthentic. According to the Scots Confession, what especially distinguishes the true or genuine church is its faithful proclamation of the gospel of Jesus Christ. To paraphrase an ancient dictum of Roman Catholicism that "where the bishop is, there is the church" (*ubi episcopos est, ibi ecclesia*) in terms that conform to this confession, the Scots Confession maintains in effect that "where the true preaching of Christ is found, there is the church."

The Belgic Confession of 1561[14]

So far as the doctrine of the preaching of the gospel is concerned, the Belgic Confession reaffirms some of the themes we have already witnessed in the Gallican Confession of 1559 and the Scots Confession of 1560. However, it also elaborates upon the official character of preaching as the calling of those whom Christ appoints in his church as pastors and ministers of the Word. Therefore, this confession deserves to be considered in its own right not only because it remains one of the great standards of the Continental Reformed churches—especially the churches of the "Lowlands," or the Netherlands—but also because of the way it emphasizes the authority of the preaching office.

The Belgic Confession takes its name from its origins in the southern provinces of the Netherlands, which are known today as Belgium. It was originally drafted by Guido de Brès in 1561 and was self-consciously patterned after the Gallican Confession of 1559. Like its predecessor, this confession was to

---

mark of the true church, an addition that is reflected in the Scots Confession and the Belgic Confession.

14. The following English translation is taken from *Ecumenical and Reformed Creeds and Confessions*, 317–36. The citations from the French are taken from Schaff, *The Evangelical Protestant Creeds*, 383–436.

articulate the main tenets of the Reformed faith and to defend the Reformed churches before the civil magistrates and others that maligned their testimony. As an "apology," or defense of the Reformed faith, it especially seeks to distinguish the teaching of the Reformed churches from that of the Anabaptists, who rejected any Christian participation in the civil order.[15] Originally presented as an apology to Philip II of Spain, the text of this confession was adopted by the Reformed churches in the Netherlands, first by the Synod of Wesel (1568) and then the Synod of Emden (1571). After a number of revisions and translations, the Synod of Dort adopted a revised text and commissioned the preparation of an official Latin translation of it.[16] Following almost exactly the structure of the Gallican Confession, the Belgic Confession takes up the doctrine of preaching in its extensive consideration of the doctrine of the church (articles 27–35).

The Belgic Confession's doctrine of preaching must be understood as an expression of its general doctrine of the church. In article 28, an important affirmation is made regarding the true church of Jesus Christ. This church or "holy congregation" (*sainte . . . congrégation*) is "an assembly of those who are saved, and outside of it there is no salvation."[17] Unlike the Gallican Confession, which qualifies this claim by noting God's freedom to save beyond the use of the ordinary means, the Belgic Confession, speaking of the church as a gathered assembly under the authority of Christ and his appointed officers, embraces

---

15. For an introduction to the Belgic Confession, see Nicolaas H. Gootjes, *The Belgic Confession: Its History and Sources* (Grand Rapids: Baker Academic, 2007); Daniel R. Hyde, *With Heart and Mouth: An Exposition of the Belgic Confession* (Grandville, MI: Reformed Fellowship, 2008); and Cornelis P. Venema, "The Belgic Confession," *Tabletalk* (April 2006): 10–13.

16. The English translations of the Belgic Confession historically in use in North America have been based upon this authorized Latin translation commissioned by the Synod of Dort. This Latin text is found in Niesel, *Bekenntnisschriften*, 119–36. However, in 1985 the Synod of the Christian Reformed Church in North America adopted a translation based upon the French text of 1619.

17. Article 28, Every One Is Bound to Join Himself to the True Church: "We believe, since this holy congregation is an assembly of those who are saved, and outside of it there is no salvation (Latin: 'atque extra eam nulla sit salus' [Niesel, *Bekenntnisschriften*, 130.41]), that no person of whatsoever state or condition he may be, ought to withdraw from it, content to be by himself; but that all men are in duty bound to join and unite themselves with it."

John Calvin's teaching that the church is the "mother of the faithful" (*mater fidelium*), the assembly within which children of God are born and nurtured in the faith. Echoing the ancient dictum of Cyprian, "outside the church there is no salvation" (*extra ecclesiam nulla salus*), and the historic conviction of the Christian church, the Belgic Confession insists that Christ is savingly present only through the ministry and communion of the church.[18]

When it comes to the particular means by which Christ saves his people through the church's ministry, however, the Belgic Confession focuses upon the ministry of the Word and sacraments. Echoing the teaching of the Gallican and Scots Confessions, the Belgic Confession distinguishes several marks of the true church, the first of which is the preaching of the "pure doctrine of the gospel."[19] In the church of Jesus Christ, Christ's authority as the "only Head of the church" comes to expression when all things are managed according to his Word and ordinances. As the Head of the church, Christ has been pleased to govern her "by that spiritual polity" taught in the Word (art. 30). Specifically, this means that there are to be three kinds of office bearers—pastors, elders, and deacons—who together comprise the spiritual council of the church and manage her affairs. By means of the ministry of these office

---

18. Calvin expresses the same conviction in his *Institutes* where he argues that the visible church is the mother of all the faithful: "But because it is now our intention to discuss the visible church, let us learn even from the simple title 'mother' how useful, indeed how necessary, it is that we should know her. For there is no other way to enter into life unless this mother conceive us in her womb, give us birth, nourish us at her breast, and lastly, unless she keep us under care and guidance. . . . Away from her bosom one cannot hope for any forgiveness of sins or any salvation" (4.1.4).

19. Article 29, The Marks of the True Church, and Wherein It Differs from the False Church: "We believe that we ought diligently and circumspectly to discern from the Word of God which is the true Church, since all sects which are in the world assume to themselves the name of the Church. . . . The marks by which the true Church is known are these: If the pure doctrine of the gospel ('la pure prédication de l'Évangile') is preached therein; if it maintains the pure administration of the sacraments as instituted by Christ; if church discipline is exercised in punishing sin; in short, if all things are managed according to the pure Word of God, all things contrary thereto rejected, and Jesus Christ acknowledged as the only Head of the Church. Hereby the true Church may certainly be known, from which no man has a right to separate himself."

bearers, provided they are lawfully called and serve in obedience to Christ, "the only universal Bishop and the only Head of the Church, true religion may be preserved, and the true doctrine everywhere propagated."[20]

According to the Belgic Confession, Christ is present as the bishop of his people through the ministry of those whom he appoints and commissions. When the minister of the Word preaches the holy gospel or administers the sacrament, he does so in the name and authority of Christ. By these means, Christ is pleased to dwell in the midst of his people, gathering them into his communion and nourishing them in the faith.

The Heidelberg Catechism of 1563[21]

With the Heidelberg Catechism of 1563, we turn to a confession that represents the development of the Reformed faith in Germany. It is called the Heidelberg Catechism because it originated in the city of Heidelberg, the capital of the German Electorate of the Palatinate. Out of a desire to promote the Reformed faith in his realm, Elector Frederick III commissioned the preparation of a catechism by Zacharius Ursinus, professor at the Heidelberg University, and Caspar Olevianus, the court preacher.[22] Following the Peace of Augsburg in 1555, the princes

---

20. Article 30, The Government of the Church and Its Offices: "We believe that this true church must be governed by that spiritual polity which our Lord has taught us in His Word; namely, that there must be ministers or pastors to preach the Word of God and to administer the sacraments; also elders and deacons, who, together with the pastors, form the council of the Church; that by these means the true religion may be preserved, and the true doctrine everywhere propagated."

21. The English translation in what follows is from *Ecumenical Creeds and Reformed Confessions*, 37–58. The German text cited is from Niesel, *Bekenntnisschriften*, 149–81.

22. I am simply representing the traditional view of the authorship of the Heidelberg Catechism. There has been considerable debate in more recent literature regarding the respective roles of Ursinus, Olevianus, Elector Frederick, and others in the authorship of the Catechism. For an introduction to this debate, see Lyle Bierma, "Olevianus and the Authorship of the Heidelberg Catechism: Another Look," *The Sixteenth Century Journal* 13, no. 4 (1982): 17–27; Lyle Bierma, "*Vester Grundt* and the Origins of the Heidelberg Catechism," chapter 15 of *Later Calvinism, International Perspectives*, ed. W. Fred Graham (Kirksville, MO: Sixteenth Century Journal Publishers, 1994), 289–309; and Fred H. Klooster, "The Priority of Ursinus in the Composition of the Heidelberg Catechism," in *Controversy and Conciliation: The Reformation and the Palatinate, 1559–1583*, ed. Kidran Y. Hadidian (Allison Park, PA: Pickwick Publications, 1986), 73–100.

of Germany who adhered to the Augsburg Confession were given imperial protection. Though Frederick III agreed with the altered Augsburg Confession, including its statement on the Lord's Supper, he wished to prod the churches of the Palatinate into a more fully Reformed position. The Heidelberg Catechism was the instrument by which he hoped to achieve this end. Little could Frederick III have realized that this catechism, augmented with a question and answer on the Lord's Supper that condemned the doctrine of the Mass as set forth at the Council of Trent, would become one of the most endearing and widely embraced confessions of the Reformation. Soon after it was first printed, it was translated into a variety of languages and was subsequently adopted by the Synod of Dort as one of the three confessional standards of the churches in the Netherlands.

The structure and distinctive content of the Heidelberg Catechism are remarkable. The Catechism is divided into three major divisions: the first deals with human sin and misery, the second with redemption in Christ, and the third with the Christian life of gratitude.[23] Some doctrines receive only minimal expression in the Catechism, particularly Scripture and election. Others, such as the doctrine of the sacraments and the Lord's Supper, receive sustained consideration. Following the ancient pattern of Christian catechesis, the Catechism includes the Apostles' Creed in the section on redemption and the Ten Commandments and the Lord's Prayer in the section on the Christian life of gratitude. Unique features of the Reformed tradition, in distinction from the Lutheran, include the treatment of the "communion of the attributes" of Christ's divine and human natures and the use of the Ten Commandments in the context of the Christian life.

The Heidelberg Catechism's structure is particularly significant when it comes to its consideration of preaching as the means of grace. After having established in the first main section that all human beings are lost in Adam, the second section deals extensively with the person and work of Christ as mediator. Christ is the only mediator through whom sinners can

---

23. The three divisions of the Catechism may reflect the influence of Melancthon's tripartite exposition of the gospel: law, gospel, and the Christian life. It certainly reflects the pattern of the apostle Paul's letter to the Romans.

be restored to communion and life in fellowship with the triune God. Without Christ's atoning work on their behalf, believers could not escape God's judgment against them on account of their sins or enjoy renewed favor with him. In the context of its exposition of Christ's work as mediator, the Catechism asserts a crucial point regarding the manner in which believers become partakers of Christ and his saving work. In answer to the question "Are all men, then, saved by Christ as they perished in Adam?" the Catechism declares, "No; but only those who by a true faith are ingrafted into Him and receive all His benefits" (Q&A 20). Only through union or fellowship with Christ can the fallen sons and daughters of Adam be restored to favor with God, and that union is effected by means of a true faith which the Holy Spirit "works in my heart by the gospel."[24]

If the only way sinners can be restored to favor with God is through faith in Jesus Christ, then this becomes the critical question: How is faith produced? In what way does the Holy Spirit, on behalf of Christ, work faith in our hearts so that we become members of Christ?

The Catechism answers this question with its doctrine of the church and the means of grace. Within the setting of its exposition of the third article of the Apostles' Creed, dealing with the Holy Spirit and the church, the Catechism maintains that salvation is mediated through the Spirit's working by means of the Word and sacraments. The Spirit of Christ works within and through the holy catholic church, gathering, defending, and preserving "a church chosen to everlasting life."[25] More specifically, the Spirit works by means of the Word of Christ. Christ gathers his church "by His Spirit and Word."[26] Thus,

---

24. Q&A 21: ". . . welches der heilige Geist durch's Evangelium in mir wirket. . ." Niesel, *Bekenntnisschriften*, 154.10–111.

25. Berkhof, *Systematic Theology*, 611–12, makes in this connection an important observation: "The Reformed indeed regarded the Word of God as always powerful, either as a savour of life unto life or as a savour of death unto death, but maintained that it becomes efficacious in leading to faith and conversion only by an accompanying operation of the Holy Spirit in the hearts of sinners. They refused to consider this efficaciousness as an impersonal power resident in the Word."

26. Q&A 54: "What do you believe concerning the holy catholic church? That the Son of God, out of the whole human race, from the beginning to the end of the world, gathers, defends, and preserves for Himself, by His Spirit and Word, in

_hrist's church-gathering work occurs neither by the Spirit apart from the Word nor the Word apart from the Spirit. Only by the Spirit working with the Word does Christ communicate himself and his saving work to those who belong to him.

Like a series of concentric circles, the order of questions and answers in the Catechism moves from asserting the necessity of faith to partake of Christ and his benefits, to the work of the Spirit through the church, to the specific means of grace. Therefore, when question 65 asks, "Since, then, we are made partakers of Christ and all His benefits by faith only, whence comes this faith?" we are at a decisive point in the Catechism's progression. This question really wants to focus upon the central and primary means, the ordinary and Christ-ordained method, by which the Spirit is pleased to work faith in our hearts. To this question, the Catechism responds, "From the Holy Spirit, who works it in our hearts by the preaching of the holy gospel, and confirms it by the use of the holy sacraments."[27] Although in subsequent questions the Catechism concentrates at length upon the doctrine of the sacraments, it is clear from this answer that the preaching of the gospel is preeminent. The sacraments, though an indispensable accompaniment of the preaching, only "confirm" faith, while the preaching of the gospel "works" faith. Without the preaching of the Word, the sacraments would be empty. They would have nothing to signify or seal. When they accompany the Word preached, however, they are gracious and visible tokens of God's grace toward us in Christ.

The one additional prominent mention of preaching in the Heidelberg Catechism occurs in connection with the doctrine of the keys of the kingdom. At the conclusion of an extensive consideration of the sacraments generally, and the Lord's Supper particularly, the Catechism raises the subject of the keys

---

the unity of the true faith, a Church chosen to everlasting life ('eine auserwählte Gemeine zum ewige Leben' [Niesel, *Bekenntnisschriften,* 162.3]), and that I am, and forever shall remain, a living member thereof."

27. Q&A 65: "Since, then, we are made partakers of Christ and all His benefits by faith only, whence comes this faith? From the Holy Spirit, who works it in our hearts by the preaching of the holy gospel and confirms it by the use of the sacraments ('wirket . . . durch die Predigt des heiligen Evangeliums, und bestätigt ihn durch den Brauch der heiligen Sacramente' [Niesel, *Bekenntnisschriften,* 164.25–27])."

of the kingdom in the context of the supervision of the Lord's Table. Because the church is obligated to bar from the Table those who "by their confession and life, show themselves to be unbelieving and ungodly," the church must exercise the keys of the kingdom by excluding such persons (Q&A 82). These keys are the preaching of the holy gospel and church discipline or excommunication.[28]

The definition the Catechism provides of preaching as the primary exercise of the keys of the kingdom is instructive.[29] God's judgment will ultimately be executed "according to the witness of this gospel." When believers embrace the gospel promise by a true faith, the ministry of the Word has the power to declare them forgiven of God for the sake of Christ's merits. This represents a legitimate administration of the holy gospel, an exercise of the power and authority of Christ through the official ministry of the gospel by his ministers. In such gospel preaching, Christ's voice resounds, and his authority is exercised. When, by contrast, unbelievers despise the gospel promise and refuse to turn from their sin in repentance, the ministry of the Word has the power to declare them to remain under the wrath and condemnation of God. Such a declaration does not merely represent the opinion or sentiment of the minister of the Word. Rather, it represents the voice and authority of Christ as administered through the preaching of the holy gospel.

The Second Helvetic Confession of 1566[30]

The Second Helvetic Confession of 1566 is not as well known as the Belgic Confession or the Heidelberg Catechism. It is

---

28. Q&A 83: "What are the keys of the kingdom? The preaching of the holy gospel, and church discipline or excommunication out of the Christian Church. By these two the kingdom of heaven is opened to believers and shut against unbelievers."

29. Q&A 84: "How is the kingdom of heaven opened and shut by the preaching of the holy gospel? By proclaiming and openly witnessing, according to the command of Christ, to believers, one and all, that, whenever they receive the promise of the gospel by a true faith, all their sins are forgiven them of God for the sake of Christ's merits; and on the contrary, by proclaiming and witnessing to all unbelievers and such as do not sincerely repent that the wrath of God and eternal condemnation abide on them so long as they are not converted. According to this witness of the gospel God will judge, both in this life and in that which is to come."

30. The English translation of the Second Helvetic Confession in what follows

called the Second Helvetic Confession because it followed and ultimately displaced the First Helvetic Confession of 1536 written by the Swiss Reformer Ulrich Zwingli. One of the most widely used and influential confessions of the Reformed churches, the Second Helvetic Confession was originally written by Zwingli's successor, Heinrich Bullinger, as a confession of his personal faith. However, from the beginning this confession was more than a private statement or testimony.[31] Not only was this confession to become the primary statement of faith of the Reformed churches in Switzerland, but it also was either adopted or approved by many other Reformed churches of the Continent and the British Isles. It shares with the Heidelberg Catechism, then, something of the distinction of being among the more catholic of the Reformed confessions.

Unlike the confessions we have considered thus far, the Second Helvetic Confession tends to be more expansive in its statement of the faith, displaying a more theological and polemical character than earlier statements.[32] This is immediately evident in the chapters devoted to the sacraments, where many of the Reformation debates regarding this subject are reflected and carefully addressed.

In the first chapter of the Second Helvetic Confession, "Of the Holy Scripture Being the True Word of God," the doctrine of preaching is set forth in the context of the doctrine of Scripture.[33] After having affirmed that Scripture is the Word of

is from *The Book of Confessions*, 5.001–5.260. The Latin text is found in Niesel, *Bekenntnisschriften*, 219–75.

31. For a defense of the view that Bullinger intended this confession to be a statement not only of his personal faith but of the "catholic" faith of the Reformed church, see Edward A. Dowey, "Heinrich Bullinger's Theology: Thematic, Comprehensive, Schematic," in *Calvin Studies V: Presented at a Colloquium on Calvin Studies at Davidson College and Davidson College Presbyterian Church*, ed. John H. Leith, January 19–20, 1990, 56.

32. See Schaff, *The Evangelical Protestant Creeds*, 233, who notes that the Second Helvetic Confession is "rather a theological treatise than a popular creed." As noted earlier, Gassmann divides the history of the Reformed confessions into five distinct periods. According to Gassmann, the Second Helvetic Confession falls somewhere between the last two periods and exhibits the tendency toward more elaborate and precise expression of thought, a tendency evident also in the development of the Reformed theological tradition.

33. Chapter 1, Of the Holy Scripture Being the True Word of God, The Preaching of the Word of God Is the Word of God (Praedicatio Verbi est Verbum

God, sufficient to teach fully all godliness, the confession makes a strong statement in a marginal heading: "The Preaching of the Word of God is the Word of God." This statement and its confessional elaboration clearly are intended to parallel the confession regarding Scripture. Just as Scripture *is* the true Word of God, so preaching, when it faithfully and expounds the scriptural text, *is* the true Word of God. Commenting on this statement, Edward A. Dowey Jr. writes:

> The dramatic and widely quoted marginal heading, "The Preaching of the Word of God is God's Word" (223.21), reflects an authentic lifelong preoccupation of Bullinger with the *viva vox* [living voice], whether the *viva vox Domini* [living voice of the Lord] to patriarchs, prophets, and apostles (*Decades* I.i), or the oral and audible passing along "as if by hand" of the gospel from Adam to Moses, or the living preaching which even "today" is the usual means of announcing the Gospel.[34]

When the minister of the Word of God explains and applies the biblical text, God himself speaks in a living voice to the congregation of Jesus Christ. God himself is heard in the preached Word.

The heading in the Second Helvetic Confession requires careful consideration. To grasp fully what the statement means by identifying preaching with the Word of God, we must note two significant qualifications.

First, though the confession clearly wants to parallel the affirmations that Scripture and preaching are the Word of God, the correspondence is not an unqualified identification of the two. The preaching of the Word of God *is* the Word of God *insofar as it faithfully expounds and applies the scriptural*

Dei [Niesel, *Bekenntnisschriften*, 223.21]): "Wherefore when this Word of God is now preached in the church by preachers lawfully called, we believe that the very Word of God is proclaimed, and received by the faithful; and that neither any other Word of God is to be invented nor is to be expected from heaven: and that now the Word itself which is preached is to be regarded, not the minister that preaches; for even if he be evil and a sinner, nevertheless the Word of God remains still true and good."

34. Edward A. Dowey Jr., "The Word of God as Scripture and Preaching," in *Later Calvinism: International Perspectives*, ed. W. Fred Graham (Kirksville, MO: Sixteenth Century Publishers, 1994), 9.

Word. Unlike the scriptural Word, which is given by inspiration and constitutes a *normative* and sufficient revelation from God, the preaching of the Word is *subnormative,* that is, subject to the norm and text of Scripture. Only those preachers who have been "lawfully called" and whose preaching does not contain any inventions that go beyond or are contrary to the Word of God deserve to be heard as those who proclaim the very Word of God. This does not mean that the efficacy or truthfulness of the preached Word depends upon the person of the preacher.[35] So long as the preaching of the Word faithfully echoes the teaching of Scripture, it deserves to be received as the very Word of God. Therefore, when the Second Helvetic Confession boldly asserts that the preaching of the Word of God is the Word of God, it does not mean to assert that the preaching of the Word of God is not subject to the supreme rule of faith, the Word of God in Scripture, or that the preacher is not subject to the regulation and governance of the church in his preaching office. The preaching of the Word of God is instrumental and reflexive when contrasted with the original and primary authority of Scripture.

Accordingly, the Second Helvetic Confession's affirmation that the preaching of the Word of God is the Word of God needs to be distinguished from Karl Barth's well-known understanding of the threefold form of the Word of God (as preached, as written, and as revealed).[36] In Barth's understanding, only Jesus

---

35. Rohls, *Reformed Confessions*, 178–79: "On the basis of Luke 10:16: 'Whoever listens to you listens to me,' Bullinger can even dare to propound the thesis that 'the preaching of the Word of God is the Word of God' (ibid.). However, this identification, carried out from the standpoint of faith, is not to be understood in such a way that preaching would be simply identical with the word of God. Instead, the purpose of making this identification as an interpretation of Luke 10:16 is to assert, in opposition to a Donatistic understanding of the office of ministry, that the validity of the proclamation of the word is independent of the subjective character of the person occupying the ministerial office. The validity of the proclamation of the word depends solely on its content: that is, it depends on whether or not the sermon does in fact give expression to God's word."

36. Barth discusses the threefold form of the Word of God in volume 1, part 1 of his *Church Dogmatics: The Doctrine of the Word of God* (Edinburgh: T. & T. Clark, 1936), 98–140. The following statement regarding preaching and Scripture is typical of his view: "To make matters clearer, note what was just called the phenomenal similarity between Church proclamation and the second element contrasted with it in the Church, the canon of Holy Scripture. It consists in the

Christ, as the Word become flesh, is in the strictest sense to be identified as the very Word of God. Both preaching and Scripture are only derivatively and instrumentally the Word of God. They become the Word of God when the Spirit is pleased to use them in their unique and privileged witness to Jesus Christ. In this construction, preaching and Scripture are equivalent forms of the Word of God. However, the Scriptures may not be directly identified as God's Word by virtue of the unique, divine inspiration of the Holy Spirit. The preaching of the Word and the inscripturation of the Word function as (become) the Word of God only in the here and now, as the Spirit sovereignly employs them as instruments to make Christ known to his people. The inspiration of Scripture and the illumination of the mind of the believer become virtual synonyms for the sovereign and free work of the Spirit that always occurs in the event of revelation. This understanding differs in important respects from the Reformed confessions, which identify Scripture as the inspired, true Word of God and speak of preaching as a form of the Word of God only so far as it faithfully administers and applies the prior and normative scriptural Word.

Second, when accompanied by the inward illumination of the Holy Spirit, the preaching of the Word of God is the ordinary means Christ is pleased to use to work faith in the hearts of his people.[37] Here too, the Second Helvetic Confession clearly compares the inward illumination of the Spirit in the believer's

---

fact that obviously even in Holy Scripture we are dealing with Scripture not in a primary but in a secondary sense: for it itself is the deposit of proclamation made in the past by the mouth of man. But even in its form as Scripture it claims to be not so much an historical monument as rather a Church document, proclamation in writing. Thus primarily *both entities stand side by side within one genus: there Scripture as the beginning, here preaching to be carried out today, as the continuation of one and the same event*; Jeremiah and Paul at the beginning, the preacher of the Gospel to-day at the end of one and same series" (114, emphasis added).

37. Chapter 1, Inward Illumination Does Not Eliminate External Preaching: "For he that illuminates inwardly by giving men the Holy Spirit, the same one, by way of commandment, said unto his disciples, 'Go into all the world, and preach the Gospel to the whole creation' (Mark 16:15). . . . At the same time we recognize that God can illuminate whom and when he will, even without the external ministry, for that is in his power; but we speak of the usual way of instructing men, delivered unto us from God, both by commandment and examples."

reception of the written and preached Word of God.[38] The external preaching, or the external ministry, is indispensable, to be sure. The Spirit does not ordinarily speak apart from the Word. However, only through the powerful working of the Spirit together *with* the Word, illuminating the heart and mind of the Word's recipient, does the Word effectively produce a true and living faith. There is, in this respect, a sense in which the preaching of the Word of God becomes the Word of God in the believer's hearing, when the Spirit unstops the heart and grants a ready reception to the Word.[39] Only as the external ministry is accompanied by the inward illumination of the Spirit does the believer recognize it to be the true Word of God. However, though God is free to "illuminate whom and when he will, even without the external ministry," in the ordinary exercise of his power, he has bound himself to the preaching ministry as the effective instrument for producing and strengthening faith.

Though we must beware of simply identifying preaching with the Word of God for the reasons mentioned, preaching remains the living voice of Christ in the church, having the

---

38. Dowey, "Word of God as Scripture and Preaching," 11, provides a helpful summary of this kind of formulation in the theology of the Reformers: "For Bullinger and the Second Helvetic Confession, as for Calvin and most Reformed Confessions, there is a twofold or two-level approach of the Spirit consisting of 'outer' words (written or spoken) and 'inner' *illuminatio, inspiratio,* or *persuasio.* The latter are elements of saving faith, of regeneration (242.47ff.), of the distinction between letter and spirit (241.8)—in short, of the redemptive work of the Holy Spirit. . . . The 'outer' and 'inner' modes through which the Spirit works are inseparably bound together, barring only the freedom of God to 'illuminate whom and when he will' (223.47). Together they constitute the *usitata ratio* (223.49), the ordinary or normal way by which the Word comes to men."

39. I am aware of the danger of subjectivism in this language. The Word of God, written or spoken, is *objectively* the very Word of God, whether it is subjectively embraced or refused by those to whom it comes. The Second Helvetic Confession even openly affirms this in the marginal statement, "Inward Illumination Does Not Eliminate External Preaching" ('Interior illuminatio non tollit externam praedicationem' [Niesel, *Bekenntnisschriften,* 223.39–40]). However, because the preaching of the Word of God finds its source and norm in the scriptural Word, there is an important sense in which that preaching only "becomes" the Word of God for us when it is received by faith as the Spirit inwardly illumines the heart. The theological expression of this distinction uses the language of "inspiration," the punctiliar (nonrepeated) work of the Spirit in the giving of scriptural revelation, on the one hand, and "illumination," the continuing work of the Spirit in the reception of the Word, on the other.

power to open and shut the door of entrance into the kingdom of God. Chapter 14 of the Second Helvetic Confession offers a striking declaration regarding the power of preaching as an administration of the keys of the kingdom.[40] When the ministers of Christ faithfully and lawfully preach the holy gospel, the ministry of reconciliation takes place. As Christ's ambassadors, the ministers of the Word are authorized to "persuade to believe and repent" and thus "reconcile men to God" (chap. 14). In the administration of the gospel of Christ, such ministers have the authority to open the door of the kingdom of heaven and declare the remission of sins to those who believe and repent.[41] Conversely, they have the authority in Christ's name to declare the door of entrance closed to those who remain unbelieving and impenitent. In this chapter, the statement regarding "how ministers absolve" sins is especially significant. Though it criticizes the practice of the Roman Catholic Church, particularly the notion that the effectiveness of the absolution pronounced depends upon its being "murmured in the ear" or "murmured singly over someone's head," it endorses a biblical practice of absolution. The minister of the Word does legitimately have the authority, as a representative and instrument of Christ in the administration of the gospel, to proclaim diligently the absolution of sins and to promise an individual believer "that

---

40. Chapter 14, Of Repentance and the Conversion of Man, Of the Keys of the Kingdom of Heaven: "Concerning the keys of the Kingdom of Heaven which the Lord gave to the apostles, many babble many astonishing things, and out of them forge swords, spears, scepters and crowns, and complete power over the greatest kingdoms, indeed, over souls and bodies. Judging simply according to the Word of the Lord, we say that all properly called ministers possess and exercise the keys or the use of them when they proclaim the Gospel; that is, when they teach, exhort, comfort, rebuke, and keep in discipline the people committed to their trust. Opening and Shutting (the Kingdom). For in this way they open the Kingdom of Heaven to the obedient and shut it to the disobedient."

41. Chapter 14, How Ministers Absolve: "Ministers, therefore, rightly and effectually absolve when they preach the Gospel of Christ and thereby the remission of sins, which is promised to the one who believes, just as each one is baptized, and when they testify that it pertains to each one peculiarly. Neither do we think that this absolution becomes more effectual by being murmured in the ear of someone or by being murmured singly over someone's head. We are nevertheless of the opinion that the remission of sins in the blood of Christ is to be diligently proclaimed, and that each one is to be admonished that the forgiveness of sins pertains to him."

the forgiveness of sins pertains to him."[42] This authority is strictly ministerial and does not include the unbiblical and oppressive features of the traditional Roman Catholic doctrine of absolution. The minister is authorized only to announce the assurance of the pardon of sins to those who embrace the gospel promise in the way of faith. But the minister has no power to require the Roman Catholic practice of the confessional or to stipulate works of satisfaction for the remission of the temporal penalty of so-called venial sins.

Summary

Though our survey of the principal Reformed confessions' doctrine of preaching will be completed in the following chapter, these earliest classical symbols of the Reformed churches uniformly affirm that the preaching of the gospel is the primary means by which Christ gathers, nourishes, and strengthens his church in the Christian faith. Unlike the sacramentalism of the medieval Roman Catholic Church, which elevated the seven sacraments above the proclamation and teaching of the gospel Word, the evangelical and Reformed churches emphasized preaching as the most basic instrument that Christ has appointed to communicate the saving benefits of his work as mediator. In the next chapter, we will consider several more confessions that were produced in the period of the consolidation of Reformed orthodoxy.

---

42. I call attention to this exposition of the role of the ministry in the pardon of sins not only because it properly reflects the classic Reformed view of preaching but also because it is liable to make many, even confessionally Reformed Christians, uncomfortable today. Ministers of the Word are authorized, as instruments through whom Christ promises the forgiveness of sins to those who believe and repent, to pronounce Christ's absolution or pardon of sins. For a recent treatment of the historic Reformed view of absolution, see Daniel R. Hyde, "Lost Keys: The Absolution in Reformed Liturgy," *Calvin Theological Journal* 46, no. 1 (2011): 140–66.

Chapter 3

Faith Comes by Hearing: Preaching in the Reformed Confessions (2)

The Reformed confessions discussed in the previous chapter all stem from the early, foundational period of the Protestant Reformation in the sixteenth century. These confessions consistently testify that the preaching of the gospel Word is a preeminent mark of the true church of Jesus Christ and the appointed means whereby Christ gathers and nourishes believers in fellowship with himself. Where the Word of Christ is faithfully proclaimed and ministered, there, you may be sure, Christ is present, calling his people to faith and equipping them for their faith and practice as citizens of his kingdom. All the Reformed confessions we have considered concur with John Calvin's striking expression that the "saving doctrine of Christ is the soul of the church."[1] Without the living preaching of the Word of God, through which Christ communes with his people and gives himself to them, the church would be utterly lifeless, however active and busy it might appear.

In this chapter, we will turn to the principal confessions that the Reformed churches in the early and middle part of the seventeenth century adopted. Compared to the earlier confessions of the sixteenth century, these symbols represent the mature expression of the faith of the Reformed churches. Like their predecessors, they clearly and uniformly express the conviction that the proclamation of the gospel is the church's central task and the means by which Christ communicates himself to his people.

---

1. Calvin, *Institutes*, 4. 12.1.

The Canons of Dort of 1618–1619[2]

With the Canons of Dort of 1618–1619, we enter upon a different period in the history of the Reformation confessions. To this point, we have considered confessional statements that express the consensus of the Reformed churches at the zenith of the Reformation and represent the formative summary of the distinctive features of the Reformed faith at its height in the sixteenth century. With the Canons of Dort, however, we are considering an early seventeenth-century confession that was written at a time not so much of *consolidation* among the Reformed churches as of *adjudication* of post-Reformation doctrinal disputes that had begun to surface among them.

The Canons of Dort are the product of a genuinely international synod of the Reformed churches convened at Dordrecht, the Netherlands, in 1618. The synod was called by the States General of the Netherlands to adjudicate the conflict raging within the Reformed churches of the Netherlands over the doctrine of election and reprobation. The two parties to this dispute were the orthodox Calvinists and the Arminians, or Remonstrants.[3] In addition to the delegates from the Dutch churches, twenty-six delegates from eight foreign countries were present for the deliberations. Rather than representing a complete or comprehensive statement of the Reformed faith, the Canons have instead the character of a judgment rendered regarding the controversy over the doctrine of election as it was expounded in article 16 of the Belgic Confession. Titled "The Decision of the Synod of Dort on the Five Main Points of Doctrine in Dispute in the Netherlands," the Canons consist of a series of doctrinal affirmations and rejections of errors touching the five disputed points of doctrine between the orthodox Calvinists and the

---

2. The English translation of the Canons of Dort was adopted by the Synod of the Christian Reformed Church in 1986 and is included in *Ecumenical Creeds and Reformed Confessions,* 59–82. The Latin text is found in Schaff, *The Evangelical Protestant Creeds,* vol. 3 of *The Creeds of Christendom,* 550–79.

3. For a brief account of this history, see Louis Praamsma, "The Background of the Arminian Controversy (1586–1618)," in *Crisis in the Reformed Churches: Essays in Commemoration of the Great Synod of Dort, 1618–1619,* ed. Peter Y. De Jong (Grandville, MI: Reformed Fellowship, Inc., 1968), 22–38; and Cornelis P. Venema, *But for the Grace of God,* 2nd ed. (Grandville, MI: Reformed Fellowship, Inc., 2011), 10–18.

Arminians. The selection and sequence of these points follow the order adopted by the Arminian party in its presentation of its statement of faith in five points as the Remonstrance of 1610.

Because the Canons of Dort address only one important doctrinal dispute, they do not deal with the doctrine of preaching as specifically as some confessions we considered in the last chapter. However, the doctrine of preaching set forth in the Canons is consistent with what we previously have seen. Furthermore, due to this confession's peculiar focus on the doctrine of sovereign election, it is all the more significant that it reiterates the consensus of the earlier Reformed confessions on the salvation of God's elect being effected ordinarily and properly through the ministry of the Word in preaching.

The Canons primarily expound on the doctrine of preaching in the third and fourth main points ("Human Corruption, Conversion to God, and the Way It Occurs"). Already in the first and second main points of doctrine, however, two aspects about preaching are emphasized: its indispensability as the means of drawing believers into the fellowship of Christ; and the obligation to preach the gospel to all nations and people without exception.

In the first main point, which examines the doctrine of divine election and reprobation, the subject of the indispensability of preaching comes up almost immediately. Since all people are sinners in Adam and liable to God's judgment, and since God has sent his only begotten Son into the world so that those who believe in him might have eternal life, the preaching of the gospel of his Son in which all are called to faith is most necessary. Quoting Romans 10:14–15, the Canons give preeminence to preaching as the appointed means by which all people have opportunity to hear the gospel and be called to repentance and faith.[4] The doctrine of unconditional election affirms that those who are saved belong to the number of those whom God chose

---

4. I/3: "In order that people may be brought to faith, God mercifully sends proclaimers of this very joyful message to the people he wishes and at the time he wishes. By this ministry people are called to repentance and faith in Christ crucified. For how shall they believe in him of whom they have not heard? And how shall they hear without someone preaching? And how shall they preach unless they have been sent? (Rom. 10:14–15)."

in Christ unto salvation before the foundation of the world (Canons of Dort, I/7).

The means to further this electing purpose are the working of the Spirit and the hearing of the Word, bestowing true faith in Christ upon all the elect of God. In the article that defines God's purpose of election, we read that God "decided to give the chosen ones to Christ to be saved, and to call and draw them effectively into Christ's fellowship *through his Word and Spirit*" (Canons of Dort, I/7, emphasis added).

A second and more controversial aspect of the doctrine of preaching in the Canons is the insistence upon the preaching of the gospel to all nations and peoples without exception. This aspect finds expression within the second main point of doctrine, which deals with the extent or design of Christ's work of atonement. Christ's atoning work is definite and particular; it was accomplished for the purpose of providing satisfaction for God's elect. However, this does not place any limitation on the value and worth of Christ's death. Christ's death is "of infinite value and worth, more than sufficient to atone for the sins of the whole world." Nor does it restrict in any way the mandate to preach the gospel to all. The promise of the gospel that whoever believes in Christ shall not perish but have eternal life, "together with the command to repent and believe, ought to be announced and declared without differentiation or discrimination to all nations and peoples, to whom God in his good pleasure sends the gospel."[5] In the third main point of doctrine, this insistence upon the universal preaching of the gospel is further explained as a serious and genuine calling. Often called the "well-meant offer" of the gospel, this call is extended through the preaching of the gospel:

> Nevertheless, all who are called through the gospel are called seriously. For seriously and most genuinely God makes known in his Word what is pleasing to him (*quid sibi gratum sit*): that those who are called should come to him.

---

5. II/5: "Moreover, it is the promise of the gospel that whoever believes in Christ crucified shall not perish but have eternal life. This promise, together with the command to repent and believe, ought to be announced and declared without differentiation and discrimination to all nations and people, to whom God in his good pleasure sends the gospel."

Seriously he also promises rest for their souls and eternal life to all who come to him and believe.[6]

The most extensive statement of the Canons regarding the doctrine of preaching is found in the third and fourth main points of doctrine, which explain the manner in which sinful people are brought to true conversion. Having set forth the doctrines of unconditional election and definite (limited) atonement, the focus in this part of the Canons is upon the means God is pleased to use in the actual salvation of his people. It is not enough to speak of God's electing purpose or of the provision of atonement

---

6. In the Latin the article reads: "Quotquot autem per Evangelium vocantur, serio vocantur. Serio enim et verissime ostendit Deus verbo suo, quid sibi gratum sit, nimi rum, ut vocati ad se veniant. Serio etiam omnibus ad se venientibus et credentibus requiem animarum, et vitam aeternam promittit." Schaff, *Creeds of Christendom,* 3:565–6. Though this is not the place to address the disputed subject of the so-called well-meant offer of the gospel, this article clearly suggests the doctrine. If God declares in the Word what *pleases* him, and if he seriously calls all through the Word to believe and repent, then it seems to follow that he is pleased to save those whom he calls. Those who reject the well-meant offer are not only uncomfortable with the language of this article but also unwilling to distinguish between God's *sovereign intention to save the elect only* and his *desire that all should be saved.* The insistence that the latter distinction amounts to a logical contradiction is born from a failure to distinguish, to borrow terms from Dabney (see below), between God's "executive volition" to save the elect only and his "propension" to show mercy to all. What to our understanding may appear to be a tension or contradiction is only due to a limited comprehension of the things of God. The supposed contradiction between God's sovereign decree of election and the well-meant offer of the gospel is what Cornelius Van Til properly termed an "apparent contradiction," something that is mysterious to us but *known by God to be fully harmonious and consistent.* For representative treatments of this issue, see Robert Lewis Dabney, "God's Indiscriminate Proposals of Mercy, as Related to His Power, Wisdom, and Sincerity," in *Discussions of Robert Lewis Dabney,* vol. 1 (1891; repr., Carlisle, PA: Banner of Truth, 1982); John Murray, "The Free Offer of the Gospel," in *Collected Writings of John Murray: Studies in Theology* (Carlisle, PA: Banner of Truth, 1982), 4:113–32; Iain H. Murray, *Spurgeon v. Hyper-Calvinism: The Battle for Gospel Preaching* (Carlisle, PA: Banner of Truth, 1995); A. C. De Jong, *The Well-Meant Gospel Offer: The Views of H. Hoeksema and K. Schilder* (Franeker: T. Wever, 1954); and David J. Engelsma, *Hyper-Calvinism and the Call of the Gospel,* rev. ed. (Grand Rapids: Reformed Free Publishing, 1994). The studies of Iain Murray and De Jong are historical in nature, though they join Dabney and John Murray in defending a doctrine of the well-meant offer. Engelsma represents the position of the Protestant Reformed Churches: though there is a universal call extended through the gospel to all, this call does not express any favorable disposition, good pleasure, or desire on God's part that all should believe and repent and so be saved.

through the work of Christ. It is also necessary to speak of the way in which believers are united to Christ and become his beneficiaries. To this question, the Canons, following the precedent of the confessions previously considered, answer by insisting that these means include principally the preaching of the gospel. Neither the "light of nature" nor "the law" is able to bestow salvation. Only through the "ministry of reconciliation" has it "pleased God [to] save sinners."[7]

In language reminiscent of the Second Helvetic Confession, the Canons of Dort distinguish, but do not separate, between the proclamation of the gospel "outwardly" and the Holy Spirit's inward enlightening of the mind so that believers "may rightly understand and discern the things of the Spirit of God."[8] The Spirit's work in regeneration is an "entirely supernatural work," as real and as incomprehensible as creation or the raising of the dead (Canons of Dort, III/IV.12). But it is nonetheless a work that the Holy Spirit is pleased to accomplish by the means of "the holy admonitions of the gospel, under the administration of the Word."[9] Thus, what God has joined together—the regeneration of his chosen people and the use of the ordinary

---

7.   III/IV.6: "What, therefore, neither the light of nature nor the law can do, God accomplishes by the power of the Holy Spirit, through the Word or the ministry of reconciliation. This is the gospel about the Messiah, through which it has pleased God to save believers, in both the Old and the New Testament."

8.   III/IV.11: "Moreover, when God carries out this good pleasure in his chosen ones, or works true conversion in them, he not only sees to it that the gospel is proclaimed to them outwardly, and enlightens their minds powerfully by the Holy Spirit so that they may rightly understand and discern the things of the Spirit of God, but, by the effective operation of the same regenerating Spirit, he also penetrates into the inmost being of man, opens the closed heart, softens the hard heart, and circumcises the heart that is uncircumcised. He infuses new qualities into the will, making the dead will alive, the evil one good, the unwilling one willing, and the stubborn one compliant; he activates and strengthens the will so that, like a good tree, it may be enabled to produce the fruits of good deeds."

9.   III/IV.17: "Just as the almighty work of God by which he brings forth and sustains our natural life does not rule out but requires the use of means, by which God, according to his infinite wisdom and goodness, has wished to exercise his power, so also the aforementioned supernatural work of God by which he regenerates us in no way rules out or cancels the use of the gospel, which God in his great wisdom has appointed to be the seed of regeneration and the food of the soul. . . . So even today it is out of the question that the teachers or those taught in the church should presume to test God by separating what he in his good pleasure has wished to closely join together."

means of preaching—may not be separated in the practice of the church.[10] Similarly, the perseverance of the saints whom God sovereignly and graciously saves is accomplished "by the hearing and reading of the gospel, by meditation on it, by its exhortations, threats, and promises, and also by the use of the sacraments" (Canons of Dort, V.14).

The Canons of Dort, therefore, clearly teach that the salvation of God's elect people is accomplished by those means he is pleased to use, namely, by the Spirit working *with* and through the preaching of the holy gospel, to which the sacraments are appended.[11] Contrary to the prejudice that the Canons so

---

10. In the history of Reformed theology, there has been a great deal of discussion whether regeneration is "immediate" or "mediate." Advocates of a doctrine of immediate regeneration maintain that the *Spirit alone is the direct and immediate Author of regeneration;* to ascribe the working of regeneration to the instrumentality of the Word would be, in this view of things, to transfer the authorship of salvation from God to a creaturely medium. On the other hand, advocates of a doctrine of mediate regeneration have maintained that the Spirit of Christ is *ordinarily pleased to effect regeneration by the use of the means of grace.* Because the Spirit grants new life in Christ to the believer through the instrumentality of the Word, regeneration is mediated through the Word. Though some of the debates regarding this subject have been rather arcane and unduly complicated, a genuine issue is at stake in this discussion. Advocates of immediate regeneration have been properly concerned to insist that the Spirit is the author of regeneration, not the Word as such. The Word of God preached does not by itself possess an inherent power that can grant new life to otherwise dead sinners. Only God by his Spirit has the power to grant the new birth. However, once this point has been granted, it has to be acknowledged that the Reformed confessions typically insist that the Spirit ordinarily grants that new birth through the use of the means of grace. Consequently, though it is proper to be clear about *who* authors the new birth, it is just as proper to be clear about *how* (by what means) that new birth is authored. As always, the Reformed insist upon a *distinction, without separation,* between the Spirit and the Word of Christ. For a discussion of the subject of immediate and mediate regeneration, see *Saved by Grace,* by Herman Bavinck, ed. J. Mark Beach, trans. Nelson D. Kloosterman (Grand Rapids: Reformation Heritage Books, 2008); Berkhof, *Systematic Theology,* 474–5; Abraham Kuyper, *The Work of the Holy Spirit,* trans. Henri De Vries (1900; repr., Grand Rapids: Eerdmans, 1979), 293–342; Robert L. Reymond, *A New Systematic Theology of the Christian Faith* (Nashville: Thomas Nelson, 1998), 712ff. In this list of authors, Kuyper argues most vigorously for the idea of an immediate regenerative work of the Holy Spirit. However, Kuyper also acknowledges that the Spirit's work of regeneration is ordinarily accomplished by means of the Word and sacraments.

11. I deliberately use the preposition *with* here because it preserves against the idea that the Word alone is sufficient to create faith and conversion in the believer. Traditionally, Reformed theologians prefer to speak of the Spirit working "with" the Word (*cum verbo*) rather than, as in orthodox Lutheran teaching, of the Spirit

emphasize the sovereign electing purpose of God as to diminish the responsible use of the God-appointed means of grace, the Canons adamantly insist on the concrete manner in which— through the proclamation of Christ—believers are brought to salvation. Far from displacing these means, the decree of election constitutes their source and dynamic. The effectiveness and power of preaching are the fruit of God's unfailing purpose to use this method to bring salvation and blessedness to his people.

The Westminster Standards[12]

It is fitting that we conclude our review of the doctrine of preaching in the Reformed confessions with a consideration of the Westminster Confession of 1647 and the Larger Catechism of 1648, for these confessional standards represent the apex of doctrinal development and formulation in historic Presbyterianism. Though these standards are not an adjudication of a doctrinal dispute as the Canons of Dort were, they do represent a rich and full statement of the Reformed faith formulated in the context of political and religious ferment on the British Isles in the early and middle part of the seventeenth century. They have been popularly characterized as the ripe fruit of the Reformation, a mature and precise statement of the Reformed position at the close of the great period of reformatory activity that commenced at the beginning of the sixteenth century and closed about the time of the writing of these great confessional documents.

The historic occasion for the calling of the Westminster Assembly is a complicated story whose details and significance lie outside the purview and focus of this study.[13] For our purpose, it is enough to note simply that the assembly met

---

working "through" or "in" the Word (*per verbum*). On this point, see Berkhof, *Systematic Theology*, 611.

12. The text of the Westminster Confession and Catechisms that I am using is found in *Ecumenical Creeds and Reformed Confessions*, 87–168.

13. Among the classic treatments of the Westminster Assembly and its work, see W. Beveridge, *A Short History of the Westminster Assembly* (Edinburgh: T. & T. Clark, 1904); A. A. Hodge, *The Confession of Faith. A Handbook of Christian Doctrine Expounding the Westminster Confession* (1869; repr., London: Banner of Truth, 1958); and Benjamin B. Warfield, *The Westminster Assembly and Its Work* (New York: Oxford University Press, 1931).

during the period of the Puritan revolution and ascendancy in England. Convened by an act of Parliament, the Westminster divines included representatives of the Church of Scotland, who attended as commissioners of their government (after the signing of the Solemn League and Covenant), and representatives of the Church of England. At the time the confession was written, certain departures from the historic consensus of the Reformed churches, the "liberal" French school of Saumur and the teaching of Arminius, were extant. The Westminster divines effectively resisted these departures in the formulations of the Westminster Standards. With the completion of the Westminster Confession of Faith, together with the Larger and Shorter Catechisms, the confessional standards of the Presbyterian churches were established. These standards were adopted in Scotland and England and have been the dominant standards of the English-speaking Presbyterian churches to the present day.

The doctrine of preaching in the Westminster Standards, consistent with their nature as mature and precise statements of the Reformed faith, represents a kind of codification of all the major emphases that we have witnessed in the Reformed confessions previously considered. The first important mention of preaching in the Westminster Confession occurs in the chapter on effectual calling, or regeneration. In this section, a series of chapters are devoted to what, in theological parlance, is known as the *ordo salutis,* the order and aspects of the application of Christ's saving work to believers. The chapter on effectual calling addresses the first of these aspects. The application of salvation begins with the Holy Spirit's work, effectually calling sinners into fellowship with Christ. So far as the doctrine of preaching is concerned, this chapter makes it clear that this effectual calling occurs "by [God's] Word and Spirit." Through "the ministry of the Word" sinners are "outwardly called" into the fellowship of Christ; and through the work of the Holy Spirit who accompanies that ministry, sinners are spiritually enlightened and made receptive to its summons. This is the usual and ordinary manner of the Spirit's working, though the confession carefully adds the qualification that, for example, in the case of "elect infants, dying in infancy," the Spirit is free to work "when, and where, and how he pleaseth." By adding this disclaimer, the confession anticipates its affirmation in chapter 25 that "there is no *ordinary* possibility of salvation" (emphasis added) outside of the communion of the visible church. This disclaimer is not added to minimize the force of the confession's insistence that effectual calling and the salvation of sinners are effected through the Spirit's use of the ministry of the Word. Rather, it only means to reserve to God the freedom to act, should he be pleased to do so, beyond the means with which ordinarily he is pleased to work.[14]

One of the distinctive features of the Westminster Standards' doctrine of preaching is the rather extended treatment given to the practice and ordinances that govern the preaching of the gospel. In chapter 21, "Of Religious Worship and the Sabbath Day," the "reading of the Scriptures with godly fear, the sound preaching and conscionable hearing of the Word, in obedience to God," are designated as essential "parts," or components, of the worship of God. How these parts of worship are to be understood and exercised receives further elaboration in the Westminster Larger Catechism of 1648. In question and answer 108, the duties required in the second commandment include "the reading, preaching, and hearing of the Word." Both in the Westminster Confession and Larger Catechism, a special point is made to distinguish between the reading and preaching of the Word. It is not enough that the Scriptures are read in public worship. The Word must especially be preached. This becomes quite explicit in question and answer 155 of the

---

14. Chapter 10: "I. All those whom God hath predestinated unto life, and those only, he is pleased, in his appointed and accepted time, effectually to call, by his Word and Spirit, out of that state of sin and death, in which they are by nature, to grace and salvation, by Jesus Christ; enlightening their minds spiritually and savingly to understand the things of God, taking away their heart of stone, and giving unto them a heart of flesh; renewing their wills, and, by his almighty power, determining them to that which is good, and effectually drawing them to Jesus Christ; yet so, as they come most freely, being made willing by his grace. . . . III. Elect infants, dying in infancy, are regenerated, and saved by Christ, through the Spirit, who worketh when, and where, and how he pleaseth: so also are all other elect persons who are incapable of being outwardly called by the ministry of the Word." We have already witnessed a similar emphasis in the Gallican Confession of 1559. This reservation of freedom to God to act beyond the ordinary use of the means of grace is a commonplace among Reformed theologians of the sixteenth and seventeenth centuries.

Larger Catechism. When the question "How is the Word made effectual to salvation?" is posed, the preaching of the Word is particularly underscored:

> The Spirit of God maketh the reading, but especially the preaching of the Word, an effectual means of enlightening, convicting, and humbling sinners; of driving them out of themselves, and drawing them unto Christ; of conforming them to his image, and subduing them to his will; of strengthening them against temptations and corruptions; of building them up in grace, and establishing their hearts in holiness and comfort through faith unto salvation.[15]

In the context of this emphasis upon the preeminent value and importance of preaching as a means of grace, the Larger Catechism also comments on the practice of preaching. The ministry of the Word of God is an *official* ministry. Only those who are "sufficiently gifted, and also duly approved and called to their office" are authorized to preach the Word of God.[16]

This official ministry of the Word places both preacher and hearer under solemn obligations and duties. The preacher is required to "preach sound doctrine" and to do so "diligently," "plainly," "faithfully," "wisely," "zealously," and "sincerely." Those who hear the Word of God preached are, for their part, obligated to "attend upon it with diligence, preparation, and prayer" and to "examine what they hear by the Scriptures." The last requirement, that believers should examine what they hear, indicates that the authority of the official ministry is carefully circumscribed and bounded by the Word of God. The preaching of the gospel grants the preacher no license to impose his opinions upon the people of God. Rather, he is under the obligation to minister the Word entrusted to him. The authority of the preaching office, therefore, is ministerial in nature, not

---

15. There is a considerable body of implication in this answer for the practice of the church and individual believers. Whereas we are tempted to think that private devotions and the reading of Scripture are of greatest value, preaching being of lesser value, the Larger Catechism says that nothing quite compares in its value and use to the public preaching of the Word of God.

16. Q&A 158: "By whom is the Word of God to be preached? The Word of God is to be preached only by such as are sufficiently gifted, and also duly approved and called to their office."

legislative so as to bind consciences beyond the Word of God

One interesting feature of the Westminster Larger Catechism's doctrine is its designation of prayer, in addition to the Word and sacraments, as a kind of means of grace. In answer to question 154, "What are the outward means whereby Christ communicates to us the benefits of his mediation?" the Larger Catechism asserts that these means include "all his ordinances; especially the Word, sacraments, *and prayer;* all which are made effectual to the elect for their salvation" (emphasis added). Does this inclusion of prayer as an outward means represent a unique, possibly novel, feature of the Westminster Standards' doctrine of the manner of the Spirit's application of the benefits of Christ's saving work? Or, to put it more sharply, does the Westminster Larger Catechism conflict at this point with the more common affirmation of the Reformed confessions that the Word and sacraments are the ordinary means of grace?

To answer this question, we must observe several points. The Larger Catechism clearly distinguishes in this answer between all the ordinances of God that he may use in bringing his people to salvation and those special ordinances that have a particular use. The Catechism does not intend to be restrictive in its answer—excluding the variety of means that God may well use in his redemptive work—but approaches the question comprehensively and inclusively. By mentioning prayer as a kind of "outward means," the Catechism need not be understood to teach that it is an objective or official means of grace in the same way that the Word and sacraments are.[17] Rather, the Larger Catechism may only be affirming here what is also taught about prayer, for example, in the Heidelberg Catechism.

---

17. Berkhof, *Systematic Theology,* 604–5, makes a useful distinction between prayer as "instrumental" in strengthening faith and the Word and sacraments as alone "objective channels" for the communication of God's grace in Christ: "Moreover, faith, conversion, and prayer, are first of all fruits of the grace of God, though they may in turn become instrumental in strengthening the spiritual life. They are no objective ordinances, but subjective conditions for the possession and enjoyment of the blessings of the covenant. Consequently, it is better not to follow Hodge when he includes prayer, nor McPherson when he adds to the Word and sacraments both the Church and prayer. Strictly speaking, only the Word and the sacraments can be regarded as means of grace, that is, as objective channels which Christ has instituted in the Church, and to which he ordinarily binds Himself in the communication of His grace."

The Heidelberg Catechism answers the question "Why is prayer necessary for Christians?" by declaring that "God will give His grace and Holy Spirit to those only who with hearty sighing unceasingly beg them of Him and thank Him for them" (Q&A 116). Because of the important and indispensable role of prayer in the Christian life, and because God has ordained to give his gifts only in the context of the practice of prayerful seeking, prayer can be termed a kind of outward means of grace. The Larger Catechism, moreover, is not alone in making this kind of affirmation. The Second Helvetic Confession also affirms that God grants faith "by the Holy Spirit by means of the preaching of the Gospel and steadfast prayer."[18] Using the language of "outward means" in this more general and loose sense, the Larger Catechism may be emphasizing the importance of prayer only as an indispensable accompaniment of preaching and sacraments. Since the means of grace are effective only through the working of the Holy Spirit, who uses them instrumentally, prayer for the Spirit's blessing upon their use may not be neglected.

Summary Observations

With this summary of the doctrine of preaching in the Westminster Standards, we conclude our survey of the principal confessions of the Reformed churches. Now that we have examined these confessions in historical order, we are in a position to set forth in more synthetic form the common emphases articulated in them with respect to preaching as a means of grace. Six themes emerge as the common confessional inheritance of the Reformed churches. It is not my purpose in this conclusion to enter into a theological analysis or evaluation of them. Rather, I intend to illustrate those key points of consensus from our consideration of the Reformed confessions.

First, the doctrine of preaching as a means of grace in the Reformed confessions is undergirded by, and is an expression of, their doctrine of the church. The holy catholic church is an assembly or congregation of believers, outside of which there is no ordinary possibility of salvation. The Reformed confessions

---

18. Latin: " . . . per spiritum sanctum, mediante praedicatione evangelii, et oratione fideli." Niesel, *Bekenntnisschriften,* 246.15–16.

breathe, in this respect, the spirit of catholic Christianity, insisting upon the church as the unique medium of Christ's dwelling and presence. Those who would have part in Christ must partake of him through the communion and ministry of his church, the common "mother of the faithful" in whose bosom Christ's members are conceived and through whose ministry they are nurtured. The individualism and parachurch methodism that so often mark contemporary evangelical practice in North America contrast remarkably with the doctrine of the church found in these confessions.

Second, the Reformed confessions are careful to safeguard God's freedom to save his people "when and where and how he pleases" on the one hand, without diminishing or neglecting a proper emphasis upon those means he is pleased to use in granting salvation on the other. Though they acknowledge God's freedom to save by other means of his choosing, they insist that God has bound himself to those ordinary means that he has appointed to this end. Accordingly, it would be foolish for the church to neglect these means because God is at liberty to act in other ways. This would be incompatible with God's faithfulness and his promise to accompany these appointed means with his blessing. The Reformed confessions do not underscore God's freedom from these means in order to diminish their importance. Rather, they acknowledge this freedom to accentuate the aspect of God's good pleasure in using precisely these means to accomplish the redemption of his people.

Third, the preeminent means that God has appointed for the communication of salvation in Christ is the preaching of the holy gospel. However important and indispensable the sacraments as visible accompaniments and confirmations of the gospel promise, they depend wholly for their content and efficacy upon the prior Word communicated through preaching. Preaching as means of grace produces and strengthens faith. The sacraments as means of grace only confirm faith. The danger lurking in this kind of formulation, of course, is that of minimizing the sacraments.[19]

---

19. Perhaps this is the place to note that, in their emphasis upon the preeminence and priority of preaching in comparison with the sacraments, the Reformed confessions never betray any hint of antisacramentalism. In some respects, this

However, the sacraments are essentially appendices to the Word, signs and tokens of God's favor and promise first proclaimed in the gospel. Though the sacraments are necessary by virtue of God's having mercifully appointed them as aids and props to our faith, they add nothing to the Word and depend wholly for their efficacy upon the Spirit working through the Word that they signify and seal. Therefore, the ministry of the Word is the first, the preeminent, means of grace, while the sacraments are the second, the subordinate, means of grace.

Fourth, when the Reformed confessions speak of preaching as the preeminent means of grace, they refer to the official administration of the Word by lawfully called and ordained ministers of the Word and sacraments. The confessions do not deny the importance and usefulness of the reading and hearing of the Word of God in other contexts and by other persons. However, the Reformed conception of preaching means that it is especially the lively ministry of the holy gospel, the faithful exposition and application of the Word of God in the context of the calling of the ordained ministry, that God is pleased to use to communicate Christ and his benefits to his people. Though the Word of God may be and is ministered in a variety of ways—all believers are partakers of Christ's anointing as prophets and have the calling to bear witness to the truth of the Word of God[20]—the official ministry of the Word is the divinely appointed means of grace. According to the confessions, the language of preaching and the ministry of the Word designates

chapter, by virtue of its concentration upon the preaching of the Word, neglects to give proper attention to the function of the sacraments as means of grace in the Reformed confessions. Suffice it to say that the danger of a diminishing of the sacraments is as great today as that of diminishing preaching. As official means of grace, both are threatened by the kind of spirit and practice mentioned only briefly in my introduction.

20. See Heidelberg Catechism, Q&A 32: "Q. But why are you called a Christian? A. Because I am a member of Christ by faith, and thus a partaker of His anointing, that I may confess His Name, present myself a living sacrifice of thankfulness to Him, and with a free and good conscience fight against sin and the devil in this life, and hereafter reign with Him eternally over all creatures." Readers of this study should not conclude from our treatment of the priority of preaching as means of grace that the Reformed tradition lacks a proper appreciation for the office of believer in the communication of God's Word. It is just that preaching alone has the official, preeminent place the confessions ascribe to it.

a particular form of administering the Word of God. Christ is pleased to use the minister as an instrument through whom his voice is sounded and grace communicated. Though the minister of the Word may preach and teach in a variety of settings and contexts, this preaching and teaching are to be regarded as an official administration of the Word of God.[21]

Fifth, the power, authority, and effectiveness of the official ministry of the Word of God is, according to the testimony of the Reformed confessions, dependent upon and inextricably joined to the working of the Spirit of Christ by these means. Christ, who is pleased to use the preaching of the holy gospel to impart himself to his people, does so not by transferring his authority or power to the minister but by the working of his Spirit through the Word. The preaching of the Word of God has, accordingly, an instrumental but not an inherent authority and power. Typically, the Reformed confessions emphasize this point by distinguishing the external ministry of the Word and the inward illumination of the Holy Spirit. The Holy Spirit, on Christ's behalf, works in and with and through the preaching of the Word to impart faith and new life to the believer.

The effectiveness of the Word as a means of grace, in a manner analogous to the effectiveness of the sacrament, is founded upon the use Christ's Spirit makes of the Word as his tool in gathering and strengthening the church. Preaching *is* the Word of God in this instrumental and derivative sense. When the Spirit accompanies the exposition and application of Scripture through preaching, creating and strengthening faith in the hearer, Christ himself speaks in a "living voice" (*viva vox*) to the church. The high view of preaching in the Reformed confessions rests upon this conviction that the Spirit works through the faithful ministry of the Word. It does not rest upon any magical view that would ascribe an inherent power and effectiveness to the person of the minister or the words of the sermon. Just as the Reformed confessions reject any view of the sacraments that ascribes an intrinsic effectiveness to the

---

21. This means, for example, that though the teaching of catechism or the counseling of a congregational member may not be preaching in the context of public worship, these acts of the ministry should nonetheless be regarded as a kind of "extension of the pulpit."

sacraments, so they reject any view of preaching that would ascribe effectiveness to it apart from the accompanying work of the Holy Spirit.[22]

Sixth, the power of the keys of the kingdom to open or close the door of entrance into the kingdom of God is primarily exercised through the preaching of the gospel. Even though the Reformed confessions warn against the abuse of ministerial authority in the Roman Catholic practice of absolution, they do not shrink back from granting an appropriate ministerial authority to the preaching of the gospel. When they do not legislate or bind consciences beyond the proper limits of scriptural authority, ministers of Christ are called to minister the gospel of reconciliation in the name of Christ. In so doing, they have the right to declare sins forgiven or sins retained and to do so in a pointed and direct manner. Preaching, therefore, has an awesome and holy responsibility to declare the grace of Christ to those who embrace the gospel promise and the judgment of Christ to those who are unbelieving.

Measured by the standard of these emphases of the Reformed confessions, the practice of many Reformed churches today belies their claim to stand in the tradition of the Reformation. Reformed churches, if they are Reformed by the measure of this confessional tradition, are convicted that Christ's dwelling with his people is principally effected through the ministry of the holy gospel. Where Christ is preached by ministers of his choosing, lawfully called and faithful in the discharge of their holy office, there the true church of Christ is to be found. Only in this way, through the ministry of the Word of God and the sacraments, does the Spirit gather, nourish, and preserve the people of God in the unity of the true faith. The uniform testimony of the Reformed confessions can be summarized in the formula "where the Word of God is, there is the church" (*ubi Verbum Dei est, ibi ecclesia*). Or, to express it in alternative terms familiar to the Reformed tradition, "the church is born of the Word of God" (*ecclesia nata est ex Dei Verbo*).

---

22. No more than in the case of the sacraments does preaching work by its simple performance (*ex opere operato*). Only when the Spirit works through the Word preached to create faith in the hearer does, as we argued earlier, the sermon become the Word of God for us.

Chapter 4

Faith Confirmed by the Sacraments

Few students of the great sixteenth-century Reformation of the Christian church would quarrel with the thesis that it restored the centrality of preaching to worship. Even a casual observer of Reformation churches will notice the central location of the pulpit in their sanctuaries and the prominence of preaching in their liturgies. Convinced that Christ communicates himself to his people through the living preaching of God's Word, the Reformers uniformly insisted upon the central and indispensable place of the ministry of the Word as a means of grace.

This emphasis upon preaching, however, was not intended to diminish the indispensable and integral role of the sacraments in imparting Christ's grace to his people in worship. Though the Reformers opposed what they regarded as an unbiblical sacramentalism, or sacerdotalism, in the medieval Roman Catholic Church, they never embraced a spirit or practice of antisacramentalism. The confessions and polemics of the sixteenth century regarding the nature and efficacy of the sacraments provide ample evidence of the Reformers' conviction that Christ is pleased to dwell among his people, not only through the preaching of the Word but also through the proper administration of the sacraments that necessarily accompany the Word.

When measured against the teaching and practice of the magisterial Reformers, the practice of many evangelical churches, even churches that stand historically in the Reformation tradition, represents a decline and impoverishment with regard to the sacraments. The architecture,[1] liturgies, and

---

1. In this connection, I am reminded of an incident from my days as a graduate student at Princeton Theological Seminary. In a course on Calvin's theology, a professor was severely critical of the architecture in Miller Chapel, especially the presence of what he labeled an "altar" in front of the pulpit. As I recall, the students' reaction to this criticism—and these students represented a fair cross-

popular piety of many contemporary evangelical churches witness to an uncertainty at best and a relative indifference at worst regarding the sacraments' role in the church's ministry. One of the factors fueling some evangelicals' fascination with the Roman Catholic and Eastern Orthodox traditions is the rich liturgical and sacramental practice of these communions.[2] Liturgical renewal for many evangelicals consists of a return to the teaching and practice of the ancient church, including all of the trappings and accoutrements of its sacramental administration. Compared to the perceived barrenness of the liturgy in many evangelical churches, the "smells and bells" of the ancient church liturgies seem attractive. Weighted with the approval of long-standing tradition, immune from the tendency to mimic the latest fashions of popular culture and piety, steeped in the rich liturgical and theological inheritance of the historic Christian church, the sacramental liturgy of these communions appeals to the sensitivities of those who have felt the absence of a genuine theology and administration of the sacraments as a means of grace in the modern Protestant church.

The problem with much of the so-called liturgical renewal movement, including the greater emphasis upon the sacraments in Christian worship, however, is that it is often born primarily out of reaction and lacks an acquaintance with the historic sacramental theology of the Reformation. Continuing reformation among the churches cannot be accomplished either by traditionalism, a return to the practices of the past uninformed by a living confession, or by progressivism,

---

section of the Protestant church in North America—mostly regarded the matter as too trivial to merit any comment and exhibited little or no interest in pursuing the subject further. I am informed that, in the recent remodeling of Miller Chapel, this architectural error has been remedied.

2. For an introduction to this phenomenon and its causes, see "'New Orthodox Attract Evangelicals," *Christianity Today* 36, no. 6 (May 18, 1992): 50, 53; Thomas Doulis, ed., *Journey to Orthodoxy: A Collection of Essays by Converts to Orthodox Christianity* (Minneapolis, MN: Light and Life, 1986); Max Thurian and Geoffrey Wainwright, eds., *Baptism and Eucharist: Ecumenical Convergence in Celebration* (Grand Rapids: Eerdmans, 1984); and Timothy Weber, "Looking for Home: Evangelical Orthodoxy and the Search for the Original Church," *New Perspectives on Historical Theology: Essays in Memory of John Meyendorff*, ed. Bradley Nassif (Grand Rapids: Eerdmans, 1996), 95–121.

introducing changes for the sake of change.[3] For a Reformed church to be ever reforming (*ecclesia reformata semper reformanda est*), particularly when it comes to the subject of the sacraments, there must first exist a substantial acquaintance with and appreciation for the confessional and historical position of the church.

Admittedly, renewal in the church's sacramental practice requires more than a consideration of these confessions' doctrine of the sacraments. Consistent with the Reformation principle of *sola Scriptura,* the primary source and authoritative standard for understanding the nature and purpose of the sacraments must be the Word of God. Nevertheless, because the confessions provide a corporate and unifying reiteration of what the churches believe the Scriptures teach regarding the sacraments, their doctrine is of more than mere historical interest. For churches that are confessional—and the Reformed churches are, if nothing else, confessional churches—a starting point for reflection upon the sacraments has to be the doctrine of the confessions. These confessions represent the distillation of the churches' historic interpretation of the Scriptures. Contrary to the modern evangelical tendency to grant greater authority to the private opinions of individual theologians and celebrity pastors, the Reformed churches have always insisted that the burden of proof, when there is a departure in practice and teaching from the historical consensus of the churches, rests with those whose positions are innovative. The choice here is not between biblicism and traditionalism but between a biblicism unconstrained by the weight of the churches' historical reading of the Scriptures and an uncritical acceptance of whatever the confessions declare.[4]

---

3. See Jaroslav Pelikan, *The Christian Tradition, A History of the Development of Doctrine, Volume 1: The Emergence of the Catholic Tradition (100–600)* (Chicago: University of Chicago Press, 1971), 9: "Tradition is the living faith of the dead; traditionalism is the dead faith of the living."

4. For a recent debate regarding the relation between the Reformed confession of *sola Scriptura* and the authority of the confessions in Christian theology, see John Frame, "In Defense of Something Close to Biblicism: Reflections on *Sola Scriptura* and History in Theological Method," *Westminster Theological Journal* 59, no. 2 (Fall 1997): 269–91; David F. Wells, "On Being Framed," *Westminster Theological Journal* 59, no. 2 (Fall 1997): 293–300; Richard A. Muller,

With this understanding, we turn now to the Reformed confessions' teaching on the sacraments as a means of grace. In this chapter, we will explore the doctrine of the sacraments in general.[5] And in the following chapters, we will examine, respectively, the two sacraments affirmed in the confessions, baptism and the Lord's Supper. At the conclusion of each section in our review of the confessions' teaching regarding the sacraments, I will summarize their teaching in a more synthetic manner by identifying the chief features of the historical evangelical and Reformed view. In the context of my summary of these features, I will also include some further comments relating to the sacramental practice of the churches today.

The Gallican (French) Confession of 1559

As with our treatment of the doctrine of preaching, we begin our consideration of the sacraments with one of the earliest statements of the faith of the Reformed churches in the sixteenth century, the Gallican (French) Confession of 1559. In its outline of the faith, this confession follows a traditional order of topics.[6] It addresses the subject of the sacraments within the setting of its consideration of the church's ministry. The redemption that has been accomplished for us by the Mediator, Jesus Christ, benefits us only when we become partakers of Christ through the ministry and communion of the church. Believers come

---

"Historiography in the Service of Theology and Worship: Toward Dialogue with John Frame," *Westminster Theological Journal* 59, no. 2 (Fall 1997): 301–10; and John Frame, "Reply to Richard Muller and David Wells," *Westminster Theological Journal* 59, no. 2 (Fall 1997): 311–18. The title of John Frame's contribution to this discussion betrays a false dilemma that pits *sola Scriptura* against a robust Reformed confessionalism. However, not only is *sola Scriptura* itself a Reformed confessional affirmation but it also shapes the Reformed understanding of the confessions: they find their source and authoritative norm in the Scriptures. Only an antihistorical and individualistic evangelicalism could find a proper respect for the historic confessions to be inimical to the principle of Scripture alone.

5. Sometimes this distinction between a general and particular doctrine of the sacraments is criticized as speculative since the Scriptures speak only of particular rites and not generally of the sacraments. For a defense of the distinction and its scriptural propriety, see G. C. Berkouwer, *The Sacraments,* trans. Hugo Bekker (Grand Rapids: Eerdmans, 1969), 9–11.

6. Unless otherwise indicated, references to a Reformed confession's use of the traditional order of topics will assume that the order of the Gallican Confession is representative.

to enjoy fellowship with Christ, not apart from the ministry of the church, but by means of the ministry of the Word and sacraments that Christ has entrusted to it. Though the Gallican Confession does not expressly affirm that outside the church there is no salvation, it clearly teaches that "no one ought to seclude himself and be contented to be alone; but that all jointly should keep and maintain the union of the Church, and submit to the public teaching, and to the yoke of Jesus Christ" (art. 26). Christ dwells among his people and communicates the benefits of his saving work through the church's ministry. Therefore, to become a member of Christ is tantamount to becoming a member of the church.

The Gallican Confession's first explicit reference to the sacraments occurs in the article dealing with the true church and the marks that distinguish it from the false church. Consistent with John Calvin's identification of two distinguishing marks by which the true church is authenticated, this confession maintains that "there can be no Church where the Word of God is not received, nor profession made of subjection to it, nor use of the sacraments."[7] Measured by the standard of these authenticating marks, the Roman Catholic Church does not rightly bear the title of church of Jesus Christ. When taking up directly the subject of the sacraments, the confession begins with an article that speaks of the sacraments in general and then continues with a series of articles that addresses the New Testament church's two sacraments in particular, baptism and the Lord's Supper.

So far as the general understanding of the sacraments is

---

7. Article 28: "In this belief we declare that, properly speaking, there can be no Church where the Word of God is not received, nor profession made of subjection to it, nor use of the sacraments (où la parole de Dieu n'est receue, et on ne fait nulle profession de s'assuiettir à ielle, et où il n'y a nul usage des Sacremens, à parler proprement, on ne peut iuger qu'il y ait aucune Eglise" [Niesel, *Bekenntnischriften*, 72.40–43].) "Therefore we condemn the papal assemblies, as the pure Word of God is banished from them, their sacraments are corrupted, or falsified, or destroyed, and all superstitions and idolatries are in them. . . . Nevertheless, as some trace of the Church is left in the papacy, and the virtue and substance of baptism remain, and as the efficacy of baptism does not depend upon the person who administers it, we confess that those baptized in it do not need a second baptism (n'avoir besoin d'un second Baptesme [Niesel, *Bekenntnisschiften*, 73.7–8]). But, on account of its corruptions, we cannot present children to be baptized in it without incurring pollution."

concerned, the Gallican Confession speaks of them as divinely ordained "pledges" (*gages*) or "seals" (*marreaux*) of the grace of God. Due to the weakness and infirmity of our faith, God has seen fit to "add" to the Word of the gospel the sacraments as a "more ample confirmation" by which our faith is strengthened and aided. These sacraments are "outward signs through which God operates by his Spirit, so that he may not signify any thing to us in vain."[8] Though we ought not to confuse the outward sign with "their substance and truth," which is in Jesus Christ— indeed "of themselves they are only smoke and shadow"[9]—God has so conjoined the sacramental sign with the grace of Jesus Christ that they are instrumental to the communication of that grace. In its summary of the doctrine of the sacraments in general, the Gallican Confession emphasizes their divine authorship and use as effective instruments to communicate God's grace. Since they have been "added to the Word," they are a subordinate and ancillary means of grace. The Word is the primary means of communicating the gospel of Christ. Nevertheless, due to God's having appointed them to this end and because of the weakness of our faith, they are indispensable instruments to convey God's saving grace in Christ to the believer.

After its opening exposition of the doctrine of the sacraments in general, the Gallican Confession takes up the particular sacraments of the new covenant, baptism and the Lord's Supper, and identifies their unique features. In three concise articles that deal with the two sacraments of the New Testament church, the Gallican Confession affirms their efficacy as visible signs of God's grace in Christ. Both in the Lord's Supper and in baptism God "gives us really and in fact that which he there sets forth

---

8. Article 34: "We believe that the sacraments are added to the Word for more ample confirmation (plus ample confirmation), that they may be to us pledges and seals of the grace of God, and by this means aid and comfort our faith, because of the infirmity which is in us, and that they are outward signs through which God operates by his Spirit, so that he may not signify any thing to us in vain (qu'ils sont tellement signes exterieurs, que Dieu besongne par iceux en la vertu de son Esprit, afin de ne nous y rien signifier en vain [Niesel, *Bekenntnisschriften,* 74.11–12]). Yet we hold that their substance and truth is in Jesus Christ, and that of themselves they are only smoke and shadow."

9. Article 34: " . . . n'est rien qu'ombrage et fume." Niesel, *Bekenntnisschriften,* 74.15.

for us"; the "true possession and enjoyment" of God's grace is given "with" the sacramental sign.[10] Even though the water of baptism is a "feeble element," nonetheless it "still testifies to us in truth the inward cleansing of our souls in the blood of Jesus Christ by the efficacy of his Spirit."[11] The sacramental signs are not to be identified with the grace they signify; the blood of Christ washes away sin, not the water of baptism. However, because God chose to appoint the sacrament of baptism as a pledge and sign of this washing, the sacrament is a genuine and effective instrument in communicating that grace to the believer. Through the sacrament, Christ is pleased to give himself to those who "bring a pure faith" as the indispensable instrument through which the grace of Christ is received.[12]

The Scots Confession of 1560

Although the order of doctrines in the Scots Confession bears some resemblance to the Gallican Confession of Faith and the Belgic Confession, some doctrines receive scant or little consideration, including the doctrines of revelation and Scripture, the Trinity, and creation and providence. Though there are some resemblances to the treatment of the doctrine of the sacraments in the Gallican Confession, this confession adds certain emphases, including a vigorous polemic against the doctrine and administration of the sacraments in the Roman Catholic Church.

As in the Gallican Confession, the Scots Confession's

---

10. Article 37: "Dieu nous donne realement et par effect ce qu'il y figure." Niesel, *Bekenntnisschriften*, 74.46.

11. Article 38: "Thus, we hold that water, being a feeble element, still testifies to us in truth the inward cleansing of our souls in the blood of Jesus Christ by the efficacy of his Spirit (nous testifier en verité le lavement interieur de nostre ame au sang de Jesus Christ, par l'efficace de son Esprit [Niesel, *Bekenntnisschriften*, 75.6–7]), and that the bread and wine given us in the sacrament serve to our spiritual nourishment."

12. The Gallican Confession insists upon the necessity of faith to a proper receiving of the grace communicated through the sacrament of the Lord's Supper. This is not, however, made explicit in the case of the sacrament of baptism. The obligation of faith is implicit nonetheless because the grace of the sacrament is the same as that communicated through the preaching of the Word and invariably demands faith on the part of the one who receives it. The efficacy of the sacrament does not reside in the mere performance of the sacrament (*ex opere operato*), but requires that the grace of Christ be appropriated through faith.

first reference to the sacraments occurs in connection with a designation of the "notes" by which the true church is distinguished from the false. According to the Scots Confession, there are three authenticating notes of the true church of Jesus Christ: "the true preaching of the Word of God"; "the right administration of the sacraments of Christ Jesus, with which must be associated the Word and promise of God to seal and confirm them in our hearts"; and "ecclesiastical discipline uprightly ministered."[13] The true church is distinguished by the proper use of the sacraments that Christ has appointed for the benefit of his people. These sacraments accompany the preaching of the gospel promise, sealing and confirming that promise to their recipients.

In its treatment of the general doctrine of the sacraments, the Scots Confession affirms that just as the fathers under the law were given two sacraments, circumcision and the Passover, so God's people in the new covenant have been given only two sacraments, baptism and the Lord's Supper. These sacraments are not provided merely "to make a visible distinction" between those who are and those who are not numbered among the people of God. They are not simply badges of a Christian profession. Rather, they have been divinely ordained "to exercise the faith" of God's people and "to seal in their hearts the assurance of his promise, and of that most blessed conjunction, union, and society, which the chosen have with their Head, Christ Jesus."[14] Therefore, we must not imagine that the sacraments

---

13. Chapter 18, The Notes by Which the True Kirk Shall Be Determined from the False: "The notes of the true Kirk, therefore, we believe, confess, and avow to be: first, the true preaching of the Word of God, in which God has revealed himself to us, as the writings of the prophets and apostles declare; secondly, the right administration of the sacraments of Christ Jesus, with which must be associated the Word and promise of God to seal and confirm them in our hearts; and lastly, ecclesiastical discipline uprightly ministered, as God's Word prescribes, whereby vice is repressed and virtue nourished. Then wherever these notes are seen and continue for any time, be the number complete or not, there, beyond any doubt, is the true Kirk of Christ, who, according to his promise, is in its midst."

14. Chapter 21, The Sacraments: "These sacraments, both of the Old Testament and of the New, were instituted by God not only to make a visible distinction between his people and those who were without the Covenant, but also to exercise the faith of his children and, by participation of these sacraments, to seal in their hearts the assurance of his promise, and of that most blessed conjunction, union, and society, which the chosen have with their Head, Christ Jesus."

are "nothing else than naked and bare signs," as though they did not actually communicate the gracious promise of saving fellowship with Christ the Mediator. The sacrament of baptism genuinely serves to "engraft" the believer into Christ, so that we are made partakers of his righteousness and recipients of the forgiveness of sins. This communication of God's grace in Christ occurs only where the sacrament is received by true faith. Where true faith apprehends Christ Jesus as he is attested in the sacramental sign and seal, we may be confident that the sacrament is no mere "symbol" of God's grace but an effective means of its communication. This does not mean, of course, that the sacramental sign should be confused or identified with Christ Jesus himself "in his eternal substance." But it does mean that God chooses to join the sign and the grace signified in the sacrament, so that the believer who receives the sign may be assured that he is also the recipient of Christ himself.

One interesting feature of the Scots Confession's treatment of the sacraments is its emphasis on "right administration." According to the Scots Confession, there are two indispensable components of a proper administration of the sacraments.[15] First, the administrant of the sacrament must be a minister of the Word who has a lawful call from a particular church. Because the sacrament is a visible confirmation of the gospel promise that is communicated initially through preaching, the administrant of the visible Word of the sacrament must be himself a minister of the Word. And second, the sacrament must be administered in accordance with the biblical provisions for its celebration. Only those elements and features that have biblical warrant are to be included. For this reason, when the Roman Catholic Church

---

15. Chapter 22, The Right Administration of the Sacraments: "Two things are necessary for the right administration of the sacraments. The first is that they should be ministered by lawful ministers, and we declare that these are men appointed to preach the Word, unto whom God has given the power to preach the gospel, and who are lawfully called by some Kirk. The second is that they should be ministered in the elements and manner which God has appointed. Otherwise they cease to be the sacraments of Christ Jesus. This is why we abandon the teaching of the Roman Church and withdraw from its sacraments; firstly, because their ministers are not true ministers of Christ Jesus (indeed they even allow women, whom the Holy Ghost will not permit to preach in the congregation to baptize) and, secondly, because they have so adulterated both the sacraments with their own additions that no part of Christ's original act remains in its original simplicity."

adds elements that are not biblically sanctioned and celebrates the sacrament in a manner not authorized by scriptural precept or precedent, believers are obliged to withdraw themselves from the use of the sacraments in it.[16]

The Belgic Confession of 1561

The doctrine of the sacraments, particularly the sacrament of baptism, receives more elaborate treatment in the Belgic Confession than in the two confessions we have already discussed. This elaboration reflects in part the continuing conflicts regarding the sacraments in the sixteenth century. Not only were the Reformed churches opposed to the sacramental teaching and practice of the medieval Roman Catholic Church, but they were also increasingly at odds with the emphases of the radical reformation, especially the Anabaptist rejection of the practice of infant baptism. The testimony of the Belgic Confession reflects these ongoing debates.

The doctrine of the sacraments in the Belgic Confession occurs in the traditional setting of the doctrine of the church. The catholic Christian church, according to the Belgic Confession, is "an assembly of those who are saved, and outside of it there is no salvation."[17] Because the redemptive work of Christ benefits believers only through the ministry and communion of the church, no one ought to separate himself from the true church. This true church may be distinguished from the false church by the presence of three marks: the preaching of the "pure doctrine of the gospel"; "the pure administration of the sacraments as instituted by Christ"; and the exercise of Christian discipline.[18]

---

16. Though we will return to the question of the validity of the sacrament of baptism in the Roman Catholic Church in the next chapter, it seems apparent that the Scots Confession differs at this point from the Gallican Confession. While the Gallican Confession identifies the sacrament of baptism as a "trace" of the true church within the Roman Catholic communion, the implication of the Scots Confession seems to be that the Roman Catholic administration of the sacrament is invalid on account of its unauthorized "additions" to the biblical elements.

17. Article 28: " . . . l'assemblée des sauvés, et qu'il n'y a point de salut hors d'elle." The language of the Belgic Confession at this point undoubtedly reflects a deliberate embracing of the ancient dictum of the church father Cyprian: "Outside the church there is no salvation" (*extra ecclesiam nulla salus*).

18. Article 29, The Marks of the True Church: "The marks by which the true Church is known are these: If the pure doctrine of the gospel is preached therein;

Where these marks are evident, Christ dwells among his people and communicates his benefits to them.

In its ordering of the marks of the church and in its treatment of the sacraments, the Belgic Confession clearly regards the sacraments as divinely ordained means, added to the preached Word, that are indispensable to the communication and confirmation of the gospel. In its doctrine of the sacraments, the Belgic Confession especially emphasizes God's gracious ordination of the sacraments for our benefit due to "our weakness and infirmities." The sacraments are added to the Word "thereby to seal unto us His promises, and to be pledges of the good will and grace of God towards us, and also to nourish and strengthen our faith."[19] Thus, the sacraments do not stand alone, nor do they have any meaning apart from the preaching of the gospel. But they are nonetheless an important means whereby God confirms the promises of the gospel and strengthens the faith of believers. The sacraments are "joined to the Word of gospel, the better to present to our senses both that which [God] declares to us by His Word and that which He works inwardly in our hearts, thereby confirming us in the salvation which He imparts to us."[20] Utilizing the traditional language of Augustine in his treatment of the sacraments, this confession defines the sacraments as "visible signs and seals of an

---

if it maintains the pure administration of the sacraments as instituted by Christ; if church discipline is exercised in punishing of sin; in short, if all things are managed according to the pure Word of God, all things contrary thereto rejected, and Jesus Christ acknowledged as the only Head of the Church. Hereby the true Church may certainly be known, from which no man has a right to separate himself."

19. Article 33, The Sacraments: "We believe that our gracious God, taking account of our weakness and infirmities (notre rudesse et infirmité), has ordained the sacraments for us, thereby to seal unto us His promises, and to be pledges of the good will and grace of God towards us (pour sceller en nous ses promesses, et nous être gages de la bonne volonté et grace de Dieu envers nous, et aussi pour nourrir et soutenir notre foi), and also to nourish and strengthen our faith; which He has joined to the Word of the gospel, the better to present to our senses both that which He declares to us by His Word and that which He works inwardly in our hearts, thereby confirming us in the salvation which He imparts to us. For they are visible signs and seals of an inward and invisible thing, by means whereof God works in us by the power of the Holy Spirit."

20. Article 33: "Il a ajoutés à la parole de l'Évangile, pour mieux représenter à nos sens extérieurs, tant ce qu'il nous donne à entendre par sa Parole, que ce qu'il fait intérieurement en nos coeurs, en ratifiant en nous le salut qu'il nous communique."

inward and invisible thing, by means whereof God works in us by the power of the Holy Spirit."[21] Accordingly, the sacraments are not "empty or meaningless," but effective instruments in presenting and communicating Jesus Christ to his church. [22]

The Heidelberg Catechism of 1563

The doctrine of the sacraments is addressed in the second major division of the Catechism, in connection with the redemptive work of Christ and the communication of Christ's saving benefits through the mediation of the church. Elaborating upon the person and work of the Holy Spirit and the third article of the Apostles' Creed, the Heidelberg Catechism defines the holy catholic church as a "community chosen unto everlasting life" which Christ is gathering by his Spirit and Word (Q&A 54). The Holy Spirit, who has been given to the believer in order to make him by true faith a partaker of Christ and all his benefits, dwells within and works through the ministry and fellowship of the church. Therefore, faith is authored and nourished by the Holy Spirit through the instrumentality of the church.

This is the immediate setting for the Heidelberg Catechism's treatment of the "means of grace," those appointed instruments Christ is pleased to use by the working of the Spirit to gather and build up his church in the unity of the true faith. In answer to the question, "Since, then, we are made partakers of Christ and all His benefits by faith only, whence comes this faith?," the Catechism maintains that the Holy Spirit "works it in our hearts

---

21. Article 33: " . . . signes et sceaux visibles de la chose intérieurement et invisible, moyennant lesquels Dieu opère en nous par la vertu du Saint-Esprit."

22. In this emphasis, the Belgic Confession follows Calvin, who insisted that the sacraments not only "exhibit" but also "confer" the grace of Christ upon believers. There is some debate whether Heinrich Bullinger, Zwingli's successor as chief pastor of the church in Zurich, embraced this instrumental view or continued the emphasis of Zwingli upon the sacraments as simply "testimonies" to God's grace. Cf. Berkouwer, *The Sacraments,* 75, who quotes the following statement of Bullinger against Calvin's instrumental view: "These sacraments (gifts) do not exhibit or confer as exhibiting or conferring instruments, but signify, testify, and seal" (Sacramenta illa [dona] non exhibent aut conferunt, ceu exhibendi et conferendi instrumenta, sed significat, testifantur, et obsignantur). When we consider the Second Helvetic Confession, authored by Bullinger, we will have occasion to see whether Bullinger moved in the direction of or even embraced this stronger, instrumental view.

by the preaching of the holy gospel, and confirms it by the use of the holy sacraments" (Q&A 65).[23] By using different verbs to describe the Spirit's work through the instruments of preaching and sacraments—preaching "produces" (*würckt*) faith, the sacraments "confirm" (*bestätiget*) faith—the Catechism clearly subordinates the sacraments to preaching. The sacraments are added to the Word, not in order to supplement what the Word promises but in order to attest and confirm the truth of the Word. Without adding anything to the Word, the sacraments have been instituted by Christ as a help to confirm and nourish faith.

According to the Heidelberg Catechism, the sacraments are divinely ordained "visible signs and seals, appointed of God for this end, that by the use thereof He may the more fully declare and seal to us the promise of the gospel."[24] The sacraments visibly represent the truth and substance of the gospel, namely, the one sacrifice of Christ accomplished on the cross by which believers are graciously granted the forgiveness of sins and life eternal. What the Word promises in preaching is sacramentally presented and communicated to believers when the Holy Spirit, using the sacrament, "assures us" that our salvation rests upon the work of Christ alone. For this purpose, Christ has instituted two sacraments in the new covenant, baptism and the Lord's Supper.[25]

---

23. Q&A 65: " . . . würckt denselben in unsern hertzen durch die predig des heiligen Euangelions und bestätiget den durch den brauch der heiligen Sacramenten." Niesel, *Bekenntnisschriften*, 164.25–27.

24. Q&A 66: "What are the sacraments? The sacraments are holy, visible signs and seals, appointed of God for this end, that by the use thereof He may the more fully declare and seal to us the promise of the gospel (sichtbare heilige warzeichen vnnd Sigill von Gott darzu eingesetzt dass er uns durch den brauch derselben die veriheissung des Euangelions desto besser zuuerstehen geb vnnd versigele); namely, that He of grace grants us the remission of sins and life eternal, for the sake of the one sacrifice of Christ accomplished on the cross."

25. Q&A 67 and 68: "Are, then, both the Word and the sacraments designed to direct our faith to the sacrifice of Jesus Christ on the cross as the only ground of our salvation? Yes, indeed; for the Holy Spirit teaches us in the gospel and assures us by the sacraments that the whole of our salvation stands in the one sacrifice of Christ made for us on the cross. How many sacraments has Christ instituted in the new covenant or testament? Two: holy baptism and the holy supper."

The Second Helvetic Confession of 1566

The structure of the Second Helvetic Confession is similar to that of the Gallican and the Belgic Confessions. God the Father, who in his electing grace purposed in Christ to save his people, has provided for our redemption through the work of the Lord Jesus Christ. The redemptive work of Christ benefits us, however, only when we are brought into communion with Christ by the working of the Holy Spirit. This is accomplished by means of the ministry and communion of the church of Jesus Christ, outside of which there is no salvation.[26] Just as "there was no salvation outside Noah's ark when the world perished in the flood," so "there is no certain salvation outside Christ, who offers himself to be enjoyed by the elect in the Church."[27] The one holy catholic and apostolic church is the singular instrument whereby the saving benefits of Christ's work are communicated to his people. This church is known by its peculiar "notes or signs" (*notis vel signis*), which, according to the Second Helvetic Confession, are "the lawful and sincere preaching of the Word of God," the true worship of God alone in spirit and in truth,[28] and participation in the sacraments instituted by Christ.

The church communicates the grace of God in Christ to believers through the preaching of the gospel and the use of the sacraments. The sacraments are "mystical symbols, or holy rites, or sacred actions, instituted by God himself, consisting of his Word, of signs, and of things signified."[29] These have been

---

26. For this reason, the heading of one section of chapter 17 of the Second Helvetic Confession that deals with the church bears the title "Outside the Church There Is No Salvation" (Extra ecclesiam Dei nulla salus). Niesel, *Bekenntnisschriften,* 251.41.

27. Latin: "extra arcam Noé, non erat ulla salus, pereunte mundo in diluvio . . . extra Christum, qui se electis in ecclesia fruendum praebet, nullam esse salutem certam." Niesel, *Bekenntnisschriften,* 251.44–46.

28. The inclusion of this "note" reflects one of the distinctives of the Swiss Reformation, particularly the emphasis of Zwingli upon the "spiritual" nature of true worship. Christian discipline is not expressly cited as a note of the true church.

29. Chapter 19, Of the Sacraments of the Church of Christ: "From the beginning, God added to the preaching of his Word in his Church Sacraments or sacramental signs. For thus does all Holy Scripture clearly testify. Sacraments are mystical symbols, or holy rites, or sacred actions, instituted by God himself, consisting of his Word, of signs and of things signified, whereby in the Church

added to the Word in order to serve several functions. By means of these sacraments, God reminds his people of the benefits of his grace toward them, "seals his promises" (*promissiones suas obsignat*), "outwardly represents" (*exterius repraesentat*) and offers to our sight those things "which he inwardly performs for us," and "distinguishes" believers from all other peoples.

There are several features of the sacraments that require special emphasis. First, because the author of the sacraments is God, the church has no authority to institute sacraments other than those that are of divine appointment.[30] In the church of Jesus Christ, there are only two such sacraments, baptism and the Lord's Supper. Among the so-called sacraments of the Roman Catholic Church, therefore, some may be "profitable ordinances" (*instituta utilia*), but they do not have the sanction of Christ's having appointed them as sacraments for the church. Second, the sacraments, though they are administered by ministers of the Lord, work to communicate the grace of God only as the Lord works in them. Thus, in the administration of the sacrament, a clear distinction must be made "between the Lord himself and the ministers of the Lord, confessing that the substance of the sacraments is given them by the Lord, and the outward signs by the ministers of the Lord."[31] Third, a proper understanding

---

he keeps in mind and from time to time recalls the great benefits he has shown to men; whereby also he seals his promises, and outwardly represents, and, as it were, offers unto our sight those things which inwardly he performs for us (quae ipse nobis interius praestat [Niesel, *Bekenntnisschriften*, 295.5]), and so strengthens and increases our faith through the working of God's Spirit in our hearts."

30. Chapter 19, The Author of the Sacraments: "The author of all Sacraments is not any man, but God alone. Men cannot institute Sacraments. Christ Still Works in Sacraments: And as God is the author of the Sacraments, so he continually works in the Church in which they are rightly carried out; so that the faithful, when they receive them from the ministers, know that God works in his own ordinance, and therefore they receive them as from the hand of God; and the minister's faults (even if they be very great) cannot affect them, since they acknowledge the integrity of the Sacraments to depend upon the institution of the Lord. The Author and the Ministers of the Sacraments to Be Distinguished: Hence in the administration of the Sacraments they also clearly distinguish between the Lord himself and the ministers of the Lord, confessing that the substance of the Sacraments is given them by the Lord, and the outward signs by the ministers of the Lord."

31. Latin: " . . . inter dominum ipsum, et domini ministrum, confitentes sacrmentorum res dari ab ipso domino, symbola autem a domini ministris." Niesel, *Bekenntnisschriften*, 259.39–41.

of the sacraments requires that a careful distinction be made between their "substance" (*substantia*), that which is signified in the sacrament, and their "signs" (*signa*). So far as the substance of the sacraments is concerned, they visibly represent to us the reality of "Christ the Savior," whose sacrifice is the only source of life and salvation for God's people. What is peculiar to the sacraments is that the "sign" takes on the name of the "thing signified," though we are not to think that "the symbols are changed into the things signified, or cease to be what they are in their very nature."[32] There is, by the Lord's choosing, a union by "mystical signification" (*significationem mystica*) between the sacramental sign and the grace to which it refers. And fourth, for those who receive the sacrament to benefit from their use, faith or a believing appropriation of the grace signified must be present. The sacrament requires a "spiritual participation" (*spiritualiter communicent*) in the things signified, so that the participant may be "spiritually cleansed" by faith from his sins and truly partake of Christ. For this reason, we may not say that the thing signified in the sacrament is "so bound to and included in the signs that whoever participate outwardly in the signs, no matter what sort of persons they be, also inwardly participate in the grace and the things signified."[33]

The Canons of Dort of 1618–1619

The Canons of Dort address the subject of the sacraments in two places. In the first main head of doctrine, which addresses the doctrine of unconditional election, an article is devoted to the question of the salvation and election of the infant children of godly parents whom God calls to himself in their infancy. Though this article does not expressly mention the sacrament of baptism, it does have indirect implications for the significance of the baptism of children of believing parents. In the next chapter, which will take up the doctrine of baptism in the Reformed confessions, we will have occasion to deal with this article at greater length.

---

32. Latin: "Non quod symbola mutentur in res significatas, et desinant esse id quod sunt sua natura." Niesel, *Bekenntnisschriften*, 261.4–5.

33. Latin: " . . . gratiam et res significatas, signis ita alligari et includi, ut quicunque signis exterius participent, etiam interius gratiae rebusque significatis, participes sint, quales quales sint." Niesel, *Bekenntnisschriften*, 261.30–33.

The second place where the Canons of Dort address the sacraments is in the fifth main head of doctrine that deals with the perseverance of the saints. In article 14, in the context of an elaboration of the means God uses in communicating his grace to the elect, the Canons affirm that the sacraments are added to the preaching of the Word as a means of preserving believers in the way of faith.[34] The perseverance of the saints, far from being an occasion for complacency or carelessness, is effected through the faithful and proper use of the preaching of the Word of God and the sacraments. These means of grace have been given by God for the purpose not only of creating faith but also of nourishing, strengthening, and preserving it. This is true for both the sacrament of baptism, which, though administered only once, continues to constitute a definitive sign and seal of God's grace in Christ for believers throughout the whole course of the Christian life, and the sacrament of the Lord's Supper, which is a continuing source of nourishment for faith.

The Westminster Standards

The Westminster Standards follow the general pattern of the Reformed confessions by insisting that the visible church of Jesus Christ is the communion through which Christ's salvation is mediated to his people. Outside of the Christian church there is no "ordinary possibility of salvation" (chap. 25.2). To this church Christ has been pleased to give "the ministry, oracles, and ordinances of God, for the gathering and perfecting of the saints . . . and doth, by his own presence and Spirit, according to his promise, make them effectual thereto" (chap. 25.3). Those who would enjoy the benefits of Christ's saving work must become partakers of him by the working of his Spirit through the ministry and ordinances of the church. The church is, consequently, the place, or the medium, of Christ's saving presence in the world. Through the preaching of the gospel and the administration of the holy sacraments, the preeminent ordinances of the church, Christ savingly communicates himself to his people.

---

34. V/14: "And, just as it has pleased God to begin this work of grace in us by the proclamation of the gospel, so he preserves, continues, and completes his work by the hearing and reading of the gospel, by meditation on it, by its exhortations, threats, and promises, and also by the use of the sacraments."

Following the pattern of the other Reformed confessions, the Westminster Standards first address the general doctrine of the sacraments and then address, respectively, the two sacraments of the new covenant, baptism and the Lord's Supper.

Several aspects of the doctrine of the sacraments receive special emphasis in the Westminster Standards. Because the sacraments are "immediately instituted by God," their efficacy and power depend upon the use Christ's Spirit makes of them in conferring God's grace upon the believer. What distinguishes the sacraments from the preaching of the Word is that they employ visible signs that God has appointed to "represent Christ, and his benefits" (chap. 27.1). Therefore, the sacraments are "holy signs and seals of the covenant of grace" that are intended to "signify, seal, and exhibit unto those that are within the covenant of grace, the benefits of [Christ's] mediation; to strengthen and increase their faith, and all other graces; to oblige them to obedience; to testify and cherish their love and communion one with another; and to distinguish them from those that are without."[35] According to the Westminster Standards, the relation between the sign and the thing signified is a "spiritual" one, where there is a kind of "sacramental union" between the visible representation of Christ and the invisible grace to which the sign points. The sign is an outward exhibition of the "inward" grace that becomes effective only through "the working of the Holy Ghost and the blessing of Christ." Furthermore, because their signs represent the truth and promise of the gospel, the sacraments require a believing reception on the part of those to whom they are administered.[36] The same faith that is required as a response to

---

35. The Westminster Larger Catechism, Q&A 162: "How do the sacraments become effectual means of salvation? The sacraments become effectual means of salvation, not by any power in themselves, or any virtue derived from the piety or intention of him by whom they are administered, but only by the working of the Holy Ghost and the blessing of Christ, by whom they are instituted." Cf. The Westminster Confession of Faith, chapter 27.1: "Sacraments are holy signs and seals of the covenant of grace, immediately instituted by God, to represent Christ, and his benefits; and to confirm our interest in him: as also, to put a visible difference between those that belong unto the church, and the rest of the world; and solemnly to engage them to the service of God in Christ, according to his Word."

36. It is interesting that the Shorter Catechism's answer (Q&A 91) to "How do the sacraments become effectual means of salvation?" is virtually identical to the

the gospel Word is a required response to the gospel sacrament. Since a sacrament is not an invention of the church but a means of grace that depends entirely upon the Lord's appointment, there are only two lawful sacraments in the church of Jesus Christ, baptism and the Lord's Supper.[37] These two sacraments replace the sacraments of the Old Testament, though their spiritual substance is the same.[38]

Summary Observations

Undoubtedly, there are a great number of historical factors and theological debates that underlie the doctrine of the sacraments set forth in Reformed confessions. In the preceding exposition and commentary on the primary confessional standards of the Reformed churches, I have largely bypassed questions regarding the development of doctrine, including the doctrine of the sacraments, during the sixteenth and early seventeenth centuries. To address these questions would require further exploration of the historical development and theological refinement of the doctrine of the sacraments during this period. The sheer extent of these confessions' articulation of the doctrine of the sacraments, particularly in the later confessions, bears witness to the era's doctrinal ferment and vigorous polemics. On no matter of Christian doctrine and practice were the debates among Roman Catholic, Reformed, Lutheran, and Anabaptist more sustained and acute than in this area.

I conclude this chapter with a series of summary observations regarding the chief points of doctrine that represent a consensus of teaching among the Reformed churches. In some instances, I will have occasion to note where there may not be a full

---

Larger Catechism's (Q&A 161), with one exception. The Shorter Catechism adds the phrase, "in them that *by faith* receive them" (emphasis added). Though it is clearly the teaching of the Westminster Standards generally that the sacraments confer grace only where they are believingly received—they do not work, in other words, *ex opere operato*, by their being performed whether the recipient believes or not—it is odd that this phrase is not part of the language of the Larger Catechism's answer, as it is in the Shorter Catechism.

37. Chapter 27.4; Westminster Larger Catechism, Q&A 164.

38. Chapter 27.5: "The sacraments of the old testament, in regard of the spiritual thing thereby signified and exhibited, were, for substance, the same with those of the new."

uniformity of teaching on a particular point.

First, the doctrine of the sacraments belongs, in the structure of the Reformed confessions, to the doctrine of the church and her ministry. Those whom God the Father elects to save in Jesus Christ become beneficiaries of his saving work in no other way than through communion with the church. Though the ancient dictum of Cyprian (*extra ecclesiam nulla salus*) is not explicitly echoed in all of the Reformed confessions, they share the conviction that saving fellowship with Christ does not ordinarily occur apart from the use of the church's official ministry of Word and sacrament. Christ's saving presence in the world is mediated through the church and her means of grace. Where the true church of Jesus Christ is manifest, there Christ is present gathering, defending, and preserving for himself a people chosen unto everlasting life. Christ is pleased to communicate himself by the working of his Spirit through the administration of the Word of God in preaching and sacrament. Where the Word of God is faithfully preached and the sacraments rightly administered—the two marks of the true church uniformly stipulated in the confessions—there we may be sure Christ is present by his Spirit imparting his saving benefits to his people. The location of the doctrine of the sacraments in the confessions, accordingly, attests to their importance as necessary marks of the presence of the true church of Christ and to their indispensable function in the communication of God's grace in Christ to his people.

Second, Christ has appointed the sacraments for the church's use in close conjunction with the preaching of the Word. The sacraments do not communicate anything other than the grace of God in Christ, the same grace and promise that are communicated through the preaching of the gospel. Apart from the Word of the gospel, which the sacrament communicates in its own peculiar manner, the visible word of the sacrament would be empty and lifeless. Therefore, there is a clear ordering of Word and sacrament, such that the sacrament follows upon, or is "added" to, the Word as an auxiliary means of grace. If the sacrament is to be administered properly, it must be preceded by an exposition of the biblical Word and promise that the sacrament signifies and seals. Failure to administer the sacrament in this kind of conjunction with the Word represents a misunderstanding of the nature of the sacraments as "appendices" to the Word.[39] For this reason, it is permissible to speak of the preaching of the Word as the "first," or "preeminent," means of grace, and of the sacrament as the "second" and "subordinate" means of grace.

This raises a question that has been disputed in the history of the Reformed tradition. Are the sacraments necessary and indispensable to the communication of God's grace in Christ? Or is the preaching of the Word of God a sufficient means of grace, apart from the sacraments? The best answer to this question, and the one that most faithfully represents the doctrine of the Reformed confessions, must be that the sacraments are ordinarily necessary and indispensable. This necessity and indispensability, however, are not absolute but consequent upon the Lord's appointment of the sacraments for the believer's benefit. Because the Lord has appointed the sacraments for the church's use and added them to the preaching of the Word, it would be disobedience to his will to neglect their use. Furthermore, because they have been added to the Word, in view of the believer's weakness and proneness to doubt the gospel promise in Christ, neglecting the sacraments would betray an ingratitude and false sense of security on the part of the church. Though it may be necessary to posit (by way of exception in extraordinary circumstances)[40] the possibility of the

---

39. The language of the sacrament as an "appendix" to the Word belongs to Calvin: "Now, from the definition that I have set forth we understand that a sacrament is never without a preceding promise but is joined to it as a sort of appendix, with the purpose of confirming and sealing the promise itself, and of making it more evident to us and in a sense ratifying it." *Institutes,* 4.14.3. When the Reformed confessions insist that the administrant of the sacrament be a lawfully ordained minister, they are setting forth one of the implications of the intimate and necessary conjunction of the ministry of the Word and the sacraments.

40. For example, the Westminster Confession of Faith, chapter 10.3, speaks of infants and others who may be elect and regenerated without the ordinary use of the means of grace, particularly the preaching of the Word. It is possible to imagine other circumstances where the sacraments could not be administered to believers or their children. For example, one reason the Reformed confessions were able to reject the practice of baptism by midwives was their assumption that the sacrament of baptism is not necessary to the infant's salvation. The Roman Catholic permitting midwives to baptize infants reflects the teaching of the necessity of baptism for salvation. For a statement of this view, see Schaff,

grace of Christ being communicated apart from the sacraments, the ordinary means Christ uses require the sacraments. To neglect the use of the sacraments represents a failure to appreciate the intimate conjunction of Word and sacraments in the divine economy of grace. For just as the sacraments require the preceding Word, so the Word requires, by virtue of Christ's appointment, the accompanying sacrament.

Third, the typical definition of the sacraments in the Reformed churches speaks of them as "visible signs and seals" of an "invisible grace." What is peculiar to the sacramental communication of God's grace in Christ is the appointment or consecration of visible elements that represent to the eye of faith the truth of the believer's saving fellowship with Christ. The water of baptism, for example, is a visible representation of the washing away of sins through the blood of Christ and the regeneration of the Holy Spirit. There is a divinely appointed correspondence between the visible sign and the grace to which it points. Moreover, the sacraments are given by God to confirm and attest the promise of the gospel. Not only are they signs that visibly represent but they are also seals that authenticate and assure the believer of the truth of the gospel promise. The Reformed confessions are fond of insisting that the believer is assured by the visible sign and seal of the sacrament that the grace of God in Christ is for the one who receives it by faith. Though the sign and seal do not add anything to the promise, they do constitute a more "full," or "open," confirmation of the gospel so that the believer's faith is nourished and fortified.[41]

Fourth, all of the Reformed confessions grope for words to

The Creeds of Christendom, vol. 2: *Greek and Latin Creeds*, "The Canons and Decrees of the Council of Trent," Seventh Session, On Baptism, Canon V (121). Though this teaching is also expressed in the Augsburg Confession (art. 9), it has always been rejected by the Reformed churches. See Calvin, *Institutes*, 4.15.20–22. Sometimes Reformed theologians have distinguished, so far as the necessity of the sacraments is concerned, between a "necessity of means" and a "necessity of precept." See Berkhof, *Systematic Theology*, 618–19.

41. To say the sacraments do not "add" anything to the Word is only to say that their "substance" is the grace of God in Jesus Christ, the same grace communicated through preaching. However, they do "add" something, namely, a visible sign and seal of this grace. If I may use an analogy, a birth certificate does not "add" anything to the evident fact of one's birth and subsequent life, but it does authenticate this fact in ways that are publicly credible and important.

express simultaneously the most *intimate conjunction* between the sacramental sign and the grace signified as well as the *necessary distinction* between them. Consistent with the nature of sacraments, the Lord has appointed the sign as a visible representation and confirmation of the gospel. However, the visible representation and confirmation are not to be confused with the spiritual reality to which they point. The water of baptism is not to be confused with the blood of Christ or the washing of the Holy Spirit. The bread and wine of the Lord's Supper are not to be confused with the body and blood of Christ. In sacramental language, we may speak of the sign as though it were the reality, so intimate is the divinely appointed connection between them. But we may not neglect to distinguish between the sign and the reality lest we fall prey to idolatry, worshiping the sacramental element rather than the Mediator, Jesus Christ, to whom the element refers. The "substance" to which the sacramental sign points can be only Christ himself in all his saving presence and power.

Fifth, the power and efficacy of the sacraments require that they be received by faith. Since the sacraments do not add anything new to the grace of Christ promised in the gospel, and since the sacramental elements are not to be confused with the spiritual reality to which they refer, the sacraments require the same response as the Word. Neither the preaching of the gospel nor the administration of the sacrament savingly communicates the grace of Christ unless the gospel promise is believed or appropriated by an active faith. The Holy Spirit, who authors faith through the preaching of the Word, also uses the sacraments to confirm and nourish faith. The sacraments function instrumentally to communicate the grace of God in Christ, but only when the Holy Spirit works through them to strengthen the believer in faith. Consistent with this emphasis upon the believing reception of the sacraments, the Reformed confessions commonly oppose any doctrine of *sacramental regeneration* apart from the Spirit's working faith through the Word. The sacraments do not work simply by virtue of their administration (*ex opere operato*) so long as the recipient does not interpose any obstacle (*obex*) to the reception of the grace they confer.[42] Though they do genuinely serve, as means of grace, to *confer* and to *communicate* the grace of God in Christ, they do so only as the Spirit is working in them and as they confirm the faith required on the part of their recipients.[43]

Jan Rohls, author of a fine commentary on the Reformed confessions, has argued that there is a subtle difference of emphasis regarding the efficacy of the sacraments in the Reformed confessions. In Rohl's estimation, some of the confessions (e.g., Gallican, Belgic) affirm a fully "instrumental" view of the sacraments as means of grace. In this view the sacraments confer grace at the time of their administration and through the means of the sacramental sign and seal itself. However, other confessions (e.g., Second Helvetic Confession, Westminster Confession of Faith) affirm that grace is conferred only "in parallel," or alongside of, the administration of the outward sign and seal. In this second view, there is a sharper disconnection between the "external reception of the sign" and the "internal reception of the signified substance." I am not persuaded that this difference of emphasis is as significant as Rohls maintains. Though it is true that some of the confessions use stronger language in linking the sign with the thing signified while others are more anxious to keep a distance between them, these differing emphases answer to different concerns. The former are anxious to stress the efficacy of the sacraments as God-appointed instruments for the communication of the grace

---

42. The teaching that the sacraments effectively confer grace upon their recipients by virtue of their administration (*ex opere operato*) was affirmed by the Council of Trent and continues to be the official teaching of the Roman Catholic Church. See "The Canons and Decrees of the Council of Trent," Seventh Session, On the Sacraments in General, Canon 8: "If any one saith, that by the said sacraments of the New Law grace is not conferred through the act performed (*ex opere operato*), but that faith alone in the divine promise suffices for the obtaining of grace: let him be anathema." Schaff, *The Creeds of Christendom*, 2.121. Though Roman Catholic teaching does acknowledge the necessity of certain "minimum conditions" (the absence of which constitutes an "obstacle" to the reception of grace) in the adult recipient of the sacraments to the realization of their "fruits," in the particular case of the baptism of infants, baptism confers grace by the simple performance of the act. For a contemporary statement of the Catholic view, see *New Catholic Encyclopedia* (Washington, D.C.: The Catholic University of America, 1967), 12:806–16 (esp. 813); and *Catechism of the Catholic Church*, 292.

43. Rohls, *Reformed Confessions*, 181–85.

of Christ to his people. The latter are anxious to stress that this efficacy requires a believing reception of the sacrament and that this believing reception finds the "substance" of the sacrament in Christ himself, not the sacramental sign. However, all of the Reformed confessions, though they distinguish between the sign and the thing signified, affirm the power of the sacraments as genuine instruments of grace. When they are administered in conjunction with the preaching of the Word, the Holy Spirit works in and through the sacrament to confirm and nourish faith. This working of the Spirit in and through the sacrament is a spiritual reality, not merely a "sign" or "testimony" to that reality.

And sixth, the sacraments are, in the nature of the case, visible signs and seals that the Lord alone can appoint for the use and benefit of the church. Because they require divine authorization, the church may not appoint as sacraments any church rite or practice, however useful, that she pleases. The Lord has appointed only two sacraments for the use of his people, holy baptism and the Lord's Supper. Therefore, the Roman Catholic doctrine and administration of seven sacraments represents an abuse of church authority and undermines its claim to be the true church of Jesus Christ.

Chapter 5

Baptism: The Sacrament of Incorporation into Christ

The Reformed confessions share a common theme in their treatment of the doctrine of the sacraments: the sacraments exist only by virtue of Christ's appointment. The church of Jesus Christ does not have any inherent authority to create a sacrament. Nor does the church have the right to administer a sacrament in whatever manner it pleases or by adding to the biblically prescribed elements. The Lord Jesus Christ, who chooses to build his church primarily through the ministry and proclamation of the gospel, has instituted the sacraments as an indispensable and subordinate means of confirming the gospel promise. Since the church is a fruit of the gracious purpose and work of the triune God, the means it employs to carry out its mission in the world must be conformed to the will of Christ, who is pleased to produce faith by the proclamation of the gospel and to confirm it by the accompanying administration of the sacraments.

The confessions understand the sacraments as an accompaniment to the preaching of the gospel, and they maintain that only two sacraments have been appointed by Christ—Christian baptism and the Lord's Supper. The first is a sacrament of incorporation into Christ and his church, and the second is a sacrament of continual nourishment by and fellowship with Christ. In this chapter, we will take up the confession's teaching regarding the first of these sacraments, Christian baptism. What distinguishes this sacrament as a means of grace and as a visible proclamation and confirmation of the gospel promise of salvation through Jesus Christ?

The Gallican (French) Confession of 1559

Earlier, we noted that the Gallican Confession first refers to the sacraments in connection with the marks of the true church. In its treatment of the distinguishing marks of the church, this confession follows John Calvin by identifying two such marks: the reception and preaching of the Word of God, and the proper use of the sacraments. It also follows Calvin's lead by speaking of traces, or vestiges, of the church that remain within the Roman Catholic communion. Even though the Roman Catholic Church lacks the distinguishing marks of the true church and believers are therefore not to take part in its assemblies and rites, some traces of the true church remain within the Roman Catholic communion. Among these traces, the Gallican Confession specifically identifies the sacrament of baptism. Though the Roman Catholic Church's corruptions of the administration of the sacrament of baptism make it inadvisable to present children to be baptized in it, those who have been baptized in the Roman communion do not need a second baptism. The baptism of the Roman Catholic Church, however irregular, retains its validity inasmuch as the "virtue and substance remain,"[1] and the "efficacy of baptism does not depend upon the person who administers it."[2] Though this conviction was common among the Reformers in the sixteenth century, the Gallican Confession is unique among the major Reformed confessions in expressly affirming the validity of baptisms administered within the Roman Catholic Church.

In the church of the new covenant, the Gallican Confession states there are only two sacraments, which it calls "common," baptism and the Lord's Supper. Baptism is given as a "pledge of our adoption" (*tesmoignage d'adoption*) and is the means by which we are "grafted into the body of Christ, so as to be

---

1. Article 28: " . . . et mesme que la substance du Baptesme y est demeuree." Niesel, *Bekenntnisschriften*, 73.4–5.

2. Article 28: " . . . l'efficace du Baptesme ne depend de celuy qui l'administre." Niesel, *Bekenntnisschriften*, 73.5–6. In rejecting the view that the sacrament's efficacy depends upon the character of the administrant, the Gallican Confession illustrates the Reformed churches' concurrence with the ancient consensus of the church against Donatism. Donatism taught that the integrity of the minister was essential to the validity of the sacramental administration, whereas Augustine and the ancient catholic church argued that the minister's role was strictly instrumental. For a brief treatment of this issue, s.v. "Donatism," *Evangelical Dictionary of Theology*, ed. Walter A. Elwell (Grand Rapids: Baker, 1984), 329–30.

washed and cleansed by his blood, and then renewed in purity of life by his Holy Spirit."[3] The water of baptism signifies and pledges to us a twofold washing: the washing away of the guilt of sin and the washing away of the corruption of sin. Though baptism is received only once as a sacrament of incorporation into Christ, its use and power "reaches over our whole lives and to our death, so that we have a lasting witness that Jesus Christ will always be our justification and sanctification" (art. 35). Without elaborating upon the biblical argument for the baptism of children of believing parents, the confession simply affirms that "as God receives little children into the Church with their fathers," the children of believing parents should be baptized (art. 35).

Both in the Lord's Supper and baptism, God "gives us really and in fact that which he there sets forth for us."[4] The "true possession and enjoyment" of God's grace is given "with" (*avec*) the sacramental sign. Even though the water of baptism is a "feeble element," nonetheless it "still testifies to us in truth the inward cleansing of our souls in the blood of Jesus Christ by the efficacy of his Spirit."[5] The sacramental signs are not to be identified with the grace that they signify; the blood of Christ—not the water of baptism—washes away sin. Because God has appointed the sacrament of baptism as a pledge and sign of this washing, however, the sacrament is a genuine and effective instrument in communicating that grace to the believer. Through the sacrament, Christ chooses to give himself to those who "bring a pure faith."[6]

---

3. Article 35: "We confess only two sacraments common to the whole Church, of which the first, baptism, is given as a pledge of our adoption; for by it we are grafted into the body of Christ, so as to be washed and cleansed by his blood, and then renewed in purity of life by his Holy Spirit. We hold, also, that although we are baptized only once, yet the gain that it symbolizes to us reaches over our whole lives and to our death, so that we have a lasting witness that Jesus Christ will always be our justification and sanctification. Nevertheless, although it is a sacrament of faith and penitence, yet as God receives little children into the Church with their fathers, we say, upon the authority of Jesus Christ, that the children of believing parents should be baptized."

4. Article 37: " . . . Dieu nous donne realement et par effect ce qu'il y figure." Niesel, *Bekenntnisschriften*, 74.46.

5. Article 38: " . . . nous testifier en verité le lavement interieur de nostre ame au sang de Jesus Christ, par l'efficace de son Esprit." Niesel, *Bekenntnischififten*, 75.6–7.

6. Like the other Reformed confessions, the Gallican Confession insists upon

The Scots Confession of 1560

Perhaps the most striking feature of the Scots Confession's treatment of the doctrine of the sacraments is its extended polemic against the improper administration of the sacraments within the Roman Catholic Church. Unlike the Gallican Confession, which singles out baptism as a trace of the true church remaining within the Catholic communion, the Scots Confession roundly condemns the use of the sacraments in the Catholic Church. Two things are necessary to a "right" administration of the sacraments: first, "that they should be ministered by lawful ministers"; and second, "that they should be ministered in the elements and manner which God has appointed."[7] Because both of these are absent from the Roman church, its sacraments must be rejected altogether. With respect to the sacrament of baptism particularly, the Roman Catholic Church permits women, in cases of necessity, to administer the sacrament. Moreover, to the sacramental sign of water, the Roman communion has joined "their own additions [so] that no part of Christ's original act remains in its original simplicity."[8] Though the Scots Confession does not directly address what to

---

the necessity of faith to a proper receiving of the grace communicated through the sacrament of the Lord's Supper. This is not, however, made explicit in the case of the sacrament of baptism. The obligation of faith is implicit nonetheless because the grace of the sacrament is the same as that communicated through the preaching of the Word and invariably demands faith on the part of the one who receives it.

7.   Chapter 22: "Two things are necessary for the right administration of the sacraments. The first is that they should be ministered by lawful ministers, and we declare that these are men appointed to preach the Word, unto whom God has given the power to preach the gospel, and who are lawfully called by some Kirk. The second is that they should be ministered in the elements and manner which God has appointed. Otherwise they cease to be the sacraments of Christ Jesus. This is why we abandon the teaching of the Roman Church and withdraw from its sacraments; firstly, because their ministers are not true ministers of Christ Jesus (indeed they even allow women, whom the Holy Ghost will not permit to preach in the congregation to baptize) and, secondly, because they have so adulterated both the sacraments with their own additions that no part of Christ's original act remains in its original simplicity."

8.   For a fine exposition of the form of the Latin baptismal rite in the period prior to the Reformation, see Hughes Oliphant Old, *The Shaping of the Reformed Baptismal Rite in the Sixteenth Century* (Grand Rapids: Eerdmans, 1992), 1–32. Old's volume is an excellent treatment of the historical and theological aspects of the Reformed understanding of the sacrament of baptism in the sixteenth century.

do about someone baptized in the Roman Catholic Church, the implication of its teaching is that such a person still needs to be baptized, since the baptism of the Roman church constitutes no sacrament at all.

When it comes to the meaning and efficacy of the sacrament of baptism, one of the two "chief sacraments" of the new covenant, the Scots Confession offers only a brief statement. Both the sacrament of baptism and the Lord's Supper were appointed by God to "make a visible distinction between his people and those who were without the covenant, but also to exercise the faith of his children and . . . to seal in their hearts the assurance of his promise, and of that most blessed conjunction, union, and society, which the chosen have with their Head, Christ Jesus" (art. 22). Far from being a mere "symbol" or a "naked and bare" sign, the Scots Confession strongly declares that "by baptism we are engrafted into Christ Jesus, to be made partakers of his righteousness, by which our sins are covered and remitted" (art. 22). Though we should not confuse the sacramental sign of water with "Christ Jesus in his eternal substance," the sacrament does serve effectively as a means to signify and seal the believer's fellowship with Christ and those who belong to the visible church.

In its concluding article on the sacraments, the Scots Confession addresses the issue of those to whom the sacraments belong. Against the "error of the Anabaptists," the confession insists that baptism belongs not only to believers but also to their children, even though the children do not yet have "faith and understanding."[9] The Lord's Supper, however, requires faith on the part of its recipients since those who receive this sacrament must do so only after having tried and examined themselves.[10]

---

9. Chapter 23, To Whom the Sacraments Appertain: "We hold that baptism supplies as much to the children of the faithful as to those who are of age and discretion, and so we condemn the error of the Anabaptists, who deny that children should be baptized before they have faith and understanding."

10. Chapter 23: "But we hold that the Supper of the Lord is only for those who are of the household of faith and can try and examine themselves both in their faith and their duty to their neighbors. Those who eat and drink at that holy table without faith, or without peace and goodwill to their brethren, eat unworthily. This is the reason why ministers in our Kirk make public and individual examination of those who are to be admitted to the table of the Lord Jesus."

The Belgic Confession of 1561

The doctrine of the sacraments, particularly the sacrament of baptism, receives more elaborate treatment in the Belgic Confession than in the two confessions we have already discussed. This elaboration reflects something of the ongoing debates and conflicts regarding the sacraments in the sixteenth century. Not only were the Reformed churches opposed to the sacramental teaching and practice of the medieval church but they were also increasingly at odds with the emphases of the radical reformation, especially the Anabaptist rejection of the practice of infant baptism. Because the Belgic Confession was written in part to distinguish the Reformed faith from that of the Anabaptists, its testimony reflects that ongoing debate.

The Belgic Confession's first mention of the sacrament of baptism occurs incidentally in a statement regarding the doctrine of original sin. This reference rejects the Roman Catholic teaching that baptism wholly removes or abolishes the corruption of original sin.[11] Though the article dealing with original sin implies that baptism is efficacious to remove some of the guilt and corruption of original sin, its explicit purpose is to oppose the Roman Catholic Church's exaggerated view of the sacrament's efficacy to expunge original sin.

In its formal consideration of the sacrament of baptism, the Belgic Confession begins by describing its divine institution and meaning. With Christ's sacrificial death upon the cross, God has made an end of "all other sheddings of blood which men could or would make as a propitiation or satisfaction for sin."[12]

---

11. Article 15, Original Sin: "Nor is [original sin] altogether abolished or wholly eradicated even by baptism; since sin always issues forth from this woeful source, as water from a fountain; notwithstanding it is not imputed to the children of God unto condemnation, but by His grace and mercy is forgiven them." The classic Roman Catholic understanding of baptism's removal of the guilt and pollution of original sin is set forth in "The Canons and Decrees of the Council of Trent," Fifth Session, Decree Concerning Original Sin, 5 (quoted from Philip Schaff, *The Creeds of Christendom*, 2.87): "If any one denies, that, by the grace of our Lord Jesus Christ, which is conferred in baptism, the guilt of original sin is remitted; or even asserts that the whole of that which has the true and proper nature of sin is not taken away; but says that is only rased [*sic*], or not imputed; let him be anathema. For, in those who are *born again,* there is nothing that God hates."

12. Article 34: "We believe and confess that Jesus Christ, who is the end of the

Circumcision, which involves a shedding of blood, has been abolished, and the ordinance of baptism has been instituted as its new covenant counterpart. By means of Christian baptism, believers are "received into the Church of God" and are separated from all others. Baptism is a "sign and ensign" that believers belong to God and that "He will forever be our gracious God and Father" (art. 34).

In the sign appointed for the sacrament of baptism ("pure water") and in the words of institution ("into the name of the Father and of the Son and of the Holy Spirit"), God intends to teach us that "as water washes away the filth of the body when poured upon it," "so does the blood of Christ by the power of the Holy Spirit internally sprinkle the soul, cleanse it from its sins, and regenerate us from children of wrath unto children of God."[13] Therefore, baptism is a sacrament of incorporation into Christ and his people, signifying and pledging the washing away of sins through the blood of Christ and the regenerating work of the Holy Spirit. By means of the sacrament, the gospel promise is visibly represented and attested to the believer. This does not mean that the water of baptism has an inherent power to remove sin, however; it remains a sign and seal of an invisible grace, which is the sprinkling with the blood of Christ. In understanding the power and significance of the sacrament, it is necessary to distinguish without separating between the "visible sign" and the "invisible grace" to which it points: "The ministers . . . on their part administer the sacrament and that

---

law, has made an end, by the shedding of His blood, of all other sheddings of blood which men could or would make as a propitiation or satisfaction for sin; and that He, having abolished circumcision, which was done with blood, has instituted the sacrament of baptism instead thereof; by which we are received into the Church of God, and separated from all other people and strange religions, that we may wholly belong to Him whose mark and ensign we bear; and which serves as a testimony to us that He will forever be our gracious God and Father" (portant sa marque et son enseigne: et nous sert de témoignage qu'il nou sera Dieu à jamais, nous étant Père propice).

13. Article 34: "The ministers, therefore, on their part administer the sacrament and that which is visible, but our Lord gives that which is signified by the sacrament, namely, the gifts and invisible grace; washing, cleansing, and purging our souls of all filth and unrighteousness; renewing our hearts and filling them with all comfort; giving unto us a true assurance of His fatherly goodness; putting on us the new man, and putting off the old man with all his deeds."

which is visible, but our Lord gives that which is signified by the sacrament, namely, the gifts and invisible grace."[14]

In the concluding section of its article on holy baptism, the Belgic Confession condemns the errors of the Anabaptists. As a sacrament of incorporation into Christ and his people (the church), baptism must be administered but once. Just as a person cannot be born twice, the sacrament of the new birth cannot be received a second time. Even though baptism is administered only once, its power and significance encompass the Christian's entire life. Throughout the whole course of the Christian life, baptism stands as a constant reminder and pledge of our fellowship with Christ and saving participation in his atoning death.[15] The Anabaptists' denial of "the one only baptism they have once received" seriously compromises this truth.

But the most serious error in Anabaptist teaching and practice is its rejection of the baptism of the children of believing parents. Because the children of believers are the recipients of the "same promises" as were made to the "children of Israel formerly," and because baptism has come in the place of circumcision as the sign and seal of the new covenant in Christ, the children "ought to be baptized and sealed with the sign of the covenant."[16] Failure to baptize such children denies the truth that "Christ shed His blood no less for the washing of the children of believers than for adult persons."[17] At this juncture, the Belgic Confession cites

---

14. "Les Ministres nous donnent de leur part le Sacrement et ce qui est visible: mais notre Seigneur donne ce qui est signifié par le Sacrement, savior les dons et grâce invisibles."

15. Article 34: "We believe, therefore, that every man who is earnestly studious of obtaining life eternal ought to be baptized but once with this only baptism, without ever repeating the same, since we cannot be born twice. Neither does this baptism avail us only at the time when the water is poured upon us and received by us, but also through the whole course of our life. Therefore we detest the error of the Anabaptists, who are not content with the one only baptism they have once received, and moreover condemn the baptism of the infants of believers, who we believe ought to be baptized and sealed with the sign of the covenant, as the children in Israel formerly were circumcised upon the same promises which are made unto our children. And indeed Christ shed His blood no less for the washing of the children of believers than for adult persons; and therefore they ought to receive the sign and sacrament of that which Christ has done for them."

16. Article 34: " . . . lesquels . . . devoir être baptisés et scellés du signe de l'alliance."

17. Article 34: "Christ n'a pas moins répandu son sang pour laver les petits

the Old Testament practice of sacrificing a lamb for the children of the covenant shortly after their birth.[18] This offering of a lamb was "a sacrament of Jesus Christ," typifying the inclusion of children under the provisions of Christ's sacrifice for them. Therefore, in the church of Jesus Christ, children of believing parents should receive the sacrament of baptism, just as children in the old covenant received the sign and seal of the covenant promises in circumcision.

The Heidelberg Catechism of 1563

In its elaboration upon the significance of Christian baptism, the Heidelberg Catechism speaks first of the connection between the sacramental sign and seal and what it signifies. Then it addresses the issue of whether the children of believers ought to be baptized.

The sacramental sign of water shows the washing away of sins through the blood of Christ and the sanctification of the Holy Spirit. Christ's appointment of the baptismal sign of water was added to "the promise that I am washed with His blood and Spirit from the pollution of my soul" in order to attest to us the truth of this promise.[19] This does not mean that the water of baptism, by itself, washes away the filthiness of sin; only the blood of Christ and the work of the Holy Spirit can accomplish this spiritual washing.[20] However, Christ is pleased to join the sacramental sign with the grace signified, so that those who are baptized may be assured of God's promise in Christ by means of the water of baptism. So intimate is the connection between the sign and the thing signified that the one baptized may be as

---

enfants des fidèles, qu'il a fait pour les grands."

18. The practice referred to here is described in Leviticus 12:3. This particular scriptural support for the practice of the baptism of infants is unique to the Belgic Confession.

19. Q&A 69: "How is it signified and sealed unto you in holy baptism that you have part in the one sacrifice of Christ on the cross? A. Thus, that Christ has appointed this outward washing with water and added the promise that I am washed with His blood and Spirit from the pollution of my soul, that is, from all my sins, as certainly as I am washed outwardly with water, by which the filthiness of the body is commonly washed away."

20. Q&A 72: "Is then, the outward washing with water itself the washing away of sin? No, for only the blood of Jesus Christ and the Holy Spirit cleanse us from all sins."

assured of the washing away of his sins by the blood of Christ as he is of receiving the outward sign of washing in baptism. This conjunction of sign and reality is confirmed by the scriptural language that calls baptism "the washing of regeneration" and "the washing away of sins."[21] Though the sign may not be identified with the thing signified—no more than a seal adds something to the pledge it confirms or authenticates—we may still speak of the sacrament as a divinely appointed instrument by which God assures us "that we are spiritually cleansed from our sins as really as we are outwardly washed with water."[22]

On the subject of whether children of believers ought to be baptized, the Heidelberg Catechism, though not as elaborate in its exposition as the Belgic Confession, is equally emphatic. The children of believing parents *must be* baptized for the same reason that adult believers are to be baptized: they are included in the covenant and church of God.[23] The promises of the gospel are for these children as well as their parents.[24]

---

21. Q&A 71: "Where has Christ assured us that we are washed with His blood and Spirit as certainly as we are washed with the water of baptism? A. In the institution of baptism, which reads thus: Go ye therefore, and make disciples of all the nations, baptizing them into the name of the Father and of the Son and of the Holy Spirit, Matt. 28:19. And: He that believeth and is baptized shall be saved; but he that disbelieveth shall be condemned, Mark 16:16. This promise is also repeated where the Scripture calls baptism the washing of regeneration and the washing away of sins, Tit. 3:5; Acts 22:16."

22. Q&A 73: "Why, then, does the Holy Spirit call baptism the *washing of regeneration* and *the washing away of sins?* God speaks thus not without great cause: to wit, not only to teach us thereby that as the filthiness of the body is taken away by water, so our sins are removed by the blood and Spirit of Jesus Christ; but especially to assure us by this divine pledge and sign that we are spiritually cleansed from our sins as really as we are outwardly washed with water." German: " . . . dass wir so warhafftig von vnsern sünden geistlich gewaschen sind als wir mit dem leiblichen wasser gewaschen werden." Niesel, *Bekenntnisschriften,* 166.19–21.

23. Q&A 74: "Are infants also to be baptized? Yes; for since they, as well as adults, are included in the covenant and Church of God, and since both redemption from sin and the Holy Spirit, the Author of faith, are through the blood of Christ promised to them no less than to adults, they must also by baptism, as a sign of the covenant, be ingrafted into the Christian Church, and distinguished from the children of unbelievers, as was done in the old covenant or testament by circumcision, instead of which baptism was instituted in the new covenant."

24. For this reason, it is not technically correct to speak of "infant baptism" as opposed to "believer's baptism," as though these were two distinct kinds of baptisms, based upon different grounds. Christian baptism, whether of adult

Through the blood of Christ, they become recipients of the promise of redemption and the Holy Spirit. Accordingly, they must be distinguished from the children of unbelievers as heirs of the gospel promise through baptism. Just as circumcision was formerly the sacramental sign of covenant membership in the old covenant, so now baptism has come in its place as the sacramental sign of the new covenant.

The Second Helvetic Confession of 1566

The Second Helvetic Confession's chapter on holy baptism is relatively brief compared to its elaborate treatment of the general doctrine of the sacraments and its subsequent detailed handling of the doctrine of the Lord's Supper. It begins by noting the institution of Christian baptism in Matthew 28:19 and the practice of the early church. Though nothing is said explicitly about the validity of baptism administered in other communions, especially the Roman Catholic Church, baptism is, as a "sign of initiation for God's people,"[25] to be administered only "once" and "continues for all of life" as a "perpetual sealing of adoption."[26] The meaning of baptism includes not only the confirmation of God's grace toward his people in Christ but also a corresponding obligation. To be baptized means that one is "enrolled, entered, and received into the covenant and family, and so into the inheritance of the sons of God" (chap. 20). Baptism also, by means of the sign of water, assures us of the washing away of sins through the blood of Christ and the Spirit of regeneration. The outward sign of water testifies to and assures us of the inward washing of regeneration, purification, and renewal through the Holy Spirit.[27] Furthermore, those who have been baptized are reminded that they now belong to God and that, as his property, they are obligated to "obedience,

---

believers or the children of believing parents, always has the same ground or basis: God's covenant promise.

25. Chapter 20, Of Holy Baptism: " . . . signum initiale populi Dei." Niesel, *Bekenntnisschriften*, 262.18–19.

26. Chapter 20, One Baptism: "There is but one baptism in the Church of God; and it is sufficient to be once baptized or consecrated unto God. For baptism once received continues for all of life, and is a perpetual sealing of our adoption (perpetua obsignatio adoptionis nostrae). Niesel, *Bekenntnisschriften*, 262.22–23.

27. "Obsignantur haec omnia baptismo." Niesel, *Bekenntnisschriften*, 262.33.

mortification of the flesh, and newness of life." They have been "enlisted in the holy military service of Christ" so that all their life long they may fight against the world, Satan, and their own flesh (chap. 20). Moreover, as members of the church, baptized persons are obligated by ties of mutual love and service to those who, with them, belong to God.

The concluding sections of this confession's statement of the doctrine of baptism rejects aberrant doctrines and practices of the sacrament. The "most perfect form of baptism" conforms to the simplicity of Christ's institution, using the sacramental sign of his appointment without the addition of such elements as "exorcism, the use of burning lights, oil, salt, spittle," and the like. Since Christ has not authorized women to administer the sacrament, this practice should be rejected. In a final brief notation regarding the baptism of children of believing parents, it is asserted that, since they belong to the covenant people of God, the "sign of God's covenant" should also be given to them (chap. 20).

The Canons of Dort of 1618–1619

Since the Canons of Dort do not expressly examine the sacrament of baptism, it would be possible to omit this confession from our survey. There is an affirmation in the Canons of Dort, however, that is significant to our purpose. I refer to article 17 in the first main head of doctrine on divine election and reprobation. This article addresses the subject of the salvation of the infants of believers, especially the confidence that believers may have regarding their salvation.[28]

To appreciate the context and occasion for this article, we must note what is said about the subject of the salvation of the children of believers in the concluding portion of the Canons of Dort, the "Rejection of False Accusations." In this rejection, the authors of the Canons refer to those who falsely

---

28. First Main Point of Doctrine: Divine Election and Reprobation. Article 17, The Salvation of the Infants of Believers: "Since we must make judgments about God's will from his Word, which testifies that the children of believers are holy, not by nature but by virtue of the gracious covenant in which they together with their parents are included, godly parents ought not to doubt the election and salvation of their children whom God calls out of this life in infancy."

accuse the Reformed churches of teaching, by their doctrine of unconditional election, "that many infant children of believers are snatched in their innocence from their mother's breasts and cruelly cast into hell so that neither the blood of Christ nor their baptism nor the prayers of the church at their baptism can be of any use to them."[29] As this statement indicates, the Arminians commonly complained against the Reformed doctrine of election, saying it implied that many infant children of believing parents were lost because they were not the objects of God's electing purpose. This complaint was especially powerful at a time when many believers lost their children in infancy. What is particularly pertinent to our purpose is that even though article 17 of the first main point of doctrine does not expressly mention baptism, the reference in the "Rejection of False Accusations" includes baptism as a confirmatory sign and seal of the promise of God to believing parents.

There is some debate regarding the meaning of article 17. Does the article merely suggest that believing parents, subjectively considered, ought not doubt the election and salvation of their children? Because the language of this article encourages parents not to doubt, some maintain that it falls short of objectively affirming the actual salvation of such children who die in infancy. The article, then, addresses only the kind of confidence that parents should cultivate on the occasion of the death of their infant children. Others insist that this inappropriately weakens, even undermines, the force of the language in this article. The confidence that believing parents are encouraged to have can only be based upon a knowledge made from the

---

29. For a more extensive consideration of this article, including a discussion of its historical occasion, see M. Meijering, *De Dordtsche Leerregels* (Groningen: Jan Haan, 1924), 79–82; J. G. Feenstra, *De Dordtsche Leerregels,* 2nd ed.(Kampen: Kok, 1950); D. W. Sinnema, "The Issue of Reprobation at the Synod of Dort in Light of the History of This Doctrine" (PhD diss., University of St. Michael's College, 1985), 413–15; N. H. Gootjes, "Can Parents Be Sure? Background and Meaning of Canons of Dort I, 17," *Lux Mundi* 15, no. 4 (December 1996): 2–6.; and Cornelis P. Venema, "The Election and Salvation of the Children of Believers Who Die in Infancy: A Study of Article I/17 of the Canons of Dort," *Mid-America Journal of Theology* 17 (2006): 57–100. For an example of a pastoral application of this article's teaching to believers who experience the loss of a little one, see Glenda Mathes, *Little One Lost: Living with Early Infant Loss* (Grandville, MI: Reformed Fellowship, Inc., 2012).

testimony of God's reliable Word. Furthermore, the article speaks directly about the children of such parents, that they are "holy, not by nature but by virtue of the gracious covenant in which they together with their parents are included."[30] Since this is adduced as the reason for the obligation parents have not to doubt the salvation of their children, it seems apparent that this article means to teach not only that parents should be confident of their children's salvation but also that such children are indeed elect of God.[31]

The principle undergirding the teaching of the Canons in this article is that "we must make judgments about God's will from his Word" (*de voluntate Dei ex verbo ipsius nobis est judicandum*). Believers, including believing parents of children whom God calls out of this life in infancy, are obligated to believe the promises of the gospel that address them and their children. These promises are communicated through the preaching of the Word of God and also through the sacrament of baptism, which God has been pleased to join to the Word as a visible sign and seal in confirmation of the gospel promise. Accordingly, if the question is rephrased—What do such parents have to go on when the question concerns the salvation of these children?—then the only legitimate answer must be the promise of God's Word, as it also is attested and confirmed to them and their children in baptism. Far from encouraging any kind of speculative inquiry regarding the salvation of such children, this article directs us to the only means available to us by which to determine God's will toward us—the gospel Word and the accompanying sacrament.[32] These are reliable bases upon which

---

30. " . . . sanctos, non quidem natura, sed beneficio foederis gratuiti, in quo illi cum parentibus comprehenduntur."

31. It should be carefully observed that the Canons are speaking only of the infant children of believing and godly parents. They are not addressing in any way the different issue of the salvation of infants generally.

32. In his *Believers and Their Seed* (Grand Rapids: Reformed Free Publishing Assoc., 1971), 146–59, Herman Hoeksema criticizes this article for being speculative by going beyond the testimony of Scripture. He argues that it only affirms the "subjective certainty" that parents may have under these circumstances, not the "objective certainty" of their children's salvation (158). Though this is not the place to evaluate Hoeksema's theology of election, it is apparent that his own speculative approach to the doctrine of the covenant (viewed from the standpoint of the divine decree) makes it impossible for him to affirm the principle enunciated

to be confident regarding our salvation and the salvation of our children. What this article affirms, then, is that the promise of God's grace that addresses believers and their children, on the basis of which they are to be baptized, constitutes a sufficient foundation for the assurance of salvation, particularly in the case of children who die in infancy.

The Westminster Standards

The Westminster Standards introduce their discussion of the sacrament of baptism following the pattern of most Reformed confessions we have considered in this chapter. After a treatment of the doctrine of the sacraments in general, the Westminster Confession of Faith (WCF) and Larger Catechism (WLC) note that baptism is the first of the two divinely appointed sacraments of the new covenant, which must be administered by a "lawfully ordained" minister of the Word.[33] By means of this sacrament, God admits believers and their children into the visible church (WCF 28.1). The baptismal sign of water, together with the words of institution, are consecrated by Christ's appointment to signify and seal to God's people their engrafting into Christ, regeneration, the forgiveness of sins, as well as their obligation to live for God. Consistent with the historic view of the Reformed churches, the Westminster Confession of Faith notes that the mode of baptism, whether by immersion, affusion, or sprinkling, is not a necessary or essential aspect of its administration, so long as the sign of water and the baptismal formula of Matthew 28:19 are used.[34] Those to whom the sacrament is to be administered include believers and

---

in this article: that we are to make judgments about the salvation of believers and their children from the Word of God (and the sacraments that signify and seal the Word's promises). The argument of the Canons is that, if our knowledge of God's grace toward us in Christ is based upon the Word and sacraments and not upon some impossible insight into the particulars of the divine decree, then we have an adequate basis for confidence regarding the salvation of the children of believing parents.

33. Chapter 27.4: "There be only two sacraments ordained by Christ our Lord in the gospel; that is to say, Baptism, and the Supper of the Lord; neither of which may be dispensed by any, but by a minister of the Word lawfully ordained." Westminster Larger Catechism, Q&A 164.

34. Chapter 28.3: "Dipping of the person into water is not necessary; but Baptism is rightly administered by pouring, or sprinkling water upon the person."

their children since the promise of the covenant embraces the children of believing parents (WCF 28.4; WLC Q&A 166). Two prominent features of the treatment of the sacrament of baptism in the Westminster Standards are a careful reflection upon the *efficacy* of the sacrament on the one hand and an emphasis upon the continual *use* of the sacrament throughout the whole course of the baptized person's life on the other.

The Westminster Confession of Faith carefully points out that the "efficacy of Baptism is not tied to that moment of time wherein it is administered" (28.6). Though baptism is to be distinguished from the Lord's Supper as a singular rite, impossible to repeat, its efficacy and power are not restricted to the moment of its administration. For the Holy Spirit will not fail to offer, exhibit, and confer the grace that the sacrament signifies and seals to all such "as that grace belongeth unto according to the counsel of God's own will, in his appointed time" (28.6). In its treatment of the efficacy of baptism, the Westminster Confession of Faith guards against a doctrine of baptismal regeneration, which either ties regeneration to the sacrament as its exclusive instrument or infers that all baptized persons are "undoubtedly regenerated." Although baptism is a meaningful and confirming sign and seal of regeneration and participation in Christ's saving work, it depends entirely for its efficacy upon the Spirit's working with the sacrament to communicate the grace of God to those to whom this grace properly belongs according to the "counsel of God's own will" (WCF 28.6). While this kind of formulation could be misused to posit too sharp a separation between the administration of the sacrament and the conferral of grace that it effects as a means of grace, it preserves against the improper presumption that all baptized persons are regenerated, whether or not they receive the sacrament in the way of faith and make proper use of it.

Though the sacrament of baptism is, in the nature of the case, only to be administered once, the sacrament of baptism must be "improved," or used, throughout the whole course of the believer's life.[35] The use of baptism, which believers often sadly

---

35. Larger Catechism, Q&A 167: "How is our Baptism to be improved by us? The needful but much neglected duty of improving our Baptism, is to be performed by us all our life long, especially in the time of temptation, and when we are

neglect, requires that in a variety of circumstances—whether in times of temptation or upon the occasion of witnessing the baptism of others—believers call to mind the privileges and responsibilities conferred and sealed to them in their baptism. These privileges and responsibilities include remembering our baptismal vow; humility in the awareness of our sinfulness in failing to live up to the grace of baptism; a greater assurance of the forgiveness of sins through the blood of Christ; living out of the power of Christ's death and resurrection; and seeking to walk in that brotherly love that answers to our incorporation into the one body of Christ. By this kind of use of our baptism, the grace of God communicated to us in the sacrament will continue to nourish and strengthen us in the faith, preserving us in fellowship with Christ and his people.

Summary Observations

The most important tenets that belong to the historic evangelical and Reformed view of baptism can be summarized in several observations.

First, holy baptism represents the first sacrament Christ has appointed for the use and blessing of the church. Baptism is not an invention or convention of the Christian church. Christ is pleased by means of this sacrament to confirm to believers and their children all the benefits of his saving mediation. By the Lord's ordinance and appointment, the sacramental sign of baptism is pure water. Only a lawfully ordained minister of the Word is authorized to administer this sacrament, and he must do so using the words of institution given by Christ in Matthew 28:19. Though the mode of baptism may differ from place to

---

present at the administration of it to others; by serious and thankful consideration of the nature of it, and of the ends for which Christ instituted it, the privileges and benefits conferred and sealed thereby, and our solemn vow made therein; by being humbled for our sinful defilement, our falling short of, and walking contrary to, the grace of baptism, and our engagements; by growing up to assurance of pardon of sin, and of all other blessings sealed to us in that sacrament; by drawing strength from the death and resurrection of Christ, into whom we are baptized, for the mortifying of sin, and quickening of grace; and by endeavoring to live by faith, to have our conversation in holiness and righteousness, as those that have therein given up their names to Christ; and to walk in brotherly love, as being baptized by the same Spirit into one body."

place—whether through immersion, affusion, or sprinkling[36]—the validity of baptism requires the use of the Christ-appointed sign of water, which accompanies the gospel Word and promise regarding the baptized member's communion with the triune God—Father, Son, and Holy Spirit.[37]

Second, the sacrament of baptism, which by its nature may be administered only once, serves to signify and seal to believers their adoption into the household of God and incorporation into Christ. The water of baptism especially represents the washing away of sin through the blood of Christ and the Spirit of regeneration. By baptism believers are not only visibly distinguished from those who remain strangers to God and Christ's church and are incorporated into the body of Christ, but they are also confirmed in the grace of reconciliation with God and purification from the pollution and guilt of sin. As members of Christ and the household of God, believers are by baptism also enlisted into the service of Christ, engaged to him as those who are his cherished possession, and called to live in selfless love with all others who enjoy communion with Christ. Though the emphasis in the Reformed confessions falls upon the privileges of grace, which are signified and sealed to believers in baptism, the Second Helvetic Confession and the Westminster Confession of Faith especially emphasize these accompanying obligations of baptism. Just as the response to the Word of the gospel includes repentance and faith, so the required response

---

36. For a thorough discussion of the Reformers' views on the mode of baptism, including a review of the history of the question in the Christian church, see Old, *Shaping of the Reformed Baptismal Rite,* 264–82. Though some of the Reformers attempted to reintroduce the practice of immersion (e.g., Zwingli), the general consensus was that the mode was an *adiaphoron* and that sprinkling was, practically, the most expedient mode.

37. The validity of Christian baptism depends upon the presence of its essential components, the sign of water and the words of institution. I am reminded, in this connection, of an anecdote my father, Dr. Richard J. Venema, told regarding a minister in his community who, upon discovering no water in the baptismal font, proceeded with the sacrament by pretending that water was present. Though the elders of the congregation did not interrupt the service, they insisted upon the administration of baptism with water to the child at a later service. The elders were correct in this insistence since, without water or the sign of the sacrament, you do not have an irregular sacrament but no valid sacrament at all. The only error of the elders was their failure to intervene immediately during the service and to insist that the minister go no further until water be obtained.

to the visible Word of the sacrament includes corresponding responsibilities. These purposes of baptism are not restricted to the occasion of its administration. Rather, throughout the whole course of the believer's life, the sacrament of baptism serves powerfully to confirm faith and stimulate obedience. To use the language of the Westminster Confession of Faith, believers must be vigilant in the constant "improvement" of their baptism, being reminded by this sacrament of their engagement to Christ and enrollment in the company of his people.

Third, though the Reformed confessions do not teach baptismal regeneration, they do ascribe a real power and efficacy to the sacrament of baptism in conferring the grace of God in Christ upon believers. A cursory reading of the descriptions of the efficacy of baptism in these confessions must impress any fair reader with the strength of the connection drawn between the sacramental sign and the spiritual reality. Again and again, the sacrament of baptism is described as effectively communicating what it visibly represents and pledges. As a divinely appointed instrument for the confirmation of faith, it could not be otherwise. For, if the sacrament were of little or no effect as a means of grace—merely a visible testimony to the believer's subjective state and disposition toward God and not a divinely given sacramental Word signifying and sealing divine grace in Christ—then it would not have been added to the Word as a more full confirmation of God's grace. Because God has been willing to join the spiritual grace communicated with its sacramental sign, the church must not weaken its understanding of the sacrament's power and efficacy by breaking asunder what God has joined together.

For this reason, the confessions encourage a continual use of and appeal on the part of believers to their baptism throughout the whole of their Christian life. This use is twofold. On the one hand, baptism ought to be a great basis and source of assurance in the Christian life. And on the other hand, baptism ought to stimulate to a responsible life of Christian obedience. Therefore, it is a strange irony that in many Reformed churches the use of baptism as a means of assurance is frequently disparaged. Out of a concern to resist complacency and presumptuousness, the assurance of God's grace toward us in Christ that the sacrament is given to nourish and strengthen is diminished. How often it is remarked that "baptism is no guarantee of your salvation." Perhaps no other word is spoken more often regarding the baptism of believers and their children. But this kind of language betrays a weakening, even a virtual denial, of the power and efficacy of baptism as a sure sign and seal of God's favor toward us in Christ. If baptism may not be used as a ground for assurance in the Christian life, then what becomes of its proper use? This disparagement and neglect of the use of baptism as a ground of assurance before God denies the truth respecting the sacrament as it is summarized in the confessions.

The concern that an appeal to baptism as a ground of assurance will encourage complacency and presumptuousness fails to reckon with the Reformed confessions' insistence that the privileges of God's grace, which are communicated through the sacrament, undergird and accentuate the responsibilities of God's grace. If baptism is a confirmatory sign of God's grace, it is also a solemn reminder that believers belong to God and, as members of Christ's church, must live accordingly. Baptism engages the church as bride to Christ the bridegroom. Baptism, to use the language of the Second Helvetic Confession, enlists the believer "in the holy military service of Christ" and places the believer under obligations of love toward God and others who belong to the fellowship of the church. Therefore, the proper and balanced use of the sacrament of baptism in the Christian life will simultaneously provide assurance of God's grace and encourage a responsible course of Christian obedience.

Fourth, in their handling of the question of who should be baptized, the Reformed confessions consistently affirm that baptism should be administered to believers and their children. The affirmation of the baptism of children of believing parents is treated more expansively in the later confessions of the Reformation era, reflecting the continuing and intensifying polemic against the Anabaptist repudiation of infant baptism.[38]

---

38. It is well known that Karl Barth severely criticized the Reformed confessions' affirmation of the baptism of children of believing parents. See Karl Barth, *Church Dogmatics,* vol. 4, part 4, *The Doctrine of Reconciliation* (Edinburgh: T. & T. Clark, 1969), 264–94. According to Barth, the Reformers failed at this point to carry through consistently their insistence upon faith as necessary to the reception

According to the confessions, the children of believing parents must be baptized for the same reason as their believing parents: God is pleased to extend the gospel promise to them. The ground for the baptism of children of believers is their divinely promised inclusion in the church and covenant of Jesus Christ. Therefore, as members of Christ and recipients of the gospel promise, their baptism has the same meaning as that of adult believers. Like the baptism of adult believers, the baptism of the children of believers includes great privileges and corresponding obligations. Consistent with the Reformed understanding of the divine initiative in election and the communication of God's grace in Christ to his people, the baptism of children of believing parents signifies and attests to their adoption into the household of God and the washing away of their sins through the blood of Christ and the Spirit of regeneration.

Several biblical considerations are adduced in the confessions to support the practice of the baptism of children of believing parents: God's gracious promise to them; their inclusion within the covenant people of God; the kingdom of God belongs to them; the Old Testament precedent of the sacrament of circumcision, which in the New Testament has been replaced by baptism; and the Old Testament practice of offering a lamb of purification at the birth of a child, which was a sacrament of Jesus Christ. No more than in the case of adult believers are children baptized on the basis of a presumed regeneration or any other subjective condition (such as an infant faith or the faith of the parents in lieu of their own). Since the power and efficacy of the sacrament

---

of the sacrament. The Reformers simply adopted a common social practice of the day and then invented ("necessity is the mother of invention") a theological justification for it. In this criticism, Barth fails to appreciate the Reformed view of the sacrament as essentially *God's sacramental signifying and sealing of his grace* to believers and their children. Though it is true that faith receives the grace that the sacrament confers, it does so as a receptive rather than constitutive act. The children of believing parents who are baptized must believe, to be sure, but their believing is a response to the gracious promise previously signified and sealed to them in the sacrament of baptism. The argument of the Reformed confessions, which is a biblical argument based upon the doctrine of the covenant and God's sovereign initiatives in salvation, underscores the sheer graciousness of God's grace in the promise he makes to the children of believing parents. For a discussion of Barth's critique and a defense of the Reformed view, see G. C. Berkouwer, *Karl Barth en de Kinderdoop* (Kampen: J. H. Kok, 1947).

of baptism, as is the case with the sacraments generally, depend upon a believing reception of the sacramentally communicated Word of grace, the baptized children of believers are under the obligation to believe and repent that accompanies the privileges of their baptism. Moreover, because the sacramental sign and seal are to be distinguished from the spiritual grace they confirm, the efficacy of baptism may not be tied to the moment of its administration.[39] This does not diminish the efficacy of baptism but acknowledges that its power may not be immediately exhibited.

And fifth, the only Reformed confession that expressly addresses the issue of the validity of baptism in the Roman Catholic communion is the Gallican Confession. Whereas the Scots Confession seems to warrant the inference that Roman Catholic baptism is invalid, the Gallican Confession expressly affirms its validity as a "trace" of the true church remaining within that communion.

Though it has been the general practice of the Reformed churches to acknowledge the validity of baptism in the Roman Catholic Church, there have been exceptions to this practice, particularly in the Presbyterian tradition. Some encouragement to regarding Roman Catholic baptism as invalid undoubtedly stems from the kind of emphases found in the Scots Confession and later Puritanism. In this tradition, much is made of the unlawful manner in which baptism is administered in the Roman Catholic Church. Perhaps this is the reason an interesting debate on this issue arose within North American Presbyterianism in the mid-nineteenth century. After the General Assembly of the Presbyterian Church in the U.S.A. (Old School) in 1845 declared Roman Catholic baptism invalid, Charles Hodge contested the decision and argued for the traditional Reformed view. Hodge maintained that, by virtue of the presence of the

---

39. This point is one we have considered previously, particularly in connection with the necessity of the sacraments. Children of believing parents who die in infancy without having been baptized may be regenerated by the Spirit without the ordinary use of the means of grace. Furthermore, since baptism is a sign and seal of regeneration, it is not to be confused with the reality of regeneration, which may, in God's sovereign grace and the working of the Spirit, precede or follow baptism. See the Westminster Confession of Faith, chapter 28.6.

essential components of the sacrament in the Roman Catholic Church, its baptism was to be regarded as valid.[40] James Henley Thornwell, one of the advocates of the General Assembly's position, responded to Hodge with an extensive article.[41] In his argument against Hodge's view, Thornwell insisted that four requirements must be fulfilled for the sacrament to be valid: one, a washing with the sacramental sign of water; two, the use of the Trinitarian name of God; three, a professed intention to comply with the command of Christ; and four, the administration of the sacrament by a lawful minister of Christ. According to Thornwell, none of these requirements is met by the Roman Catholic sacrament of baptism.

In my judgment, the position of Hodge in this debate best represents the historic doctrine and practice of the Reformed churches. In the Reformed churches, the sacrament of baptism in the Roman Catholic communion is acknowledged to be valid, however irregular may be some of its features. So long as the essential elements of water and the Trinitarian words of institution are present, the sacrament constitutes a "trace" of the true church of Jesus Christ, to use the language of the Gallican Confession. This practice not only acknowledges the presence in the Roman Catholic Church of "traces" of the true church but it also helps to preserve the principle that baptism is an initiatory rite to be performed only once. It is also consistent with a common affirmation in the Reformed confessions that the validity of the sacrament does not depend upon the integrity of the minister. Therefore, if a Reformed church should choose in a particular case not to acknowledge the validity of Roman Catholic baptism, it should do so in such a way as to preserve the principle that baptism is never repeated. As a practical matter, this would require the decision that the person had not in any valid sense previously been baptized.

When all of these observations regarding the sacrament of baptism in the Reformed confessions are taken seriously, it

40. See Charles Hodge, "Romish Baptism," in *The Biblical Repertory and Princeton Review for the Year 1845,* 17: 444–71.

41. James Henley Thornwell, "The Validity of the Baptism of Rome," in *The Collected Writings of James Henley Thornwell* (1875; repr., Carlisle, PA: Banner of Truth, 1986), 3:283–412.

should be evident that there is a continuing need for Reformed churches to live up to their confession in the way they teach about and administer the sacrament of baptism. The doctrine of the sacrament of baptism in the Reformed confessions needs to be given far greater emphasis in the teaching and preaching ministry of the churches. If there is to be genuine renewal in the Reformed churches, so far as the administration and use of the sacraments are concerned, pastors and teachers must give themselves self-consciously to the instruction of their congregations in the doctrine of the sacraments set forth in the confessions. How many pastors have thoroughly studied the confessions on the doctrine of the sacraments and of baptism? And how many have taught courses whose primary topic was the sacraments as means of grace? If the confession of the churches is to be a living confession, one that gives birth to a corresponding practice, then it must be a confession that is known and owned by those who are members of the church.

But such instruction of the congregation is by itself inadequate. Much greater attention also needs to be given to the visibility of the sacraments in the life of the congregation. By the visibility of the sacrament, I refer to such things as the architecture and furnishing of the sanctuaries or places of worship, the location of the baptismal font and the Communion table, the care with which the sacrament is administered, and the seriousness with which the sacraments are viewed. It is not uncommon today to find Reformed churches where the baptismal font or Communion table is barely visible to the congregation. Nor is it uncommon to find pastors and elders who do not provide careful instruction for believers on the occasion of their baptism or the baptism of their children. Particularly problematic is the practice of delaying the baptism of children of believing parents for considerations which have little to do with and often diminish the importance of the sacrament itself.[42] Seldom are congregants

---

42. In the practice of the Reformed churches historically, baptism of the children of believing parents was usually administered as soon as feasible. Some church orders of Reformed communions still stipulate this practice. Admittedly, pastors need to be sensitive to considerations that might delay the administration of the sacrament. But they ought to resist unnecessary delay that only reinforces a diminished view of the sacrament's importance.

reminded of their baptism, for example, as a defining reality so far as their Christian life and communion with the triune God is concerned. The privileges and responsibilities that accompany Christian baptism do not figure prominently in the preaching and teaching ministry of the church. In each of these areas, the Reformed churches need to restore a practice that corresponds to their confession that the sacraments are an indispensable means of grace, accompanying the preaching of the Word and appointed of Christ for the nourishing and strengthening of faith.

Chapter 6

The Lord's Supper: The Sacrament of Nourishment in Christ (1)

In his fine biography of the life of the Reformer Martin Luther, Roland Bainton offers a vivid account of Luther's first celebration of the Mass. At the time, Luther was fully persuaded that he was about to reenact the sacrifice of Christ on the cross, which would involve the miracle of the bread and wine of the sacrament becoming his body and blood. This was a holy act unlike any performed on the earth, superior to any other in its spiritual efficacy to communicate eternal salvation to sinners. Luther was about to stand as a priest before the altar and prepare to enjoy sacramental communion with the crucified and risen Christ. Bainton records Luther's description of his anxiety when he came to the words "We offer unto thee, the living, the true, the eternal God" in the introductory portion of the Mass:

> At these words I was utterly stupefied and terror-stricken. I thought to myself, "With what tongue shall I address such Majesty, seeing that all men ought to tremble in the presence of even an earthly prince? Who am I, that I should lift up mine eyes or raise my hands to the divine Majesty? The angels surround him. At his nod the earth trembles. And shall I, a miserable little pygmy, say "I want this, I ask for that"? For I am dust and ashes and full of sin and I am speaking to the living, eternal and the true God.[1]

In our profane and post-Christian culture, we are apt to smile condescendingly at Luther's pre-modern fear of Christ's holy presence in the Mass. Not only do few people fear the holy presence of the triune God, but even fewer believe that presence is mediated in any significant fashion through the church's

---

1. Roland Bainton, *Here I Stand: A Life of Martin Luther* (1950; repr., New York: Abingdon Press, 1978), 30.

sacraments. Moreover, Protestant believers who repudiate the Roman Catholic doctrine of transubstantiation, which teaches that in the priest's act of consecration the elements of bread and wine become in "substance" (though not in "accidents," to use the traditional language of the Roman Catholic Church) the actual body and blood of Christ, will attribute Luther's anxiety on this occasion to his improper identification of the sacramental sign and the reality signified.[2] If Luther had known, as we know, that the sacramental elements are *merely* visible tokens or symbols of an invisible grace, then he would not have trembled in holy awe before the altar. Perhaps the kind of awe and fear Luther experienced at the altar would be appropriate in the presence of the preaching of the Word, which for Reformed believers is the preeminent means of grace, or the God-appointed instrument for communicating the gospel of God's grace in Christ.[3] But it seems inappropriate and exaggerated in the context of the sacraments, including the sacrament of the Lord's Supper.

I do not refer to this episode from Luther's life in order to suggest that his understanding of the sacrament of the Mass at the time was a valid one. Nor do I mention it in order to argue that the sacraments, which accompany as visible signs and seals the preaching of the Word of the gospel, are on a par with preaching as means to communicate the grace of Christ. As I have argued in previous chapters, the lively preaching of the Word of God has always had pride of place in an evangelical and

---

2. The classic Roman Catholic doctrine of transubstantiation was first formulated at the Fourth Lateran Council in 1215 and later was given dogmatic form at the Council of Trent. See "The Canons and Decrees of the Council of Trent," Thirteenth Session, Decree Concerning the Most Holy Sacrament of the Eucharist, 1 (from Philip Schaff, *The Creeds of Christendom,* 2.126): "In the first place, the holy Synod teaches, and openly and simply professes, that, in the august sacrament of the holy Eucharist, after the consecration of the bread and wine, our Lord Jesus Christ, true God and man, is truly, really, and substantially contained under the species of those visible things." For a more recent statement of the doctrine, see *Catechism of the Catholic Church,* para. 1373–81.

3. See James Daane, *Preaching with Confidence: A Theological Essay on the Power of the Pulpit* (Grand Rapids: Eerdmans, 1980), 8, who makes the point that the pulpit is the holy place in a Reformed understanding of worship and the communication of the gospel. If there is a place for trembling in Reformed worship, then, it should be at the pulpit.

Reformed understanding of the God-appointed means of grace. The sacraments do not stand alone, but accompany and confirm the Word first communicated through preaching. Therefore, apart from the preaching of the gospel, the sacraments would be empty and meaningless signs.

However, the preeminence of preaching is not to be understood in a way that diminishes the importance and use of the sacraments. The sacraments of the new covenant in Christ, Christian baptism and the Lord's Supper, are instruments that Christ has appointed for use in the power of his Spirit to initiate and maintain fellowship with his people. Christian baptism is an effective means by which Christ through the Spirit signifies and seals to believers and their children their incorporation into him and the body of his church. In baptism believers receive a powerful, visible attestation of the promise of salvation through Christ and of their membership in the visible fellowship of his church. Baptism as Christ's visible sign and seal is not to be diminished in significance throughout the whole course of the believer's life. Moreover, to this sacrament Christ has added another, the Lord's Supper, as an equally powerful means to nourish and strengthen believers in their fellowship with him. Though the Reformed churches do not teach that Christ's presence in the Supper is effected by a miracle of transubstantiation, they certainly maintain, as we shall see in the following survey of the classical Reformed confessions, that Christ is truly present through the sacrament when it is received by the mouth of faith.

The difference, then, between the Roman Catholic view of the sacraments and a Reformed view is not that the former emphasizes the sacraments while the latter diminishes them. The difference, rather, is that the Roman Catholic view fails to appreciate properly the first and preeminent use of preaching as a means of grace. And in so doing, the Roman view misunderstands the nature and function of the sacraments. But the Reformed view, though it rightly emphasizes preaching, does not thereby belittle the sacraments. Even though the practice of many Reformed churches may belie their profession, the confessions of the Reformed churches make quite clear the indispensable role of the sacraments in the Christian life. The preaching of the

Word is a holy and awesome affair, for Christ dwells among his people through the preaching of the gospel. But no less holy and awesome are the sacramental signs and seals that accompany the gospel. In the sacraments Christ is pleased to give himself to his people in a manner distinct from that of preaching but not to be ignored. Indeed, the problem with the Roman Catholic doctrine of the Eucharist, or the Mass,[4] is not that it stresses the *presence* of Christ in the sacrament. *That* Christ is present in the sacraments of baptism, and most especially in the sacrament of the Lord's Supper, is the common testimony of the Reformed confessions. The mode of Christ's presence is understood rather differently, as is the manner in which Christ is received through the sacrament. However, here the Reformed churches echo the conviction of the holy catholic and apostolic church: Christ communes with his people under the veil of the earthly elements of the sacrament. This communion is genuine and vital.

In the following exposition of the Reformed confessions on the sacrament of the Lord's Supper, I will be using the same approach as in my chapters on the doctrine of preaching and the sacrament of baptism. Rather than attempting to describe the complex historical setting within which these confessions were written, I will be examining them as a distillation of the official teaching, on the basis of Scripture, of the Reformed churches on the doctrine of the Lord's Supper.[5] Though these confessions are

---

4. In the Reformed tradition, the sacrament is ordinarily referred to as the Lord's Supper, though reference is also often made to Holy Communion or simply the Supper. In the Roman Catholic tradition, the language of the Mass is most common, though the sacrament is also called Holy Communion or the Eucharist (which means "thanksgiving"). The term *mass* comes from a Latin root and is based in the ancient language used for the dismissal (*Ite, missa est*) of communicant members from the service of worship after the sacrament was administered. In the Eastern Orthodox tradition, the sacrament is often termed the Divine Liturgy or Union (*syntaxis*). Among the Reformed confessions, we will see that the Second Helvetic is unique in its special consideration of the various names for the sacrament. For a recent consideration of the different terms for the sacrament, see Michael Welker, *What Happens in Holy Communion?*, trans. John F. Hoffmeyer (Grand Rapids: Eerdmans, 2000), 2–3, 55–68.

5. For a broad overview of the history of the doctrine of the Lord's Supper prior to the Reformation, see Keith A. Mathison, *Given for You: Reclaiming Calvin's Doctrine of the Lord's Supper* (Phillipsburg, NJ: P&R, 2002), 325–52. For an extensive historical study of the conflicts in the sixteenth century over the doctrine of the Lord's Supper, see Ernst Bizer, *Studien zur Geschichte des*

subordinate to Scripture, something they also attest, and need to be tested continually by the study of the biblical Word, this will not be my purpose. My aim is to summarize the traditional doctrine of the Lord's Supper that has shaped the ministry of Reformed churches since the time of the Reformation.[6]

The Gallican (French) Confession of Faith of 1559

The Gallican (French) Confession of 1559 addresses the sacrament of the Lord's Supper in a relatively brief manner, without any significant elaboration of the doctrine in the context of the extensive debates of the sixteenth century.[7] Though this confession distinguishes its teaching from the Roman Catholic and Anabaptist alternatives, it presents a simple summary of the Reformed view, which reflects the profound influence of Calvin's teaching. When considering the doctrine of the Lord's Supper in this confession, it is important to remember that John Calvin was the primary author of its original draft. When he wrote an early draft of this confession, Calvin was coming to the close of his reformatory labor during which he had on numerous occasions polemically engaged the subject of the sacrament.[8] Thus, the confession's doctrine

---

Abendmahlsstreits im 16. Jahrhundert (Gütersloh: Verlag C. Bertelsmann, 1940).

6.   There are at least two studies in English of the Reformed confessions and their doctrine of the Lord's Supper that take a more synthetic or topical approach. They are Jan Rohls, *Reformed Confessions: Theology from Zurich to Barmen* (Louisville, KY: Westminster John Knox Press, 1997); and B. Gerrish, "Sign and Reality: The Lord's Supper in the Reformed Confessions," in *The Old Protestantism and the New: Essays on the Reformation Heritage,* 118–30 (Edinburgh: T. & T. Clark, 1982).

7.   See Rohls, *Reformed Confessions,* 219: "An extensive critique of the Mass is to be found only in the early confessions, for an understandable reason. After the Mass was completely done away with in the Reformed church, its treatment no longer had an object." Not only is the Gallican Confession something of an exception to this rule, but Rohl's observation also seems overstated. As we shall see, all of the classic Reformed confessions, including the Westminster Standards of the seventeenth century, offer a considerable critique of the Roman Catholic doctrine of the Mass.

8.   It is hardly possible to overstate the influence of Calvin's doctrine of the Lord's Supper upon the magisterial Reformed tradition embodied in its confessions. Though we shall have occasion to contrast this doctrine with that of Zwingli in the following, there can be no doubt that Calvin's, not Zwingli's, view of the Lord's Supper prevailed. For Calvin's statement of his view of the sacrament, see his following works: *Institutes,* 4.14, 17–18; "Short Treatise on the Lord's Supper," in

represents an epitome of Calvin's view.

According to the Gallican Confession, Christ is pleased to communicate himself and his saving graces through the ministry and fellowship of the church. The church is distinguished by the two marks of the ministry of the Word and the sacraments: "There can be no Church where the Word of God is not received, nor profession made of subjection to it, nor use of the sacraments" (art. 28). God has added the sacraments to the Word "for more ample confirmation, that they may be to us pledges and seals of the grace of God, and by this means aid and comfort our faith, because of the infirmity which is in us" (art. 31). In the new covenant church, there are two sacraments the Lord has appointed, holy baptism and the Lord's Supper (art. 35). The first of these, holy baptism, is a pledge and seal of the believer's incorporation into Christ and his church. Because of its significance as an initiatory rite, baptism is administered only once, though its use and efficacy encompass the whole life of the believer.

What distinguishes the Lord's Supper as a sacrament is that it continually nourishes and strengthens faith. It is "a witness of the union which we have with Christ, inasmuch as he not only died and rose again for us once, but also feeds and nourishes us truly with his flesh and blood, so that we may be in him, and that our life may be in common."[9] In the sacrament of

---

Selected Works of John Calvin, ed. Henry Beveridge (1849; repr., Grand Rapids: Baker, 1983), 2.163–98; "Second Defense of the Sacraments," in *Selected Works,* 2:245–345; "Last Admonition to Joachim Westphal," in *Selected Works,* 2.346–494; and "True Partaking of the Flesh and Blood of Christ," in *Selected Works,* 2.495–572. For a treatment of Calvin's view, see G. S. M. Walker, "The Lord's Supper in the Theology and Practice of Calvin," in *John Calvin: A Collection of Distinguished Essays,* ed. G. E. Duffield (Grand Rapids: Eerdmans, 1966), 131–48; W. Niesel, *Calvin's Lehre von Abendmahl* (Munich, 1935); Ronald S. Wallace, *Calvin's Doctrine of the Word and Sacrament* (Grand Rapids: Eerdmans, 1957); Brian A. Gerrish, *Grace and Gratitude: The Eucharistic Theology of John Calvin* (Minneapolis: Fortress, 1993); B. A. Gerrish, "Gospel and Eucharist: John Calvin on the Lord's Supper," in *The Old Protestantism and the New,* 106–17; and Thomas J. Davis, *The Clearest Promises of God: The Development of Calvin's Eucharistic Teaching* (New York: AMS Press, Inc. 1995).

9. Article 36: "We confess that the Lord's Supper, which is the second sacrament, is a witness of the union which we have with Christ, inasmuch as he not only died and rose again for us once, but also feeds and nourishes us truly with his flesh and blood, so that we may be one in him, and that our life may be

the Lord's Supper, believers are repeatedly confirmed in their fellowship with Christ, whose body and blood are their spiritual food and drink.

Two emphases stand out in the Gallican Confession's brief exposition of this sacrament: the genuineness of the sacrament's communication of Christ himself to those who participate, and the necessity of faith to a proper reception of what the sacrament imparts.

On the question of the nature of Christ's presence in the sacrament, the confession uses language that is distinctly Calvinian: "Although he be in heaven until he come to judge all the earth, still we believe that by the secret and incomprehensible power of his Spirit he feeds and strengthens us with the substance of his body and his blood."[10] Christ is "spiritually" present through the sacrament, not in the sense of "imagination and fancy" but in that of "fact and truth."[11] The Spirit of Christ working through the sacrament grants it efficacy and accounts for the miracle of Christ's presence. Indeed, though the "greatness of this mystery exceeds the measure of our senses and the laws of nature," it is no less real than were it effected by alternative means.[12] This presence is not "local" in the sense that Christ's body is brought from heaven to earth or, through a miracle like that of transubstantiation or consubstantiation, that it becomes present "in" the sacramental elements.[13] But neither

---

in common. Although he be in heaven until he come to judge all the earth, still we believe that by the secret and incomprehensible power of his Spirit he feeds and strengthens us with the substance of his body and of his blood. We hold that this is done spiritually, not because we put imagination and fancy in the place of fact and truth, but because the greatness of this mystery exceeds the measure of our senses and the laws of nature. In short, because it is heavenly, it can only be apprehended by faith."

10. Article 36: "Or combien qu'il soit au ciel iusques à ce qu'il viene pour iuger tout le monde: toutesfois nous croyon que par la vertu secrete et incomprehensible de son Esprit, il nous nourrit de vivifie de la substance de son corps et de son sang." Niesel, *Bekenntnisschriften*, 74:35–39.

11. Article 36: " . . . non pas pour mettre au lieu de l'effect et de la verité, imagination ne pensee." Niesel, *Bekenntnisschriften*, 74.40–41.

12. Article 36: " . . . mais de'autant que ce mystere surmonte en sa hautesse la mesure de nostre sens, et tout ordre de nature." Niesel, *Bekenntnisschriften*, 74.41–43.

13. Though the Gallican Confession teaches that the substance of Christ's body is given "with" the sacramental elements, it implicitly rejects the Lutheran

is it spiritual in the sense that the "substance" of Christ's body and blood is not truly communicated to the believing participant. Therefore, it is not simply the power or efficacy of Christ's saving work that is imparted sacramentally through the Lord's Supper. Christ himself is communicated, and a real sacramental union is effected between him and those who belong to him. Those who disparage the sacrament by emptying the signs and elements, separating too much between the sacramental sign and the thing signified, are to be condemned. Accordingly, the Gallican Confession concludes with an explicit criticism of the Anabaptist's belittling of the sacrament and obliquely refers to the Zwinglian reduction of the sacrament to a mere visible symbolization of the believer's faith communion with Christ.[14]

In order for the sacramental sign and seal of Christ's body and blood to be a means of communion with Christ, the sacrament must be received with a "pure faith" that functions "like a vessel" in appropriating Christ.[15] Just as bread and wine

---

teaching of a local presence of the body of Christ "in, with, and under" the elements. This Lutheran doctrine, especially as it was to be formulated in the Formula of Concord, reflects a certain Christological viewpoint in which, by virtue of the "communion of the attributes" (*communicatio idiomatum*), the glorified body of Christ has the quality of "ubiquity." For a statement of the classic Lutheran view of Christ's presence in the Supper, see the Formula of Concord, article 7, "Of the Lord's Supper," and article 8, "Of the Person of Christ." Schaff, *The Creeds of Christendom*, 3.135–59. For a discussion of the history and debate among Roman Catholic, Lutheran, and Reformed regarding the Christological implications of Christ's presence in the Lord's Supper, see G. C. Berkouwer, "The Unity of the Person," in *The Person of Christ*, 271–304, trans. J. Vriend (Grand Rapids: Eerdmans, 1954).

14. The Gallican Confession identifies Zwinglians or those who affirm a merely symbolical view of Christ's presence in the Supper as "Sacramentarians," or "sacramentaires" (art. 38). This language may have been used first by Luther against the Zwinglian view and was later used by Lutherans in the Formula of Concord as a term of opprobrium against the Reformed view in all of its forms. It is instructive, therefore, that the Gallican Confession seeks to disassociate its view of Christ's real presence from that of the "sacramentarians." See Christopher Elwood, *The Body Broken: The Calvinist Doctrine of the Eucharist and the Symbolization of Power in Sixteenth-Century France* (New York: Oxford University Press, 1999), 181n25: "The term 'sacramentarian' was coined probably by Martin Luther in his controversy with the Swiss over the manner of Christ's presence in the eucharist and the interpretation of Christ's words of institution as a derogatory description of the position of those who denied the bodily presence of Christ in the sacrament."

15. Article 37: "And thus all who bring a pure faith, like a vessel (comme un

nourish the body, so the body and blood of Christ, sacramentally signified and visibly exhibited to faith, are the nourishment of the believer's soul. Faith serves, therefore, as an instrument to receive Christ as he is communicated sacramentally in the same way that the preaching of the Word calls for faith on the part of the one who hears.

The Scots Confession of 1560

Compared to the relatively concise statement of the doctrine of the Lord's Supper in the Gallican Confession, the Scots Confession of 1560 is far more expansive and detailed. It draws sharp lines of distinction between the Reformed and alternative views of the sacrament. In that respect, the Scots Confession attests to the vigor of the sixteenth-century debates regarding the sacraments in general and the sacrament of the Lord's Supper in particular more openly than the Gallican Confession .

In its extended statement outlining the general doctrine of the sacraments, the Scots Confession steers a careful course between two alternatives. On the one hand, the Scots Confession emphasizes that the two sacraments the Lord Jesus has instituted for his church are not "naked and bare signs."[16] The sacraments truly effect the believer's engrafting into Christ (baptism) and nourish through their continual use (Lord's Supper) the believer's fellowship and union with him. Through the Lord's Supper believers are "so joined" with Christ that he becomes "the very nourishment and food of [their] souls." This confession is eager to reply to the slander of those who maintain that the Reformed church teaches that the sacraments are mere "symbols and nothing more" (art. 21). On the other hand, the Scots Confession is at some pains to distinguish its understanding of Christ's real presence in the sacrament from

---

vaisseau [Niesel, *Bekenntnisschriften,* 75.1]), to the sacred table of Christ, receive truly that of which it is a sign; for the body and the blood of Jesus Christ give food and drink to the soul, no less than bread and wine nourish the body."

16. Chapter 21: "And so we utterly condemn the vanity of those who affirm the sacraments to be nothing else than naked and bare signs. No, we assuredly believe that by Baptism we are engrafted into Christ Jesus, to be made partakers of his righteousness, by which our sins are covered and remitted, and also that in the Supper rightly used, Christ Jesus is so joined with us that he becomes the very nourishment and food of our souls."

the view commonly taught in the Roman Catholic Church.

Negatively stated, Christ's presence in the Lord's Supper is not to be accounted for by a doctrine of transubstantiation. The sacramental signs of bread and wine, however closely united to the body and blood of Christ that they signify and represent, are not to be identified with the actual body and blood of Christ. Rather than accounting for the presence of Christ in the sacrament by means of this doctrine, the Scots Confession ascribes the "union and conjunction which we have with the body and blood of Christ Jesus in the right use of the sacraments" to the working of the Holy Spirit.[17] The Spirit is the one "who by faith carries us above all things that are visible, carnal, and earthly, and makes us feed upon the body and blood of Christ Jesus, once broken and shed for us but now in heaven, and appearing for us in the presence of his Father" (art. 21). By this "mystical action" of the Holy Spirit, believers "do so eat the body and drink the blood of the Lord Jesus that he remains in them and they in him." Despite the "distance between [Christ's] glorified body in heaven and mortal men on earth," Christians who partake of the sacrament enjoy a genuine communion with the body and blood of Christ, their spiritual food. Though the sacramental signs are not to be identified with what they signify, neither may they be separated so as to become "symbols and nothing more" (art. 21).

After this ringing affirmation of the real presence of Christ in the Lord's Supper, the Scots Confession addresses the subjects of the right administration of the sacraments and the identity of their recipients. The sacraments, because they accompany and confirm the gospel, which is preeminently communicated

---

17. Article 21: "Not that we imagine any transubstantiation of bread into Christ's body, and of wine into his natural blood, as the Romanists have perniciously taught and wrongly believed; but this union and conjunction which we have with the body and blood of Christ Jesus, in the right use of the sacraments is wrought by means of the Holy Ghost, who by true faith carries us above all things that are visible, carnal and earthly, and makes us feed upon the body and blood of Christ Jesus, once broken and shed for us but now in heaven, and appearing for us in the presence of his Father. Notwithstanding the distance between his glorified body in heaven and mortal men on earth, yet we must assuredly believe that the bread which we break is the communion of Christ's body and the cup which we bless the communion of his blood."

through preaching, must be administered by "lawful ministers" and "in the elements and manner which God has appointed" (art. 22). Neither of these essential components are present in the Roman Catholic administration of baptism and the Lord's Supper. In the sacrament of the Mass, the consecrated elements are adored or venerated, as if they were identical to the body and blood of Christ they signify. Furthermore, one of the two indispensable elements, the blessed cup, is withheld from the people. Rather than confirming the pure Word of the gospel, the Mass is administered by priests who teach false doctrine and act as "mediators" between Christ and his church. When the Mass is celebrated, the priests offer to God a "propitiation for the sins of the living and the dead," a propitiation that, in the nature of the case, "is blasphemous to Jesus Christ and would deprive his unique sacrifice, once offered on the cross for the cleansing of all who are to be sanctified, of its sufficiency" (art. 22).[18]

In a closing chapter that addresses to whom the sacraments appertain, it is noted that the sacrament requires faith, particularly a believing apprehension of the grace signified and sealed in it. This requires that in any proper administration of the sacrament of the Lord's Supper the recipients "try and examine themselves both in their faith and their duty to their neighbors" (art. 23). Such self-examination is a prerequisite to a believing reception of the sacramental elements and demands that those who present themselves for the sacrament undergo a "public and individual examination" by the ministers of the church. Unless such an examination is undertaken prior to the reception of the sacrament, the recipients would partake unworthily, whether because of the absence of proper faith or the absence of a proper

---

18. Though the Council of Trent endeavors to treat the Mass not so much as a repetition of Christ's sacrifice upon the cross as its re-presentation or reenactment, it nonetheless regards it as an "unbloody" sacrifice that merits or obtains additional grace for its beneficiaries. This is evident from the following statement of the Council in its Twenty-Second Session, "Doctrine on the Sacrifice of the Mass": "And forasmuch as, in this divine sacrifice which is celebrated in the mass, that same Christ is contained and immolated in an unbloody manner who once offered himself in a bloody manner on the altar of the cross; the holy Synod teaches, that this sacrifice is truly propitiatory, and that by means thereof this is effected, that we obtain mercy." Schaff, *The Creeds of Christendom*, 2.179.

relationship of "peace and goodwill to their brethren."[19]

Belgic Confession of 1561

Compared to the relatively brief statement of the Gallican Confession, the Belgic Confession follows closely the pattern of the Scots Confession of 1560 in its elaboration of the doctrine of the Lord's Supper. Guido de Brès, the primary author, used the Gallican Confession as a prototype in formulating this confession. On the doctrine of the Lord's Supper, however, he chose to provide a vigorous and extensive statement of the real presence of Christ's body and blood in the sacrament. Perhaps more emphatically than any of the standard symbols of the Reformed churches, this confession articulates a bold and unambiguous affirmation of the manner in which Christ communicates himself to his people in the Lord's Supper.

In the article on the Lord's Supper, the Belgic Confession begins by noting the difference between the sacrament of baptism, which is administered only once as a sign and seal of incorporation into Christ, and the Lord's Supper, which Christ ordained to "nourish and support those whom He has already regenerated and incorporated into His family."[20] Baptism is a sacrament of initiation into the company of Christ's church. The Lord's Supper is a sacrament of continual nourishment and strengthening of believers. Drawing upon the imagery of the John 6 discourse regarding the eating of Christ's body and drinking of his blood, the Belgic Confession distinguishes two kinds of life, the one "corporal and temporal," the other

---

19. The question of what is sometimes termed the "fencing" or "guarding" of the Table of the Lord is one that, as we shall see, is addressed in several of the Reformed confessions. I will return to this question in my conclusion and comment on the implications of the teaching of the confessions for the practice of fencing the Table of the Lord. For a treatment of the administration of the Lord's Supper, including the practice of fencing the table, in the Scottish and English Presbyterian tradition, see Horton Davies, *The Worship of the English Puritans* (1948; repr., Morgan, PA: Soli Deo Gloria, 1997), 204–16; and George B. Burnet, *The Holy Communion in the Reformed Church of Scotland* (Edinburgh: Oliver and Boyd, 1960), esp. 64–87, 158–200.

20. Article 35: "We believe and confess that our Savior Jesus Christ did ordain and institute the sacrament of the holy supper to nourish and support those whom He has already regenerated and incorporated into His family, which is His Church."

"spiritual and heavenly" (art. 35). Just as the former kind of life is sustained by "earthly and common bread," so the latter is sustained by "living bread." Jesus Christ, who descended from heaven as the spiritual bread for his people, is given to believers through the sacrament of the Lord's Supper "when they appropriate and receive Him by faith in the spirit." He becomes thereby the source and fountain of the spiritual vitality of those who belong to him and who receive him through the sacramental means he has appointed.

Particularly significant in the Belgic Confession's handling of the sacrament of the Lord's Supper is its statement of the real presence of Christ in the sacrament. As signs and seals of Christ's body and blood, the sacramental elements of bread and wine are a visible attestation that believers receive by their means "the true body and blood of Christ."[21] This reception of Christ is "by faith," since faith is the "hand and mouth of our soul." Indeed, without faith there can be no reception of the sacrament's truth, however closely linked may be the sacramental signs and the thing they signify. But where faith actively receives Christ communicated through the sacrament, we may be sure that "He works in us all that He represents to us by these holy signs." Though the "manner" of Christ's sacramental presence may surpass our understanding and comprehension—"as the operations of the Holy Spirit are hidden and incomprehensible"—we may nonetheless affirm that "what is eaten and drunk by us is the proper and natural body and the proper blood of Christ."[22] Though Christ is presently seated

---

21. Article 35: "In order that He might represent unto us this spiritual and heavenly bread, Christ has instituted an earthly and visible bread as a sacrament of His body, and wine as a sacrament of His blood, to testify by them unto us that, as certainly as we receive and hold this sacrament in our hands and eat and drink the same with our mouths, by which our life is afterwards nourished, we also do as certainly receive by faith (which is the hand and mouth of our soul) the true body and blood of Christ (le vrai corps et le vrai sang de Christ) our only Savior in our souls, for the support of our spiritual life."

22. Article 35: "Now, as it is certain and beyond all doubt that Jesus Christ has not enjoined to us the use of His sacraments in vain, so He works in us all that He represents to us by these holy signs, though the manner surpasses our understanding and cannot be comprehended by us, as the operations of the Holy Spirit are hidden and incomprehensible. In the meantime we err not when we say that what is eaten and drunk by us is the proper and natural body and the proper

at the right hand of the Father in heaven, this does not prevent his communicating himself with all his benefits to believers by means of the sacrament. When believers receive the sacramental signs and seals of Christ's body and blood by the mouth of faith, they truly enjoy a strengthening and nourishing fellowship with Christ. They sacramentally eat Christ's flesh and drink his blood.

In a closing paragraph, the Belgic Confession emphasizes the proper ecclesiastical setting for the sacrament of the Lord's Supper. This sacrament belongs, in the nature of the case, to the whole body of the church, representing the communion that believers have with Christ and thereby with each other. It is to be administered, accordingly, "in the assembly of the people of God, with humility and reverence, keeping up among us a holy remembrance of the death of Christ our Savior, with thanksgiving, making there confession of our faith and of the Christian religion" (art. 35). Those who partake of this Supper must do so only after having examined themselves, in order that they might be moved by the sacrament to a greater love for God and their neighbor.

Heidelberg Catechism of 1563

The Heidelberg Catechism's treatment of the sacrament of the Lord's Supper clearly reflects the polemical context in which it was written. The history of the sixteenth-century Reformation includes not only a number of disputes between Protestants and Roman Catholics over the Lord's Supper but also vigorous debates among different branches of the Reformation church. The Heidelberg Catechism, written at the request of Elector Frederick III in 1562, was prepared to further confessional unity among the churches of the Palatinate in Germany. The need for the furtherance of confessional unity was especially pressing due to a history of disagreement between the Lutheran and Reformed parties. This disagreement focused significantly

---

blood of Christ (est mangé est le propre et naturel corps de Christ, et son propre sang)." The strength of this affirmation of Christ's real presence in the sacrament was impressed upon me a number of years ago when, to my embarrassment, I identified this language as Roman Catholic during an oral examination for my bachelor of divinity degree at Calvin Theological Seminary.

upon the doctrine of the Lord's Supper and related issues. In the Palatinate, Elector Frederick III was confronted by the inflexibility of strict Lutherans like Hesshus, who worked to win the churches to the Lutheran view of the Lord's Supper, particularly its understanding of the nature of Christ's presence in the sacrament and the corollary doctrine of the ubiquity of Christ's glorified body.[23] Also, disputes among the Reformed arose between those who held to Calvin's view of the Supper and others who were influenced by Zwingli. The history of these disputes accounts for the catechism's extensive and detailed handling of the subject.[24]

The catechism's treatment of the Lord's Supper can be distinguished into three general parts. In the first set of questions and answers regarding this sacrament, the catechism provides a positive statement of what it signifies and seals to believers. In the second set of questions, the nature of Christ's presence in the Supper, particularly as this is distinguished from the Roman Catholic view, is addressed. Then in the third set of questions, the catechism considers the issue of the proper recipients of the sacrament and the need for church discipline in excluding unbelieving and impenitent persons from participation.

In the opening exposition of the meaning and significance of the Lord's Supper, the Heidelberg Catechism stresses its function as a visible representation of Christ's sacrifice on the cross and the saving benefits of his mediatorial work. When believers partake of the Supper, they are provided a visible token and pledge that Christ's body was offered and his blood shed for them. The sacrament visibly confirms believers in their participation in Christ; his sacrifice benefits them, and his

---

23. For a firsthand account of these disputes, particularly Calvin's answer to the arguments of the Lutherans, Westphal, and Hesshus, see John Calvin, "True Partaking of the Flesh and Blood of Christ in the Holy Supper," in *Selected Works,* 2.495–572.

24. For a treatment of the history and background of the Heidelberg Catechism, see Fred H. Klooster, *The Heidelberg Catechism: Origin and History* (Grand Rapids: Calvin Theological Seminary, 1987/1988); Schaff, *Creeds of Christendom,* 1.52–54; Bard Thompson, "Historical Background of the Catechism," in *Essays on the Heidelberg Catechism,* ed. Bard Thompson et al. (Philadelphia: United Church Press, 1963), 8–30; John Williamson Nevin, *History and Genius of the Heidelberg Catechism* (Chambersburg, 1847), 9–56; and Bizer, *Studien zur Geschichte des Abendmahlsstreits,* 300–62.

crucified body and shed blood are their spiritual food. Because of the intimate conjunction of the sacramental sign and the grace signified, believers may be persuaded that they are members of Christ "as certainly" as they see the sacramental elements with their eyes and "as assuredly" as they receive them from the minister's hand.[25] Furthermore, since the sacrament visibly represents the gospel, which is firstly and chiefly administered through lively preaching, it demands a believing reception on the part of its recipient. Unless the recipient acknowledges the truth of the gospel promise, which is visibly signified in the sacrament, it is not possible that the sacrament should serve as a means to nourish and strengthen faith. However, when believers "embrace with a believing heart all the sufferings and the death of Christ," they obtain a greater assurance of the forgiveness of sins and eternal life and grow into a deeper and more intimate fellowship with Christ. Through the sacrament, the believer becomes "more and more united to [Christ's] body, by the Holy Spirit, who dwells both in Christ and in us, so that, though Christ is in heaven and we are on earth, we are nevertheless flesh of his flesh and bone of his bones, and live and are governed by one Spirit, as members of the same body are by one soul" (Q&A 76).

When it comes to the disputed question of the nature of Christ's presence in the Supper, the Heidelberg Catechism frames its doctrine between the alternatives of Roman Catholicism and Lutheranism. Though Elector Frederick III hoped to unite the churches of the Palatinate in their confession of the catholic Christian faith, his Reformed sensitivities on the subject of the presence of Christ in the Lord's Supper clearly influenced the

---

25. Q&A 75: "How is it signified and sealed unto you in the holy supper that you partake of the one sacrifice of Christ, accomplished on the cross, and of all His benefits? Thus, that Christ has commanded me and all believers to eat of this broken bread and to drink of this cup in remembrance of Him, and has added these promises: first, that His body was offered and broken on the cross for me, and His blood shed for me, as certainly as I see with my eyes the bread of the Lord broken for me, and the cup communicated to me; and further, that with His crucified body and shed blood He Himself feeds and nourishes my soul to everlasting life as assuredly as I receive from the hand of the minister, and taste with my mouth, the bread and cup of the Lord as sure signs of the body and blood of Christ."

formulations of the catechism. In its exposition of the local presence of the body of the ascended Christ, for example, it gives an answer that implicitly rejects the Lutheran doctrine of the ubiquity of Christ's glorified body. Because the Lutheran doctrine of consubstantiation requires the local presence of Christ's body wherever the sacrament is administered, it represents, from the point of view of the Heidelberg Catechism, a failure to maintain the distinct properties of the human and divine natures of Christ.[26] To affirm that by virtue of the union of the exalted Christ's human nature with the divine that the body of Christ becomes ubiquitous is to move in the direction of a Eutychian Christology by confusing the properties of humanity and deity. Moreover, question and answer 80, which expressly condemns the Roman Catholic understanding of the Mass, was added to the second edition of the catechism at

---

26. The Reformed view of the local presence of Christ's body, which denies the Lutheran teaching of its ubiquity, is clearly expressed elsewhere in the catechism, Q&A 48: "But if His human nature is not present wherever His Godhead is, are not then these two natures in Christ separated from one another? Not at all; for since the Godhead is illimitable and omnipresent, it must follow that it is beyond the bounds of the human nature [German: ausserhalb ihrer angenommen; Latin: extra humanum naturam] it has assumed, and yet none the less is in this human nature and remains personally united to it." The Latin translation and expression *extra humanum naturam* (beyond the human nature) became the occasion historically for Lutheran theologians to speak of "that Calvinistic extra" (*extra-calvinisticum*). For a treatment of this Christological issue and its significance in the debates between Reformed and Lutheran theology historically, see Calvin, *Institutes,* 2.13.4 and 2.16.14; Berkouwer, *Person of Christ,* 93–95; Berkouwer, *The Work of Christ,* trans. C. Lambregste (Grand Rapids: Eerdmans, 1965), 234–41; E. David Willis, *Calvin's Catholic Christology* (Leiden: E. J. Brill, 1966); Thomas F. Torrance, "Calvin and the Knowledge of God," *The Christian Century* 81, no. 22 (May 27, 1964): 696–99; Richard Muller, s.v. "communicatio idiomatum/communicatio proprietatum," in *Dictionary of Latin and Greek Theological Terms* (Grand Rapids: Baker, 1985), 72–75; and Karl Barth, *Church Dogmatics,* trans. G. W. Bromiley, vol. 4, part 1, *The Doctrine of Reconciliation* (Edinburgh: T. & T. Clark, 1956), 180–81. In his study of Calvin's Christology, Willis argues that the Reformed insistence upon the local, nonubiquitous presence of Christ's human nature was no innovation of Calvin or of the Reformed tradition. It was truly an *extra catholicum,* which affirms the presence of the whole person of Christ (*totus Christus*) in all his words and works, but not the presence of the whole of Christ's two natures (*totum Christi*). This Christology accords with the formulation of the Council of Chalcedon in AD 451 (the two natures are neither to be confused nor separated, but retain their respective properties in the union of the one person). It finds expression in a long tradition spanning the writings of Augustine, John of Damascus, and Peter Lombard (*Sentences*).

Elector Frederick's direction.[27] By identifying the sacramental elements with the body and blood of Christ that they signify, the Roman Catholic view encourages the adoration of Christ in the elements. This, in the strong language of the catechism, makes the Mass an "accursed idolatry."[28]

The rejection of Lutheran and Roman Catholic doctrine of the real presence of Christ in the sacrament does not mean that the Heidelberg Catechism provides no positive statement of this presence. After denying that the bread and wine become the "real body and blood of Christ" in question and answer 79, the catechism emphasizes the close sacramental conjunction of the sign and the thing signified. The "visible signs and pledges" of the sacrament do assure us "that we are as really partakers of [Christ's] true body and blood, through the working of the Holy Spirit, as we receive by the mouth of the body these holy tokens in remembrance of Him."[29] Christ, by the working of the Spirit in and through the sacramental signs, genuinely imparts himself to believers and thereby becomes more intimately joined with them. The problem with the Roman Catholic understanding of Christ's presence in the Mass is that it involves a new and daily offering of Christ's body in an unbloody manner. The Mass teaches that the priest, who ministers at the altar, offers Christ anew as a sacrifice for sin and that Christ, inasmuch as he is "bodily present under the form of bread and wine," "is therefore to be worshipped in them" (Q&A 80). According

---

27. For an account of the addition and significance of this question and answer, see Klooster, *The Heidelberg Catechism*, 180–89; and Schaff, *Creeds of Christendom*, 1.535–36. Schaff notes that "this question was inserted by the express command of the Elector, perhaps by his own hand, as a Protestant counter-blast to the Romish anathemas of the Council of Trent, which closed its sessions Dec. 4, 1563." For a defense of the retention of this question and answer, which some Reformed churches (e.g., the Christian Reformed Church in North America) no longer include as part of their subscription to the Heidelberg Catechism, see Cornelis P. Venema, "The Lord's Supper and the Popish Mass: Does Q. & A. 80 of the Heidelberg Catechism Speak the Truth?" *The Outlook* 55, no. 5 (May 2005): 17–22; and Cornelis Venema, "The Lord's Supper and the 'Popish Mass': An Historical and Theological Analysis of Question and Answer 80 of the Heidelberg Catechism, *Mid-America Journal of Theology* 24 (2013): 31–72.

28. Q&A 80: " . . . ein vermaledeyte Abgötterey."

29. Q&A 79: " . . . dass wir so warhafftig seines waren leibs vnd bluts durch würckung des heiligen Geists theilhafftig werden / als wir diese heilige warzeichen / mit dem leiblichen mund zu seiner gedechtnuss empfangen."

to the catechism, this is tantamount to a denial of "the one sacrifice" of Christ and represents an idolatrous worship of the earthly elements of bread and wine. Rather than Christ being present under the form of bread and wine, we should recognize that the Spirit, by means of the sacrament, lifts the believer up to Christ, "who according to His human nature is now not on earth but in heaven, at the right hand of God His Father, and wills there to be worshipped by us."[30]

In its consideration of the proper recipients of the sacrament, the catechism offers a clear statement regarding those for whom the sacrament was instituted. Only those who are "truly displeased with themselves for their sins and yet trust that these are forgiven them for the sake of Christ" may partake of the Lord's Supper.[31] Moreover, believers who find forgiveness through the passion and death of Christ must also "desire more and more to strengthen their faith and amend their life." By contrast, hypocrites and those who do not turn to God with sincere hearts must abstain from participation lest they eat and drink judgment to themselves. Indeed, the unbelieving and ungodly must be disciplined by the church and warned to keep themselves from the Table of the Lord unless and until they show amendment of life (Q&A 82). For this reason, after the catechism treats the subject of the proper recipients of the sacrament, it turns to the subject of church discipline, with which the second part of the catechism concludes.

Conclusion

Though we have not completed our survey of the doctrine of the Lord's Supper in the Reformed confessions, the confessions we have examined in this chapter allow us to offer a preliminary conclusion.

The considerable attention given to the Lord's Supper in these

---

30. Q&A 80: " . . . der jetzund mit seinem waren leib im Himmel zur Rechten des Vatters is / vnd daselbst wil angebettet werden."

31. Q&A 81: "For whom is the Lord's supper instituted? For those who are truly displeased with themselves for their sins and yet trust that these are forgiven them for the sake of Christ, and that their remaining infirmity is covered by His passion and death; who also desire more and more to strengthen their faith and amend their life. But hypocrites and such as turn not to God with sincere hearts eat and drink judgment to themselves."

confessions attests to the importance of the sacrament to the evangelical and Reformed churches. Although these confessions take serious issue with some features of the traditional Roman Catholic doctrine of the Mass, they clearly view the sacrament as an important means of grace. Through the sacrament believers are confirmed and strengthened in their fellowship with Christ, who is the spiritual food and source of every saving blessing for his people. Christ, by the working of his Spirit, is truly present in the sacrament and communicates himself to those who eat the bread and wine with the "mouth of faith." By means of the sacrament, believers are joined more intimately to Christ and to those who are Christ's, called to greater love and devotion to all those who belong to Christ, and stimulated in their eager expectation for the fullness of communion with Christ in the age to come. The sacrament is a true Eucharist for the people of God, an offering of thankful praise and celebration of the finished, perfect sacrifice on the cross. But it is not, as in Roman Catholic teaching, an "unbloody sacrifice" that continues or in some sense re-presents the priestly sacrifice of Christ on the cross.

Chapter 7

The Lord's Supper: The Sacrament of Nourishment in Christ (2)

The extensive treatment of the Lord's Supper in the Reformed confessions of the sixteenth and seventeenth centuries allowed us only to begin our summary of their teaching in the previous chapter. The wide-ranging and complex handling of the doctrine of the Lord's Supper in the confessions mirrors the many controversies that arose regarding the sacrament within the ferment of the sixteenth-century Reformation. Due to these controversies, the Reformed confessions take great pains to articulate the biblical meaning and significance of the sacrament while at the same time repudiating features of the medieval Roman Catholic doctrine and practice that do not meet the test of Scripture. It would be a mistake, however, to ascribe the considerable attention the confessions devote to the sacrament of the Lord's Supper solely to the controversies of the period. The confessions' extensive treatment of the Lord's Supper also demonstrates the importance of the sacrament to the ministry and practice of the Reformed churches.

In this chapter, we will continue our summary of the Reformed confessions' understanding of the sacrament of the Lord's Supper, beginning with a particularly important confession so far as the Reformed view of the Lord's Supper is concerned. The Second Helvetic Confession is especially rich in its affirmations regarding the Lord's Supper. This richness represents the fruit of a series of vigorous debates within the Swiss Reformed churches on the nature of the sacraments in general and the disputed issue of Christ's presence in the Lord's Supper. In the Second Helvetic Confession, the Swiss Reformed churches adopted what might be termed a mediating position on the doctrine of the Lord's Supper, distancing themselves from some of Zwingli's earlier emphases while cautiously embracing a more Calvinian view.

The Second Helvetic Confession of 1566

When it comes to determining the consensus of Reformed doctrine on the sacrament of the Lord's Supper, the Second Helvetic Confession is particularly important. It was written by Heinrich Bullinger, who succeeded Ulrich Zwingli as a leading pastor of the Swiss Reformed churches in Zürich and the Rhinelands, so it provides important testimony regarding the extent to which Calvin's doctrine prevailed over that of Zwingli, even among those churches originally influenced by Zwingli's view. Though cautiously and moderately stated, the doctrine of the Lord's Supper set forth in this confession evidences more affinity with Calvin than Zwingli. It reflects especially the influence of the compromise formula, the *Consensus Tigurinus,* which was written as a consensus statement on the doctrine of the Lord's Supper by ministers of Zurich and John Calvin of Geneva.[1]

---

1. The *Consensus Tigurinus* distinguished the position of the Swiss Reformed churches from that of Luther, on the one hand, and of Zwingli on the other. For an English translation, see "Mutual Consent in Regard to the Sacraments," in *Selected Works,* 2.212–20. For a historical study of the consensus, see Bizer, *Studien zur Geschichte des Abendmahlsstreits,* 234–99. For Zwingli's view of the sacrament, see Ulrich Zwingli, "On the Lord's Supper," in *The Library of Christian Classics: Zwingli and Bullinger,* ed. John Baille et al. (Philadelphia: Westminster Press, 1953), 24:176–238; and Brian Gerrish, *Grace and Gratitude,* 163–69. Gerrish notes that for Zwingli the sacramental signs are "not instrumental, but indicative or declarative. They have a twofold use: they signal the fact that something has already been accomplished by the activity of God, and they declare the commitment of the redeemed to live in faithfulness to God who has redeemed them" (164). Therefore, the sacrament of the Lord's Supper does not serve instrumentally to communicate Christ to the recipient but declaratively to remind believers of Christ's work and to profess their faith in this work (as a "badge" of profession). Gerrish, "Sign and Reality: The Lord's Supper in the Reformed Confessions," 128–30, argues that there are three principal Reformed views of the sacraments expressed in the confessions: "symbolic memorialism" (Zwingli); "symbolic parallelism" (Bullinger); and "symbolic instrumentalism" (Calvin). He finds the second of these views, symbolic parallelism (Christ is given alongside the sacramental elements) represented in the Second Helvetic Confession and the Heidelberg Catechism. According to Gerrish, this is a mediating position between Zwingli's memorialism and Calvin's doctrine of Christ's presence *with* and especially *through* the sacramental elements. For our purpose, however, it is important to note that Gerrish places the second and third views together as representing the consensus of the Reformed confessions over against the Zwinglian view: Christ is communicated by means of the sacrament. He concludes that "*all* the leading confessions place the emphasis on communication rather than

The Second Helvetic Confession opens its consideration of the Lord's Supper with a comment on the names and author of the sacrament. It is commonly called a "supper" because it was instituted by Christ at his last supper and "because in it the faithful are spiritually fed and given drink" (chap. 21). It is also called a "Eucharist" because it is a thanksgiving for the spiritual blessings that belong to believers through Christ. The sanctity of the Supper derives from its divine origin. No angel or man has instituted this meal as a sacrament of the new covenant, but Christ alone has consecrated it to its proper and holy use as a means of grace. For this reason, the ministers of the church are obligated to administer the sacrament in accordance with the Lord's words of institution and in a manner conformed to the teaching of the Word of God.

In its first paragraph outlining the significance of the Lord's Supper, the Second Helvetic Confession appears to emphasize the Zwinglian view of the sacrament as a memorial feast. By means of this "sacred rite," the confession declares in chapter 21,

> The Lord wishes to keep in fresh remembrance that greatest benefit which he showed to mortal men, namely, that by having given his body and shed his blood he has pardoned all our sins, and redeemed us from eternal death and the power of the devil, and now feeds us with his flesh, and gives us his blood to drink, which, being received spiritually by true faith, nourishes us unto eternal life.

If this were all the confession taught regarding the sacrament, it would reduce it to little more than an act of faith, remembering and declaring that Christ's body was given and his blood shed for the sake of acquiring the forgiveness of sins. However, after this paragraph, the Second Helvetic Confession affirms that there is an intimate conjunction between the sacramental sign and reality, so that believers receive Christ himself with the sacramental elements.

In order to account for the manner in which Christ is present and received through the sacrament, the confession distinguishes—without separating—between the outward,

---

commemoration, but *some* reflect a certain shyness toward the idea of the means of grace" (128, emphasis original).

visible sign and the inward, invisible reality. "At the same time" that believers receive the elements of bread and wine, "by the work of Christ through the Holy Spirit they also inwardly receive the flesh and blood of the Lord, and are thereby nourished unto life eternal."[2] Christ is the "principal thing" communicated through the sacrament, and therefore the believer is invited to look beyond the visible tokens of his body and blood and eat "spiritually" of Christ himself. This does not mean that Christ is "eaten corporeally and essentially with a bodily mouth,"[3] as in the Roman Catholic teaching. This is the ancient error of the Capernaites, who taught a "corporeal eating whereby food is taken into the mouth, is chewed with the teeth, and swallowed into the stomach."[4] Rather, we should conceive of the eating and drinking of Christ in the sacrament as a "spiritual eating." In this kind of spiritual eating, the "body and blood of the Lord, while remaining in their own essence and property, are spiritually communicated to us, certainly not in a corporeal but in a spiritual way, by the Holy Spirit, who applies and bestows upon us these things which have been prepared for us by the sacrifice of the Lord's body and blood."[5]

Though this language could be taken to suggest that Christ's presence in the Supper is merely a presence of the power or

---

2. Chapter 21: "Therefore the faithful receive what is given by the ministers of the Lord, and they eat the bread of the Lord and drink of the Lord's cup. At the same time by the work of Christ through the Holy Spirit they also inwardly receive the flesh and blood of the Lord, and are thereby nourished unto life eternal (intus interim opera Christi per spiritum sanctum, percipiunt etiam carnem et sanguinem domini, et pascuntur his in vitam aeternam [Niesel, *Bekenntnisschriften*, 264.7–9]). For the flesh and blood of Christ is the true food and drink unto life eternal; and Christ himself, since he was given for us and is our Savior, is the principal thing in the Supper, and we do not permit anything else to be substituted in his place."
3. Chapter 21: " . . . corpus Christi manducari ore corporis corporaliter, vel essentialiter." Niesel, *Bekenntnisschriften*, 264.24–25.
4. Chapter 21: " . . . manducatio corporalis, qua cibus in os percipitur ab homine, dentibus atteritur, et in ventrem deglutitur." Niesel, *Bekenntnisschriften*, 264.16–17.
5. Chapter 21: " . . . manente in sua essentia et proprietate corpore et sanguine Domini, ea nobis communicantur spiritualiter, utique non corporali modo, sed spirituali, per spiritum sanctum, qui videlicet ea, quae per carnem et sanguinem Domini pro nobis in mortem tradita, parata sunt." Niesel, *Bekenntnisschriften*, 264.28–32.

virtue of his sacrifice and saving work, a subsequent paragraph in the Second Helvetic Confession, which is specifically addressed to the nature of his presence, makes clear that it is a substantial or real presence of Christ himself. To be sure, the Roman Catholic doctrine that the bread and wine become the actual body of Christ, not in form but in substance, confuses the sacramental elements with Christ, whom they represent. When the bread and wine are denominated the body and blood of Christ, this is said "in a sacramental way," the sign being taken for the thing signified. In the Roman Catholic view, the sign becomes an improper object of worship and is so identified with Christ that "whoever receives the sign, receives the thing itself."[6] Contrary to this view of Christ's presence, the Second Helvetic Confession, following the pattern previously seen in other Reformed confessions, insists that it is effected through an inexpressible work of the Spirit. By virtue of Christ's Spirit working in the sacrament, "the Lord is not absent from his Church when she celebrates the Supper." Even though the body of Christ remains "in heaven at the right hand of the Father," Christ is truly and effectually present when believers' hearts are "lifted up on high" as they receive the sacramental elements. In order to aid our understanding of this sacramental presence, the Second Helvetic Confession employs the analogy of the Sun: "The sun, which is absent from us in the heavens, is notwithstanding effectually present among us. How much more is the Sun of Righteousness, Christ, although in his body he is absent from us in heaven, present with us, not corporeally, but spiritually, by his vivifying operation."[7] In this way the Supper is not "without Christ," but is an "unbloody and mystical Supper" in which Christ is truly present and received by believers as their spiritual food and drink.

One point that is especially developed in the Second Helvetic Confession is the necessity and work of faith in the right

---

6. Chapter 21: " . . . quicunque signum percipiat, idem et rem percipiat ipsam." Niesel, *Bekenntnisschriften,* 265.46.

7. Chapter 21: "Sol absens a nobis in coelo, nihilominus efficaciter praesens est nobis: quanto magis sol iustitiae Christus, corpore in coelis absens nobis, praesens est nobis, non corporaliter quidem, sed spiritualiter per vivificam operationem. . . ." Niesel, *Bekenntnisschriften,* 266.2–5.

use of the sacrament. Christ, who is the spiritual food and drink communicated through the sacrament, is not received "corporeally, but spiritually by faith."[8] The appropriation of Christ by faith, moreover, is a basic and necessary act whereby believers become members of Christ and partake of his saving benefits. This appropriation of Christ by faith occurs "wherever a man believes in Christ" (chap. 21). Therefore, it cannot be restricted to or become wholly dependent upon the administration of the sacrament and the believing reception of what it administers. The sacrament, however, has been provided for the purpose of nourishing and strengthening faith. When the believer receives the sacrament, he "progresses in continuing to communicate in the body and blood of the Lord, and so his faith is kindled and grows more and more, and is refreshed by spiritual food" (chap. 21). The believing reception of the sacrament is performed in obedience to the institution and commandment of Christ and truly grants believers an enjoyment of Christ himself. As an act of faith, this reception is a eucharistic act of thanksgiving, "a faithful memorial to the Lord's death," and a "witness before the Church" (chap. 21).[9]

In the concluding sections of its summary of the doctrine of the Lord's Supper, the Second Helvetic Confession addresses several issues relating to its administration and use. In addition to its purpose as a means of communicating Christ and his saving benefits to believers, the Lord's Supper serves the purposes of uniting believers with each other in mutual service, consecrating them to a holy life, and preserving them in true faith to the end of their lives. Because the sacrament requires a spiritual eating and drinking of Christ by faith, believers are obligated to prepare themselves for its reception. Preparation for the sacrament includes self-examination "as to the kind of faith we have, whether we believe Christ has come to save sinners and to call them to repentance."[10] It also requires that the believer

---

8. Chapter 21: " . . . non corporaliter, sed spiritualiter per fidem." Niesel, *Bekenntnisschriften*, 265.6.

9. Though the Second Helvetic Confession is not, as we noted above, Zwinglian in its doctrine, these kinds of statements echo Zwingli's emphases.

10. Chapter 21: "It is therefore fitting that when we would come to the Supper, we first examine ourselves according to the commandment of the apostle,

consider whether he acknowledges Christ as his own deliverer, resolves to live a holy life, and endeavors to live in harmony with other believers.

When the sacrament is administered, it must be done in careful conformity to the Bible's teaching and the Lord's institution. The Roman Catholic practice, consequently, of withholding the cup from believers must be condemned as a serious offense against the Lord's institution, which included the express commandment, "Drink ye all of this." Moreover, the unbiblical elements, which have been added to the administration of the Roman Catholic Mass, must be eliminated. Among the most objectionable of these elements are the practices of turning the sacrament into a "spectacle," "celebrating it for a price," and using it as a "means of gaining merit" (chap. 21). In no respect should the sacrament be conceived as a kind of unbloody sacrifice, in which the priest effects the presence of Christ's body or offers it to God for the remission of the sins of the living and the dead.

Canons of Dort of 1618–1619

Unlike the Reformed confessions that we have previously considered, the Canons of Dort do not claim to be a comprehensive statement of the faith of the church. Written to address the five opinions (*Sententiae*) of the Remonstrant or Arminian party, particularly in respect to the proper interpretation of article 16 of the Belgic Confession on the subject of divine election, the Canons of Dort offer no specific doctrine of the sacraments. It would be possible, therefore, to pass over this symbol of the Reformed churches without comment.

However, it is significant that the Canons of Dort speak of the use of the sacraments, including the Lord's Supper, in their consideration of the doctrine of the perseverance of the saints.[11]

---

especially as to the kind of faith we have, whether we believe that Christ has come to save sinners and to call them to repentance, and whether each man believes that he is in the number of those who have been delivered by Christ and saved; and whether he is determined to change his wicked life, to lead a holy life, and with the Lord's help to persevere in the true religion and in harmony with the brethren, and to give due thanks to God for his deliverance."

11. V/14: "And, just as it has pleased God to begin this work of grace in us by the proclamation of the gospel, so he preserves, continues, and completes his work by the hearing and reading of the gospel, by meditation on it, by its exhortations,

By mentioning the use of the sacraments in this context, the Canons of Dort underscore their importance as a means of grace. After commencing his work of grace in the believer's life by means of the proclamation of the gospel, God continues to complete his saving work not only by the hearing and reading of the gospel but also by the use of the sacraments. Believers persevere in the faith until God's work is completed in them, not because of any inherent capacity for steadfastness and faithfulness on their part but because of God's persistence in grace and provision of those means that prevent believers from falling away in unbelief and disobedience. This means that the sacraments are divinely instituted and effective instruments to preserve, continue, and complete God's work in believers. Or, to state the matter somewhat negatively, believers may not dispense with the proper use of the sacraments, including the Lord's Supper, without despising God's grace and arrogantly presuming a strength to persevere that they do not possess. Only in the way of God's persisting grace, and in the proper use of the means he has mercifully instituted for this purpose, can believers be confident of their perseverance in the faith.

The Westminster Standards

The Westminster Confession of Faith and Catechisms provide as thorough and careful a statement of the doctrine of the Lord's Supper as any of the great confessions of the Reformed churches. Consistent with its general doctrine of the sacraments, the Westminster Standards especially emphasize the regular use of the sacraments and the manner of their administration and reception. These emphases correspond to the particular concern of the Presbyterian and Puritan tradition with the careful regulation of worship by the teaching of God's Word.[12] If The Word of God must regulate the entire worship of the church, then the administration of the sacraments, as an integral aspect

---

threats, and promises, and also by the use of the sacraments."

12. For a treatment of the historical context for the Westminster Standards, including the debates between Puritan and Anglican parties on the subject of the sacraments, see Horton Davies, *Worship and Theology in England: From Cranmer to Hooker* (Grand Rapids: Eerdmans, 1996), esp. 1:76–126; and Burnet, *The Holy Communion in the Reformed Church of Scotland.*

of worship, must likewise conform to scriptural precept and example.[13]

The opening section of the Westminster Standards on the Lord's Supper notes that the sacrament was instituted by the Lord himself to serve several purposes. These purposes include not only the communication of Christ himself to his people but also the proclamation and remembrance of his death. By means of the sacrament, Christ has set apart the elements of bread and wine from a common to a sacred use to represent his body and blood as the believer's spiritual food and to confirm the believer's participation in and union with him. When believers receive the sacrament, moreover, they are reminded of their engagement to Christ and to those who are members of his body. The sacrament is a communion, then, with Christ and, by virtue of this communion with Christ, with those who belong to him. It obligates believers to live in relation to fellow believers in "mutual love and fellowship each with others, as members of the same mystical body."[14]

The sacrament of the Lord's Supper is to be administered by ministers of the Word who follow the pattern set forth in the Lord's institution of the Supper. The sacrament requires the consecration of the elements of bread and wine to a sacred use by means of a recitation of the words of institution, the giving of thanks, and prayer. Believers who partake of the sacrament are obligated to receive both of the elements and to do so with "thankful remembrance that the body of Christ was broken

---

13. The regulative principle, as it is termed in the Presbyterian tradition, is classically stated in chapters 1.6, 20.2, and 21.1–8 of the Westminster Confession of Faith. The statement in chapter 21.1 captures the principle well: "But the acceptable way of worshiping the true God is instituted by himself, and so limited by his own revealed will, that he may not be worshiped according to the imaginations and devices of men, or the suggestions of Satan, under any visible representation, or any other way not prescribed in the holy Scripture."

14. Confession of Faith, chapter 29.1: "Our Lord Jesus, in the night wherein he was betrayed, instituted the sacrament of his body and blood, called the Lord's Supper, to be observed in his church, unto the end of the world, for the perpetual remembrance of the sacrifice of himself in his death; the sealing all benefits thereof unto true believers, their spiritual nourishment and growth in him, their further engagement in and to all duties which they owe unto him; and, to be a bond and pledge of their communion with him, and with each other, as members of his mystical body."

and given, and his blood shed, for them."[15] By contrast to this biblical administration, the sacrament of the Roman Catholic Mass involves a number of unbiblical practices. The Confession of Faith asserts: "Private masses, or receiving this sacrament by a priest, or any other, alone; as likewise, the denial of the cup to the people, worshiping the elements, the lifting them up, or carrying them about, for adoration, and the reserving them for pretended religious use; are all contrary to the nature of this sacrament, and to the institution of Christ" (chap. 29.4). These practices violate the nature of the sacrament as a participation or communion with Christ either by transferring to the sacramental sign the adoration that is owed to Christ alone or by preventing believers from a full reception of the sacramental elements. They also are contemptuous of the sufficiency and perfection of Christ's one sacrifice upon the cross, which the sacrament proclaims and commemorates but does not in an unbloody way repeat as a renewed sacrifice. For this reason, the Confession of Faith explains, "the popish sacrifice of the mass . . . is most abominably injurious to Christ's one, only sacrifice, the alone propitiation for all the sins of his elect" (chap. 29.2).

In their summary of the nature of Christ's presence in the Lord's Supper, the Westminster Standards follow, for the most part, the precedent of the classic Reformed confessions of the sixteenth century. On the one hand, the Roman Catholic and Lutheran doctrines of transubstantiation and consubstantiation, respectively, are rejected. And on the other, Christ's real, albeit spiritual and sacramental presence, is affirmed. In the Westminster Confession of Faith, the Roman Catholic view is explicitly identified and repudiated: "That doctrine which maintains a change of the substance of the bread and wine, into the substance of Christ's body and blood (commonly called transubstantiation) by consecration of a priest, or by any other

---

15. Larger Catechism, Q&A 169: "How hath Christ appointed bread and wine to be given and received in the sacrament of the Lord's Supper? Christ hath appointed the ministers of his Word, in the administration of this sacrament of the Lord's Supper, to set apart the bread and wine from common use, by the word of institution, thanksgiving, and prayer; to take and break the bread, and to give both the bread and the wine to the communicants: who are, by the same appointment, to take and eat the bread, and to drink the wine, in thankful remembrance that the body of Christ was broken and given, and his blood shed, for them."

way, is repugnant, not to Scripture alone, but even to common sense, and reason; overthroweth the nature of the sacrament, and hath been, and is, the cause of manifold superstitions; yea, of gross idolatries" (chap. 29.6). Likewise, in a manner that is uniquely explicit among the Reformed confessions, the Larger Catechism adds a condemnation of the Lutheran doctrine of consubstantiation, though without using the name: "the body and blood of Christ are not corporally or carnally present in, with, or under the bread and wine in the Lord's Supper" (Q&A 170). These critical statements regarding the presence of Christ's body and blood in the sacrament are as strong as any in the classic confessions of the Reformed churches. However, they do not follow the pattern of other confessions we have considered by identifying the particular Christological questions that doctrines of Christ's local, bodily presence in or with the sacramental elements entail.

In their positive statements of the way we are to construe Christ's presence in the sacrament of the Lord's Supper, the Westminster Standards are somewhat more reserved than, for example, the Gallican Confession or the Belgic Confession. The "outward elements" of bread and wine are related "sacramentally only" to Christ, and are not to be confused with the spiritual reality they represent (chap. 29.5). Though they may be identified in a sacramental manner by speaking of them as the body and blood of Christ, they "still remain truly and only bread and wine, as they were before." When believers receive the sacramental signs of Christ's body and blood, however, they truly receive Christ "spiritually." They are given a sacramental participation in "Christ crucified, and all the benefits of his death." Though this language is similar to that of the Second Helvetic Confession, which distinguishes a carnal from a spiritual eating and drinking of Christ, nothing is said about the work of the Holy Spirit in effecting Christ's presence through the sacrament.[16] Nor is there language that speaks

---

16. The reserve of the Westminster Standards at this point may reflect the difference that Gerrish ("Sign and Reality," 128) posits between "symbolic parallelism" and "symbolic instrumentalism" on the manner of Christ's presence. Similar to the Second Helvetic Confession, the Westminster Standards affirm that Christ is imparted *along with* the sacramental elements, but not *through* the

of the presence of Christ's "natural" body and blood (Belgic Confession) or the presence of the "substance" of his body and blood (Gallican Confession). In these respects, the Westminster Standards affirm the presence of Christ in the sacrament but refrain from any significant elucidation of the nature of that presence.

One theme that comes to particular prominence in the Westminster Standards is the necessity of a proper preparation for and reception of the sacrament. Though all of the Reformed confessions insist upon the believing reception of the grace signified and confirmed through the sacrament, the Westminster Standards are quite detailed in their description of the kind of faith required for participation in the sacrament. This is especially the case in the Larger Catechism. In answer to question 171, "How are they that receive the sacrament of the Lord's Supper to prepare themselves before they come unto it?" the Larger Catechism declares:

> They that receive the sacrament of the Lord's Supper are, before they come, to prepare themselves thereunto, by examining themselves of their being in Christ, of their sins and wants; of the truth and measure of their knowledge, faith, repentance; love to God and the brethren, charity to all men, forgiving those that have done them wrong; of their desires after Christ, and of their new obedience; and renewing the exercise of these graces, by serious meditation, and fervent prayer.

Before coming to the Table of the Lord, the believer is obligated to examine his faith. This self-examination includes an acknowledgment of sin and the necessity of Christ's saving work, a recognition that salvation depends upon fellowship

---

sacramental elements. This subtle difference of emphasis does not change the fact that the Westminster Standards affirm the sacramental communication of Christ to his people. It may explain, however, why Charles Hodge, in his expositions of the Lord's Supper, sought to articulate a mediating position between Zwingli and Calvin, in which Christ's presence in the Supper is one of his "virtue" and "benefits," but not of his body and blood. See Charles Hodge, "Doctrine of the Reformed Church on the Lord's Supper," in *Essays and Reviews* (New York: Robert Carter & Brothers, 1857): 341–92; and Peter J. Wallace, "History and Sacrament: John Williamson Nevin and Charles Hodge on the Lord's Supper," *Mid-America Journal of Theology* 11 (2000): 171–201.

with Christ, and a readiness to live in keeping with the gospel. In connection with this process of self-examination and preparation for the sacrament, the Larger Catechism adds a question regarding the propriety of participation on the part of those who may have doubts regarding their "being in Christ." Though some believers may not enjoy the full assurance of their salvation in Christ, this ought not to prevent them from receiving the sacrament, so long as they have an awareness of their sin, a desire to be found in Christ, and a readiness to "depart from iniquity" (Q&A 172).[17]

The question of who may receive the sacrament of the Lord's Supper is not merely to be answered by the individual believer. Next to the obligation of self-examination that the recipient assumes, the ministers of the church, who are obliged to administer the sacrament according to the Lord's institution, have a responsibility to supervise the Table. In reply to the question whether any "who profess faith, and desire to come to the Lord's Supper" may be kept from it, the Larger Catechism maintains that "such as are found to be ignorant or scandalous, notwithstanding their profession of the faith . . . may and ought to be kept from that sacrament, by the power which Christ hath left in his church, until they receive instruction, and manifest their reformation" (Q&A 173). The officers of the church of Christ are required to ensure the sanctity of the sacrament and to see to it that it is administered according to the requirements of the Word of God. Because the sacrament was ordained to nourish and strengthen the faith of believers, it can only be received by those whose faith is competent to proclaim and remember the death of Christ and to embrace the benefits of Christ communicated by the sacramental means.

Consistent with its pattern of extensive commentary on the doctrine of the Lord's Supper, the Larger Catechism

---

17. This acknowledgment that true believers may sometimes lack full assurance corresponds to the affirmations of chapter 18 ("Of the Assurance of Grace and Salvation") of the Westminster Confession of Faith. For example, chapter 18.3 states that "infallible assurance doth not so belong to the essence of faith, but that a true believer may wait long, and conflict with many difficulties before he be partaker of it: yet, being enabled by the Spirit to know the things which are freely given him of God, he may, without extraordinary revelation, in the right use of ordinary means, attain thereunto."

addresses two further issues. One of these concerns the particular obligations of participants in the sacrament during its administration and thereafter. Believing participants in the sacrament are required to receive it in a spirit of reverence and careful attention. In order for the sacrament to nourish faith, it must be actively received in a believing manner by recipients who meditate on and acknowledge the significance and benefits of Christ's saving work. Moreover, after receiving the sacrament, believers are called to exercise their faith and walk in a manner conformed to communion with Christ and fellow believers.

The other issue concerns the agreement and difference between the sacraments of baptism and the Lord's Supper. These sacraments agree in respect to their divine Author, their reference to Christ and his saving benefits, their sealing of the covenant of grace, their administration by lawful ministers, and their continuance until Christ's coming again (Q&A 176). However, they differ in respect to their frequency of administration, their sacramental signs, and their proper recipients. Unlike the sacrament of baptism, which signifies and seals to believers and their children their incorporation into Christ, the sacrament of the Lord's Supper, because it requires a believing and active reception, may only be administered to "such as are of years and ability to examine themselves" (Q&A 177).[18]

Summary Observations

I began my treatment of the doctrine of the Lord's Supper in the Reformed confessions by recounting Martin Luther's anxiety at celebrating his first Mass as a priest in the Roman Catholic Church. Luther was overwhelmed by the thought that he was about to offer an unbloody sacrifice of Christ upon the altar. When Protestants contemplate this episode in Luther's life, they are apt to regard it as little more than the product of his mistaken view of the nature of Christ's presence in the sacrament. For many evangelical and Reformed believers, the sacraments in

---

18. I will briefly return to the topic of the proper recipients of the sacrament of the Lord's Supper in my conclusion and offer a comment on the issue of paedocommunion (the admission of young children to the sacrament). The Westminster Standards are most clear in their implication that this practice is unwarranted.

general, and the Lord's Supper in particular, have undergone a process of desacralization. What matters in Christian worship are such things as the preaching of the gospel, the singing of God's praise, and the presentation of the worshiping community's offerings of thanksgiving. There is little place for holy reverence and exultation in the administration of the grace of Christ through the sacraments of the church.

If nothing else, our survey of the confessions of the Reformed churches and their doctrine of the Lord's Supper should confirm that there is a gap between the present practice of many Reformed churches and their historic confessions. Whatever criticisms these confessions offer against the Roman Catholic doctrine of the Mass—and these criticisms, as we have seen, are considerable—they are not offered on the basis of a diminished view of the sacraments to the life of the church and her members. Nothing could be further from the truth. These confessions wholeheartedly embrace the catholic conviction of the Christian church that the sacramental meal of Holy Communion plays an integral role in Christ's imparting himself to his people. The confessions' understanding of the Lord's Supper has significant implications for the renewal and reformation of Reformed sacramental practice in our day. Upon the basis of this conviction, I offer the following summary observations regarding the confessions' teaching on the sacrament of the Lord's Supper.

First, with respect to the frequency of its administration and reception, the Lord's Supper is clearly distinguished in the Reformed confessions from baptism. While baptism is a rite of initiation into Christ and his body, the church, the Lord's Supper is a rite of continual confirmation, nourishment, and strengthening of believers' faith. Baptism is by its nature a one-time ordinance. The Lord's Supper is by its nature a sacrament that needs to be repeated and continually used by believers.

Though the Reformed confessions do not explicitly comment on the frequency of the administration of the Lord's Supper, they encourage a practice where the sacrament ordinarily accompanies the preaching of the gospel.[19] Stated negatively,

---

19. The desirability of a frequent use of the sacrament was already set forth in

there are no clear confessional reasons that the sacrament of the Lord's Supper should not regularly be appended to the administration of the gospel in preaching. The requirements for a proper participation in the Supper—self-examination and guarding the Table against its profanation by unworthy participation on the part of the unbelieving and impenitent—might well present practical impediments to the regular, even weekly, celebration of the Supper. But, with the exception of the Westminster Larger Catechism, which provides a detailed description regarding the preparation for and use of the sacrament, none of the great confessions of the Reformed churches offer any argument against frequent Communion. Indeed, the burden of the confessions' statements respecting this sacrament argues for a practice that, in obedience to Christ's institution, administers the Supper as a regular accompaniment of the preaching of the Word.

Throughout the history of the Reformed churches, a number of practical and pastoral obstacles have limited the frequency of the celebration of the Lord's Supper. These considerations include such practices and convictions as the preaching of preparatory and applicatory sermons before and after the celebration of the Lord's Supper; the use of prescribed liturgical forms that are often lengthy and didactic expositions of the

---

Calvin's Draft Ecclesiastical Ordinances of 1537 (in *Calvin: Theological Treatises,* 66): "Since the Supper was instituted for us by our Lord to be frequently used, and also was so observed in the ancient Church until the devil turned everything upside down, erecting the mass in its place, it is a fault in need of correction, to celebrate it so seldom." Cf. G. W. Bromiley, *Sacramental Teaching and Practice in the Reformation Churches* (Grand Rapids: Eerdmans, 1957), 74: "The general view of the Reformers was that, considering scriptural precedent and the purpose and meaning of the sacrament, it ought to be administered each week, or monthly at the very least." For a recent defense of a more frequent celebration of the Supper, which argues on the basis of Calvin's doctrine and the standpoint of the Reformed confessions, see Michael J. Horton, "At Least Weekly: The Reformed Doctrine of the Lord's Supper and Its Frequent Celebration," *Mid-America Journal of Theology* 11 (2000): 147–69. It is an irony of history that, whereas several of the church orders of the Reformed churches stipulate the administration of the sacrament *at least* four times per year, this became the standard practice. Historically, this stipulation was a compromise intended to *increase* the frequency of participation in the face of the medieval practice going back to the Fourth Lateran Council of 1215 requiring reception of the Mass at least once per year (the normal practice of many).

biblical meaning and significance of the sacrament; the weight of long-standing practice among Reformed churches since the time of the sixteenth-century Reformation; and the concern on the part of many Reformed believers that a frequent celebration of the sacrament may diminish its value as a means of grace. Though the Reformed confessions may be consistent with a more frequent celebration of the sacrament, these considerations are sufficiently weighty to caution against an unpastoral imposition of a practice of more frequent Communion in the face of historic practice and custom. Considering these factors, as well as the confessional view that the sacrament of the Lord's Supper is an appendix to the preaching of the Word, perhaps a wise policy for many Reformed churches would be to administer the sacrament monthly rather than weekly. In this way, the confessional emphasis upon the priority and supremacy of the preaching of the gospel will be honored, and the prospect of an incipient sacramentalism resisted. If the history and customary practice of the Reformed churches serve as a witness, then it seems clear that weekly Communion, though commendable, is not demanded by the Reformed confessions.

Second, in the Reformed confessions the Lord's Supper is variously described, and several purposes are identified as integral to its institution. Perhaps the most basic metaphor governing the descriptions of the Lord's Supper is that of a sacred meal, which was instituted to confirm and nourish believers in their communion with Christ. The sacramental elements of bread and wine were consecrated to serve as tokens and pledges of Christ himself, whose body given and blood shed are the spiritual sustenance and life of believers. By sharing this sacramental meal, believers enjoy a rich communion with Christ and all his members. They commune with Christ under the veil of the sacramental elements and acknowledge him to be their food and drink unto life eternal. Reflecting this emphasis upon the sacrament as a nourishing meal, the Reformed confessions typically denominate the sacrament as the Lord's Supper or the Lord's Table. Even as the physical body is strengthened by bread and wine, so the spiritual life of believers is strengthened by the eating and drinking of Christ, who is the spiritual food of those who belong to him by faith.

Consistent with the understanding of the Lord's Supper as a spiritual meal in which the believer enjoys communion with and is nourished by the Lord, the Reformed confessions also speak of the sacrament as a memorial of Christ's death and sacrifice upon the cross. Though the sacrament of the Lord's Supper is not merely a memorial or occasion for thanksgiving to God—the Zwinglian doctrine of the sacrament is uniformly, though often only implicitly, repudiated as inadequate—through it the church commemorates and proclaims Christ's death until he comes again at the end of the age. The sacrament is an occasion for thanksgiving and praise—a Eucharistic meal whose character is not only one of reverent commemoration but also of joyful thankfulness. When believers receive the elements as tokens of Christ's body and blood, they do so in gratitude to God for all of the benefits of salvation that are theirs through Christ. The Lord's Supper involves a festive fellowship with the living Christ into whose presence believers are lifted up by the Spirit working through the sacrament. As a sacramental means of visibly confirming to believers the promises of the gospel, the Lord's Supper fortifies faith in Christ's death as a perfect atonement for sin. These features of the sacrament, regrettably, are often diminished in many Reformed churches by an overemphasis upon its commemorative purpose.[20] Were they to be restored to their proper place, a more balanced (confessionally speaking) understanding and administration of the sacrament would likely result.

The sacrament, which as a visible sign of an invisible grace strengthens faith in the gospel promises, also evokes thanksgiving by assuring believers of their participation in Christ and his saving work. The Lord's Supper is a Eucharist, a thanksgiving meal that assures believers of Christ's work on their behalf. To use confessional language, as assuredly as believers take the bread and wine from the hand of Christ's ministers, so assuredly

---

20. The practice of some Reformed churches of celebrating the Lord's Supper during their Good Friday services rather than on the following (Easter) Lord's Day may be symptomatic of this imbalance. Similarly, the somber mood that marks the administration of the sacrament may reflect not simply a proper reverence in the remembrance of Christ's great sacrifice for our sins but also a largely commemorative focus to the service.

may they believe that Christ's work was for them. Indeed, it was for this reason that the Lord graciously appointed the sacrament. Knowing the weakness and uncertainty that often characterize the faith of believers, the Lord instituted this sacramental meal as a visible representation of his work on their behalf. Lest the gospel promise, first announced through the preaching of the Word, be doubted, God has graciously condescended to our weakness in providing this means to aid our faith.

Because the sacramental meal of the Lord's Supper is a holy communion with Christ, it also serves the purposes of uniting believers more intimately with him and calling them to a life of loving obedience and holy consecration. When they commemorate and proclaim the reconciling work of Christ in the sacrament, believers are reminded of their calling to be united to and reconciled with fellow believers. Those who are joined through the sacrament in communion with Christ are likewise joined with all who are his members. Furthermore, as members who enjoy the most intimate and full communion with Christ, they are engaged to a life that is marked by love and obedience to him. Those who share this meal with Christ are called to live in greater intimacy with Christ and his members. Failure to live in communion with Christ or to love those who share this communion with him is a manifest denial of the nature and significance of this sacred meal.

Third, on the much-disputed question of the nature of Christ's real presence in the sacrament, the Reformed confessions typically affirm this presence in strong terms. But they do so with an accompanying denial of the explanations of that presence offered by the Roman Catholic Church or the Lutheran tradition.

According to the Reformed confessions, those who receive Christ through the sacrament with the mouth of faith genuinely partake of him. Through the sacrament believers enjoy a true participation in and reception of the body and blood of Christ. The sacramental signs of bread and wine, though not to be confused with the actual body and blood of Christ, genuinely communicate Christ to believers. The sacramental acts of eating and drinking are instrumental to a communication of Christ *with* the sacramental signs. In several of the confessions we have considered, the language used to describe Christ's presence is quite robust. Believers are said to partake through the sacrament of the "substance" of Christ's body and blood (Gallican Confession). What is eaten and drunk in the sacrament is said to be nothing other than "the proper and natural body and the proper blood of Christ" (Belgic Confession). The spiritual eating and drinking that takes place in the sacrament involves such an intimate participation in Christ that the believer becomes altogether one with him, bone of his bone, flesh of his flesh (Scots Confession of 1560, Heidelberg Catechism).

However, when it comes to explaining the manner of Christ's presence in the Lord's Supper, the Reformed confessions object vigorously to the Roman Catholic doctrine of transubstantiation and the Lutheran doctrine of consubstantiation. The Roman Catholic doctrine of transubstantiation improperly identifies the sacramental elements with the spiritual reality that they represent. The earthly elements of the sacrament become the actual body and blood of Christ, though remaining under the form or appearance of bread and wine. Whether received by faith or not, the consecrated elements are objectively the body and blood of Christ and remain what they have become until they are properly consumed.[21] Moreover, in this doctrine the eating and drinking of Christ is a physical act, an "eating with the mouth" (*manducatio oralis*), which is a physical rather than a spiritual participation in Christ. Likewise, though the Lutheran doctrine of consubstantiation does not improperly identify the sacramental signs with the thing signified, nonetheless it teaches that the actual body and blood of Christ are *locally* present in the sacrament. This doctrine also affirms an "eating with the mouth" (*manducatio oralis*) that fails to appreciate the

---

21. This kind of objectivism in the understanding of Christ's presence in the sacramental elements is clearly expressed in the decisions of the Council of Trent on the sacrament of the Mass. See "The Canons and Decrees of the Council of Trent," Thirteenth Session, Decree Concerning the Most Holy Sacrament of the Eucharist, Canon IV, in Schaff, *The Creeds of Christendom*, 1.137: "If any one saith, that, after the consecration is completed, the body and blood of our Lord Jesus Christ are not in the admirable sacrament of the Eucharist, but only during the use, whilst it is being taken, and not either before or after; and, in the hosts, or consecrated particles, which are reserved or which remain after communion, the true body of the Lord remaineth not: let him be anathema."

spiritual nature of the believer's participation in Christ through the sacrament. Contrary to these doctrines of Christ's presence, therefore, the Reformed confessions simply affirm the believer's eating and drinking of the natural body and blood of Christ. This occurs through an incomprehensible working of the Spirit, who draws believers through the sacrament to Christ, who is in heaven, in order that they might be joined in communion with him.

Fourth, in their criticism of the Roman Catholic doctrine of Christ's presence in the sacrament of the Lord's Supper, the Reformed confessions typically express several key objections to the Mass. The objection to the doctrine of transubstantiation addresses not only the problem of the adoration of the consecrated elements, which is a form of idolatry and an inappropriate identification of the sign with the thing signified, but also the idea that Christ's presence in the sacrament is the basis for his unbloody sacrifice in the Mass. The priest who ministers at the altar in the Roman Catholic Mass offers Christ himself as a propitiation and sacrifice for sin. Though this sacrifice is an unbloody representation of Christ's sacrifice upon the cross, it obtains further grace and merit for those who participate and even for those who may not be present, the dead. Furthermore, the administration of the Mass permits a number of unbiblical practices: the elevation and adoration of the host, the withholding of the cup from the laity, the communing of the clergy without the presence or participation of the laity, and private masses for individuals or portions of the whole body of the church. These and a host of additional ceremonies constitute an affront to the exclusive priesthood of Christ, whose one sacrifice is sufficient to the needs of his people, and betray a superstitious view of the working of the sacrament.

Fifth, the sacrament of the Lord's Supper, because it is a visible representation and confirmation of the gospel promise in Christ, requires faith on the part of its participants. Because the sacrament visibly signifies and seals the promises of the gospel, it demands the same response as the gospel. No more than the gospel Word does the sacrament work merely by virtue of its administration (*ex opere operato*). Only by a spiritual eating and drinking by the mouth of faith does the sacrament communicate Christ to his people. Therefore, the

Roman Catholic teaching of an objective presence of Christ in the sacramental elements, irrespective of a believing response to the gospel Word which the sacrament confirms, is rejected. Not only does this Roman Catholic view improperly identify the sacramental sign and the spiritual reality it signifies, but it also maintains that Christ is objectively present before, during, and even after the administration of the elements whether or not those participating or not participating actively accept the gospel in faith and repentance.

In the Reformed confessions, the kind of faith that is competent to remember, proclaim, and receive Christ through the Lord's Supper is carefully defined. Before members of the church may receive the sacrament, they have a biblical mandate to engage in self-examination. This self-examination involves the believers' testing of their faith against the normative requirements of the Word of God. Essential to such faith are the acknowledgment of our sin and unworthiness, the recognition that Christ alone by his mediatorial work has made atonement for the sins of his people, and a resolution to live in holiness and obedience to his will. In this way believers are called to embrace actively the promises of the gospel that the sacrament visibly confirms in the same way they respond to gospel preaching. Furthermore, it is the duty of the ministers and elders of the church to oversee the sacrament's administration, preventing so far as they are able those from participating who are unbelieving and living an ungodly life. Since Christ has instituted the sacrament for the purpose of nourishing the faith of believers, it would violate the nature of the sacrament to invite the unbelieving or the impenitent to partake. Unworthy participation, that is, participation on the part of those who have not properly examined themselves or who are unbelieving, would profane the Table of the Lord and be contemptuous of its ordained purpose.

In recent years, a number of Reformed denominations and churches have debated the issue of paedocommunion.[22] Should

---

22. For examples of the kinds of arguments employed for and against this practice, see Christian L. Keidel, "Is the Lord's Supper for Children?," *Westminster Theological Journal* 37, no. 3 (Spring 1975): 301–41; Roger T. Beckwith, "The Age of Admission to the Lord's Supper," *Westminster Theological Journal* 38, no. 2 (Winter 1976): 123–51; Leonard J. Coppes, *Daddy, May I Take Communion?*

the children of believing parents, by virtue of their inclusion within the covenant people of God, receive the sacrament? Though it is not my purpose to enter into this debate here, the confessions of the Reformed churches clearly speak to this issue. As we have seen in our exposition of these confessions, they uniformly maintain that the sacrament of the Lord's Supper is distinguished from the sacrament of baptism as a means of regularly nourishing the faith of church members. It belongs to the nature of this sacrament that those who participate *actively receive with the mouth of faith* the sacramental communication of Christ. Accordingly, the obligations of self-examination on the part of its recipients and the supervision of the Table by the ministers and elders prevent any practice that would invite all members of the congregation to participate without exception. Believers whose faith measures up to the biblical norms of self-examination and discerning the body of Christ are graciously summoned to come to the Table of the Lord. The children of believing parents, therefore, are obligated to profess that kind of faith before the church prior to their admission to the Table. This constitutes the biblical warrant for the practice of requiring a public profession of faith, in which the believer openly embraces the gospel promise and resolves to live a gratefully obedient life, before the privilege of full communion with Christ and his church may be exercised. Though there may be some debate respecting the optimum age for making such a profession or the

---

(Thornton, CO: Leonard J. Coppes, 1988); and A. A. Langdon, *Communion for Children? The Current Debate* (Oxford: Latimer Studies, 1988). For recent studies that defend the historic view and practice of the Reformed churches, which are opposed to the admission of nonprofessing members to the Lord's Supper, see Cornelis P. Venema, *Children at the Lord's Table? Assessing the Case for Paedocommunion* (Grand Rapids: Reformation Heritage Books, 2009); and Guy Waters and Ligon Duncan, eds., *Children and the Lord's Supper* (Ross-shire, Scotland: Christian Focus Publications, 2011). The only church communion that has historically practiced paedocommunion in the sense of infant communion is the Eastern Orthodox Church. The strict view of paedocommunion, which argues that membership in the covenant community is a sufficient basis for admission to the Lord's Table and members should partake so soon as they are able, should be distinguished from the view that maintains that younger children are able to make the kind of profession of faith that qualifies them for communicant membership. The former idea advocates participation as soon as the child is physically able; the latter may maintain only that the practice of delaying profession of faith until late adolescence is problematic.

quality of the faith required for admission to the Table, there can be no doubt that the Reformed churches are committed confessionally to a practice that demands faith as a prerequisite to participation. The advocacy of paedocommunion, at least in some of its forms, is inconsistent, therefore, with the confessions of the Reformed churches.

The topic of paedocommunion relates to one final matter that our survey of the confessions raises in respect to the reformation of Reformed practice—the supervision, in particular what is often called the fencing, of the Table. Among the Reformed churches historically there has been a considerable divergence of approach to this practice. Some churches simply supervise the Table by means of a verbal admonition and warning to those who partake that they must examine themselves by the standards of Scripture, lest they eat and drink judgment to themselves. In this practice, which is sometimes called open Communion, the onus falls almost exclusively upon the participant to refrain from an unworthy and improper participation.

Other churches, believing that this practice does not adequately guard the Table against abuse, practice a form of supervised, or close Communion. In this practice, the ministers and elders of the church seek in various ways to ascertain whether those who partake are believers whose faith answers to the biblical requirements and who are members in good standing of a true church of Jesus Christ.[23]

Still other churches, anxious that the sacrament be properly administered and the Table of the Lord preserved from profanation, practice an even more restricted policy of what is sometimes called closed Communion. The practice of closed communion admits to the Table only those who are members in good standing of the local congregation or of another congregation that is in close fellowship with it. For church members to be

---

23. There are, of course, various ways in which this supervision could be exercised, including such practices as the distribution of Communion tokens; the provision of letters of attestation by the elders of a local church; the request that visitors fill out a written statement of church membership and profession; an interview by elders of visitors to the service who request permission to partake. There are no foolproof means of fencing the Table. When attempts are made to devise such means, the tendency is to make the invitation to partake too restrictive.

admitted to the Table of the Lord, they have to offer attestation that they are members of a church that is in full communion with the local congregation and that they are not under any formal discipline by the ministers and elders of that church.

Though it is not possible to sort through all the differences of practice regarding the supervision of the Table of the Lord among the Reformed churches, the confessions do shed some light on the subject. If these confessions are interpreted in their historical context, taking into account the practice of the Reformed churches since the Reformation, then they commend an approach to the supervision of the Lord's Supper that is represented by the second of these practices. All of these confessions require, minimally, that those who come to the Table of the Lord be reminded of its nature and significance and called to careful self-examination. However, they also affirm the need for the ministers and elders of the church to make sure, so far as they are competent to do so, that those who participate are not under the official discipline of the church. Because the first formal step of discipline ordinarily bars church members from the use of the sacraments, those responsible for the discipline and government of the church must insist that this disciplinary measure be honored. The supervision of the Table of the Lord includes, therefore, a verbal fencing and an official oversight of the ministers and elders.

It is not evident, however, that the practice of closed communion is commended by these confessions. This practice shifts the burden too much from the participant in the Lord's Supper to the ministers and elders who oversee its administration. Though it rightly seeks to prevent the profaning of the Lord's Table, it expects too much from the ministers and elders. No method of guarding the Table, however restrictive, can ensure that only true believers will participate. What is most problematic with this approach, however, is that it risks acting contrary to the very nature of the sacrament as a sacrament of *communion*. The Table of the Lord, it must always be remembered, is the Table *of the Lord*. It belongs to the Lord, and because it belongs to the Lord, it likewise belongs to all who belong to him. To exclude from the Table of the Lord those who are genuine believers and members of the true church is to risk making it the Table of a particular church or denomination. This compromises what is essential to the sacrament: the union and communion of believers with Christ and with all who are members of Christ. However objectionable may be the practice of what is known as intercommunion in more liberal, ecumenical church contexts, it is not consistent with the Reformed confessions for any church to treat the Lord's Supper in a sectarian manner.

And sixth, one of the evident concerns in the Reformed confessions is that the sacrament of the Lord's Supper be administered in accord with its biblical institution. When the ministers of the church administer the sacrament, they ought to do so according to the biblical pattern. For this reason, the service of Holy Communion, to the extent that it is described in the confessions, reflects a kind of biblical simplicity, without the addition of unbiblical elements and practices. The sacrament should be administered in both kinds, the bread and the wine, and these should be distributed to the congregation with appropriate prayers, expressions of thanksgiving, and particularly the use of the biblical words of institution. Because the sacrament is a sacred meal with Christ as its host and substance, the ministers are required to speak and act in Christ's name, inviting believers to lift up their hearts to him and receive him with the bread and wine.[24] Such ministers are not to act as priests ministering at an altar, but as servants of Christ who minister at a table, which represents the once-for-all and sufficient sacrifice of Christ for his people upon the cross.[25]

---

24. See Rohls, *Reformed Confessions,* 223–24, who notes that though the confessions typically assume the use of "natural" bread and wine, the Church Order of Julich and Berg "observes that 'those who by nature are put off by wine, so that they can tolerate neither the smell nor the taste, ought to receive from the hand of the church's minister, along with the bread, the kind of drink to which they are accustomed.'" The substitution of another element for the bread or the wine, so long as it represented one of the "basic means of nourishment," would be irregular but would not necessarily invalidate the sacrament's administration.

25. This has implications for the furnishing of the place of worship. Not only should the Communion table find its place in front of (or near) the pulpit, but it should also be a table, not an altar. For a treatment of the traditional liturgy and administration of the Supper in the Reformed churches, see Howard G. Hageman, "A Tale of Two Cities," in *Pulpit and Table: Some Chapters in the History of Worship in the Reformed Churches* (Richmond, VA: John Knox Press, 1962). The title of Hageman's chapter reflects his thesis that Geneva (Calvin) and Zürich (Zwingli) represent two distinct views of the Lord's Supper and its liturgical

No doubt these comments on the implications of the Reformed confessions for the practice of the Reformed churches are merely suggestive. They may raise as many questions as they provide answers. What they do, however, is illustrate the need for a greater appropriation of the biblical insights and riches of the confessions for the churches' practice. One place to begin is at the Table of the Lord, where believers are continually invited to taste and see that the Lord is good and that his mercies in Christ are never failing.

---

administration. In Hageman's view, despite the predominance of Calvin's doctrine of the sacrament, historic Reformed liturgies were significantly influenced by the Zwinglian pattern. This includes the separation of pulpit and table in the practice of infrequent Communion.

Chapter 8

Conclusion:
The Medium Is the Message

I introduced this study with the observation that the Christian church today does not enjoy a good reputation. When North Americans are asked to rank institutions, the church often does not fare well. Critics of the church abound, both within and outside its membership. While today's loss of respect for the church is lamentable, it is not surprising, particularly when you consider the church's evident failures and weaknesses. If critics are looking for a convenient punching bag, they do not have far to search. It's easy to list a litany of the church's failings, especially the scandalous conduct of some leaders.

I return to the church's dismal reputation in our day to highlight the contrast between how the church is viewed in popular society and how it is viewed in the confessions that have been our study's focus. In our survey of the confessions, we have discovered quite a different approach to and understanding of the church. In these confessions, the church is not viewed from below, as a merely human institution with all the obvious weaknesses of any human endeavor. In contrast, the church is viewed from above, as a divinely authored institution with a commission from its risen and ascended Lord. While the authors of these confessions were keenly aware of the church's sins and shortcomings—after all, the church is made up of justified sinners who are simultaneously righteous and sinful (*simul iustus et peccator*)—they speak of the church in the language of faith. Rather than concentrating on the church's apparent failures, the confessions direct our attention to the church-gathering work of Christ, who is pleased to gather his people by his Spirit and Word. The church of Jesus Christ is a fellowship of elect sinners, whom God the Father loved from before the world's foundation, whom Christ purchased with his precious blood, and whom the Holy Spirit draws through the gospel Word and vivid sacraments into communion with the living God.

The Reformed confessions paint a portrait of the church as the beloved bride of Christ, the heavenly bridegroom. Though Christ's bride may display many blemishes and possess little obvious beauty of her own, she is nonetheless loved by her heavenly husband with a perfect and invincible love. Christ, who gave himself up for her upon the cross, will sanctify and wash her until she is perfect, without spot or wrinkle or any such thing (Eph. 5:27). The confessions view the church entirely in terms of Christ's gracious work by his Spirit and Word, gathering, defending, and preserving his people in the salvation he grants to them. Christ dwells with and communicates himself to his people through the means of grace that he has been pleased to appoint for the gathering of the church, the gospel Word and the sacraments. In this respect, it would not be improper to say that the confessions celebrate the glory and splendor of the church, which is Christ's body and appointed instrument for the communication of himself to the world.

The gulf between the church's popular reputation and its confessional splendor requires our return to the place where our study began. What accounts for the loss of the church's reputation and identity, even among professing believers? And how can Reformed Christians simultaneously embrace the language of their confessions regarding the church while they answer contemporary challenges such as the church growth movement, the seeker-sensitive movement, and the more recent emergent church conversation? Are the biblical themes sounded in the classic symbols of the Reformed churches adequate to meet present challenges? Or do the confessions set forth an outdated doctrine of the church, one more focused on the preservation and maintenance of the church as an institution than on God's redemptive mission in and for the world?

The Medium Is the Message

The most important feature of the confession's teaching about the church can be stated in Marshall McLuhan's simple and well-known adage: "The medium is the message." Though McLuhan employed this expression to describe the nature and influence of the modern medium of television communication, I would like to conscript it into service to the doctrine of the church. McLuhan's point was that you may not separate the visual nature of television communication from the message that it conveys. The visual medium of television profoundly influences the way modern people think and communicate. Compared to the medium of language, or the spoken word, which has the ability to communicate rich, complex, and cognitively challenging content, the medium of television is visual, dramatic, and often cognitively challenged in its content.

When the Reformed confessions emphasize the central role of preaching and sacraments to communicating the gospel of Jesus Christ, they remind us of the strangely paradoxical nature of Christ's church-building work: the method the church employs must correspond to and not belie the message it wishes to convey. If the message is the saving work of Jesus Christ, especially his atoning death upon the cross, then the method God chooses to use in communicating this message must be consistent with it. You can scarcely commend the foolishness of the cross of Christ in the face of worldly wisdom when you employ a method in gospel communication that is worldly wise. Nor can you commend the gospel of Christ's cross, which is in the eyes of the world an ignoble, shameful, and weak thing, when you enlist worldly strategies of power to carry out the church's commission to make disciples of all nations. In the church of Jesus Christ, the medium is the message. The foolishness of the preaching of the cross is God's preferred means to display his wisdom, to confound the wise, and to demonstrate his power. God's power is made perfect through weakness (2 Cor. 12:9), and nowhere is this more evident than in God's chosen method for gathering and nourishing his people in the Christian faith (cf. 2 Cor. 4:7).

> For since, in the wisdom of God, the world did not know God through wisdom, it pleased God through the folly of what we preach to save those who believe. For Jews demand signs and Greeks seek wisdom, but we preach Christ crucified, a

> stumbling block to Jews and folly to Gentiles, but to those
> who are called, both Jews and Greeks, Christ the power of
> God and the wisdom of God. For the foolishness of God is
> wiser than men, and the weakness of God is stronger than
> men. (1 Cor. 1:21–25)

Perhaps the greatest folly in the modern church's affection for
worldly strategies and methods is the self-defeating nature of
the whole enterprise. If the church adopts a pragmatic method
in order to be successful in fulfilling its mission, it fails to rely
upon Christ's Spirit and Word. Whenever the church adopts
a method for achieving success in its mission that does not
conform to the one Christ is pleased to use, the church ceases
to trust Christ's promise that he will build his church upon the
foundation of the apostles' testimony (Matt. 16:13–20; cf. Eph.
2:20). If Christ is the one who builds the church, then he is
also the one who has the right to determine the strategy that he
wishes to use to build it. Otherwise, the church will assume that
the gathering of God's people depends upon its clever strategies
and preferred methods. Christ is not only the substance of
the church's message; he is also the substance of the church's
method. You cannot preach the Christ of the Scriptures while
relying on your own clever schemes to accomplish what he has
promised to bring about in his own way.

In the Old Testament story of the Lord's victory over the
Midianites through Gideon, we witness something typical
regarding the Lord's redemptive work for his people throughout
history. In the account in Judges 6 and 7, it is clear that the
Lord deliberately devises a strange and paradoxical strategy for
securing victory for his people. The Lord's chosen instrument,
Gideon, is a young and unimpressive sort, the youngest son in
a no-account family from one of the least of the tribes of Israel.
When Gideon is commissioned to lead Israel in battle against
the Midianites, we are told the Spirit of the Lord "clothed"
him (Judg. 6:34). Amazingly, when thirty-two thousand men
heed Gideon's call to arms, the Lord intervenes and whittles the
number of men down to a meager three hundred. Furthermore,
the weapons with which Gideon and his little band of three
hundred enter the fray are clay pots and trumpets. Never in the

history of human warfare has there been a more lopsided set of combatants: on the one side, young Gideon with three hundred novices, armed only with pots and trumpets; on the other side, a vast number of Midianite armed men who fill the valley like locusts overrunning a field in midsummer. But the key to the whole story, and to the miraculous victory that Gideon wins over the Midianites, lies in the Lord's deliberate strategy to employ human weakness to achieve his redemptive purposes and thereby magnify his own power and grace. In the words of the Lord to Gideon, "The people with you are too many for me to give the Midianites into their hand, lest Israel boast over me, saying, 'My own hand has saved me'" (Judg. 7:2). God chooses a strategy of weakness to shame the strong and to cause his people to boast alone in his power.

I rehearse this Old Testament story of God's work of redemption in the days of the judges in order to illustrate the most important feature of the Reformed confessions' doctrine of the church and the means of grace: the church of Jesus Christ is no human project, but a work of God's grace from first to last. No member of the church may take credit for the building of the church. No member of the church is at liberty to undertake to build the church by any means other than those the Lord himself has appointed. And, if the Lord has chosen to employ means—gospel preaching and teaching, the administration of the sacraments of baptism and the Lord's Supper—that appear to the world foolish and weak, so be it. The simple truth is that the Lord is jealous for his glory and wants his people to boast in him and his work. This simple truth is sufficient to sweep aside all the folly and proud presumption of those who undertake to build the church in their own strength and by means of their own devices. However strong, wise, and clever the strategies and methods of the modern church, if they depart from the chosen means that the Lord is pleased to use to gather his people to himself, they will inevitably prove to be weak and foolish. Only when the church seeks to employ the means Christ has appointed, and to do so in reliance upon the power of his Spirit, will the church be able to rest its faith in the power of God rather than the wisdom of men (1 Cor. 2:5).

Though the confessions we have considered in this study stem from many centuries ago, they continue to express in a fresh way this fundamental aspect of the Bible's teaching about the church. The church, like the gospel it ministers, is all about the person and work of Jesus Christ, Lord and King of the church. When the church loses sight of the fact that the means of grace, the preaching of the gospel and the administration of the sacraments, are Christ's chosen strategy for gathering and nourishing his people in the faith, the church ceases to be the church. The confession of the evangelical and Reformed churches is that the church is born of the Spirit and Word of Christ, abides in them, and does not listen to the voice of any stranger. That confession is not the dead faith of the living, but the living faith of those who bequeathed it by God's grace to the church as it continues to witness to God's saving grace in Christ.

Answering the Challenges

While the most important response to the challenges the church faces in our day is a return to the principal work of the church, the ministry of the gospel of Jesus Christ in preaching and sacrament, this does not suffice as an adequate answer. To paraphrase a searching comment of B. B. Warfield, one of the most gifted theologians in the Reformed tradition in North America, the foolishness of preaching is no excuse for foolish preaching. The foolishness of Christ's appointed method for building his church is no excuse for a foolish employment of this method. Simply to affirm the truth that the church must carry out its ministry in humble reliance upon the Spirit and Word of Christ does not constitute a sufficient reply to the challenges of the church growth, seeker-sensitive, and emergent church movements. More needs to be said about the manner in which the church today is called to minister the Word of the gospel and the sacraments of baptism and the Lord's Supper. How can the church effectively minister the gospel and fulfill its mission to disciple the nations? Since one of the principal complaints against the historic Reformation doctrine of the church is that it leads to a preservation, or maintenance ministry in which the church becomes little more than a "holy huddle," it is not enough simply to echo the language of the confessions without answering this complaint.

What about a Strategy for Church Growth?

Often, when evangelical and Reformed believers emphasize the point that Christ builds his church by his Spirit and Word, they are quick to condemn an emphasis upon church growth. In the opinion of many Reformed believers, the church need only preach and teach the gospel, and everything will then simply fall into place. If God uses these means to add to the church's number those whom he is pleased to save, so be it. But if the church experiences little growth either in depth of knowledge and commitment or in numbers, that must simply be God's will for the church at this time. Any focus on church growth is frequently viewed as symptomatic of a loss of confidence in the ordinary means of grace. If the church focuses too much attention upon whether it is effective in gathering believers into its fellowship through the work of evangelism or gospel preaching, the worry arises that it will be tempted to succumb to a pragmatic spirit that elevates success above faithfulness. Within the framework of the confessions' doctrine of the means of grace, it is felt that no attention needs to be devoted to strategic planning for gospel outreach, church planting, and missionary endeavor. Since God is pleased to save his people through the means that he has appointed, the church only needs to maintain a faithful ministry of the gospel and sacraments, and God will use this ministry as he chooses to draw his people to himself.

Perhaps the most significant contribution of the church growth movement to the doctrine of the church in our day is that it pricks the bubble of complacency that often plagues the ministry of the church. Though it is relatively easy to decry the unbiblical pragmatism of the church growth movement, it is more difficult to answer its complaint that many churches are not focused upon finding lost sinners and evangelizing them. What the church growth movement demands of evangelical and Reformed churches is an awareness of the interplay between gospel ministry and church growth, between preaching and the work of evangelism, between good theology and practical savvy. It is not enough to say that Christ will build his church with the tools that he has appointed for this purpose. It is also necessary to ask whether these tools are being effectively used to achieve their purpose. If the church is not being built and the people of God are not being gathered and discipled, it is hardly possible to say that the Great Commission is being fulfilled and the means of grace are achieving their appointed end.

The church growth movement presents the Reformed churches with an inescapable challenge to show the intimate connection between doing Christ's work *properly,* that is, in the manner that he has appointed, and doing Christ's work *effectively,* that is, in a way that gathers and disciples believers into growing churches. In the Great Commission of Matthew 28:16–20, Christ mandates that the church "make disciples of all the nations." In the Heidelberg Catechism's confession regarding the "holy catholic church," Christ is said to be "gathering" his people throughout all history, from the beginning of the world until its end, by his Spirit and Word. The language of Scripture and of the confessions is the language of a church that is being gathered, and not of a church that has already been gathered. The accent falls upon the present, ongoing activity of Christ, who by the working of his Spirit and lively ministry of his Word is busy throughout the world and among all the nations, gathering, preserving, and defending his elect people. This language leaves no room for a false dichotomy between good theology and effective evangelism. Nor is there any place for the idea that nourishing believers whom Christ has already gathered into his church should take priority over gathering new believers into the church. The ministry of the church is one comprehensive ministry of gospel preaching and teaching that embraces mature and immature alike—that feeds the sheep who already belong to the fold while at the same time going outside the fold to restore the wandering and wayward. The challenge of the church growth movement requires that Reformed churches seek to be as faithful and effective in gathering and enfolding new disciples as they often are in nurturing and maturing the gathered community.

A significant dimension of the challenge facing Reformed churches today is the need to combine rich biblical and confessional teaching about the church's mission with wise and savvy strategy. There is no inherent contradiction between an approach to church growth that endeavors to build the church according to Christ's blueprint and to do so in the wisest, most winsome, and strategically effective way possible. The people of God are to be as "wise as serpents and as harmless as doves" in all of their endeavors, not the least of which are gospel ministry and church growth. D. A. Carson, remarking on the "strange dichotomy" in contemporary evangelicalism between theology and practical savvy, offers what seems to be a painfully accurate portrait of some theologically rich, yet ineffective Reformed churches:

> The latter group, whose theology may be as orthodox as that of the apostle Paul, sometimes gives the impression that once you know a lot of the Bible and have read a lot of theology, everything will work out smilingly—as if there were no need for the practical advice of pastors who are no less committed to theology than they, but who are equally reflective on steps that must be taken, priorities, pastoral strategies, and the like.[1]

Identifying the unhealthy and self-defeating pragmatism that often infects the church growth movement is necessary. But it is not enough to meet the challenge. Reformed churches need a laser-like focus upon what it takes to carry out with fruitfulness the great mission that Christ effects through the church's ministry.

What about Being Seeker Sensitive?

In the same way that evangelical and Reformed believers dismiss out of hand the challenge of the church growth movement, so they often dismiss wholesale the challenge of the seeker-sensitive movement. Since the seeker-sensitive movement is in many respects an extension of the church growth movement, it comes under the same indictment. If the gospel message and method are accommodated to the felt needs of so-called seekers, the evangelistic and missionary calling of the church will not be

---

1. D. A. Carson, foreword to *The Deliberate Church: Building Your Ministry on the Gospel,* ed. Mark Dever and Paul Alexander (Wheaton, IL: Crossway, 2005), 14. This book is a companion to an earlier volume by Mark Dever, *Nine Marks of a Healthy Church* (Wheaton, IL: Crossway, 2004). Both volumes are fine examples of the endeavor to combine theological integrity with practical savvy in the ministry of the local church.

carried out in the way Christ has mandated that it should be. Rather than calling sinners through the gospel to conversion, genuine faith in Christ, and repentance from sin, the church will allow the desires of seekers to trump its message and reshape its method. When the church accommodates its message and method to those whom it seeks to reach with the gospel, it inevitably abandons its proper calling and shamelessly caters' to the desires of "unchurched Harry." The irony of the seeker-sensitive approach is that once seekers are drawn with a method and message that belies the truth of the gospel of Jesus Christ, they will only be confirmed in their native attraction to what is a less-than-biblical method and message.

While it is tempting to excoriate the seeker-sensitive movement for its faults, it would be better for evangelical and Reformed churches to reflect with more humility upon this movement's challenge to the church's ministry today. Rather than repeat the obvious complaints that may be registered against the seeker-sensitive movement, we would do well to ponder what it may tell us about the weaknesses of some Reformed churches.

The moment of truth in the seeker-sensitive movement is this: the gospel the church ministers is a gospel of a seeking Savior, one who leaves the ninety-nine sheep who have not strayed from the sheepfold in order to reach the one lost, wayward sheep (Luke 15:3–7). The gospel the church ministers is the gospel of a "prodigal God,"[2] who leaves his heavenly home and birthright behind to go in the person of his Son to a far country to find and lovingly restore his lost son (Luke 15:11–32). According to the gospel that the church ministers in Word and sacrament, God is a hospitable God who welcomes sinners and enjoys table fellowship with them. The God and Father of Jesus Christ is a covenant God who desires to fill his house with redeemed children who rejoice because they are no longer orphans, but cherished members of their heavenly Father's household. The seeker-sensitive movement is wrong, of course, in its suggestion that there is a single member of God's household who, strictly speaking, seeks out or understands the things of God without

---

2. The evocative language of "the prodigal God" is from Tim Keller, *The Prodigal God: Recovering the Heart of the Christian Faith* (New York: Riverhead, 2008).

a mighty work of grace in his or her heart (Rom. 3:11). But the seeker-sensitive movement is not wrong when it emphasizes the church's need to seek out and find the lost and then welcome them home to the Father's house. If the church does not look upon the lost with compassion, and if the church does not eagerly welcome sinners in Christ's name, then the church belies the core of its gospel message. The church can scarcely minister the gospel message the way Christ wants it ministered when it lacks interest in and compassion for lost sinners. The question the seeker-sensitive movement puts to the church is whether it is as keen to communicate the gospel to the lost sheep as to those who have already been found.

This legitimate challenge of the seeker-sensitive movement is expressed in the apostle Paul's well-known words:

> For though I am free from all, I have made myself a servant to all, that I might win more of them. To the Jews I became as a Jew, in order to win Jews. To those under the law I became as one under the law (though not being myself under the law) that I might win those under the law. To those outside the law I became as one outside the law (not being outside the law of God but under the law of Christ) that I might win those outside the law. To the weak I became weak, that I might win the weak. I have become all things to all people, that by all means I might save some. I do it all for the sake of the gospel that I may share with them in its blessings. (1 Cor. 9:19–23)

These words require careful interpretation. Clearly Paul is not commending a feckless ministry of the gospel that diminishes any of its sharp edges, substituting worldly wisdom and power for divine foolishness and weakness. He is not advocating a strategy that would craft or tailor the gospel to the whims of those to whom it is ministered. The author of these words is also known for his warning to his spiritual son, Timothy, that "people will not endure sound teaching, but having itching ears they will accumulate for themselves teachers to suit their own passions, and will turn away from listening to the truth and wander off into myths" (2 Tim. 4:3–4). What the apostle Paul is commending, however, is a gospel ministry that goes out of its way to reach people where they are and in a manner that is appropriate to their unique circumstances. In the communication of the gospel, it is necessary to cultivate a sympathetic awareness of those whom the church wishes to reach.

At the very least, honoring the apostle's teaching in this passage requires that the church's ministry sensitively and sympathetically address people in terms that connect with the world in which they live. If the ministry of the church is shaped exclusively to address those who are already its members, it is not likely to be effective in reaching the lost. The implications of this for the church's ministry are far-reaching. Whether it be the way the minister crafts his sermon or the way the church's members welcome strangers in Christ's name, the obligation to be sensitive to the circumstances of the unchurched is inescapable, though often ignored. Every facet of the life and ministry of the local church should be scrutinized not only for its biblical faithfulness but also for its helpfulness to the task of enfolding the lost into the fellowship of the church. The preaching of the gospel should nourish the gathered people of God. But it should also call the unconverted to faith and repentance in a way that, without blunting the sharp edges of the gospel, warmly and graciously seeks to draw them to Christ.

The challenge of the seeker-sensitive movement boils down to this question: Does the church display a heartfelt interest in the lost in the way it carries out its ministry? Though the church has no freedom to forego its calling to minister the gospel in the manner Christ has appointed, through gospel preaching and the administration of the sacraments, it does have the freedom to lose itself in service to others in Christ's name. In the final analysis, the church's effectiveness in fulfilling the Great Commission requires only two ingredients: lively, engaging gospel preaching and teaching on the one hand, and a gospel-produced compassion for lost sinners on the other.

The first of these ingredients, gospel preaching, is obviously most important. The work of evangelism, strictly speaking, is gospel preaching. The English term *evangelism* stems from the common Greek term in the New Testament for preaching (*euangelizomai*). To evangelize is, literally, "to gospelize," that is, to declare in words the biblical gospel or evangel. Therefore, the work of evangelizing is essentially the work of preaching the biblical Word, or gospel. Evangelism consists of the ministry of the biblical gospel and may not be defined primarily in terms of the people who are the gospel's recipients. For this reason, in Acts 14:7 we read that "there they evangelized," or "continued to preach the gospel" Word. Likewise, in Acts 8:4 we are told that they "went about [evangelizing] the word," and, in verse 12, that Philip in Samaria evangelized concerning "the kingdom of God and the name of Jesus Christ." The Reformed confessions are, accordingly, on solid biblical ground when they emphasize that the preaching of the Word of God is the means by which Christ gathers and builds his church. Therefore, to the extent that the seeker-sensitive movement diminishes the faithful preaching and teaching of the Word of God, it fails to understand what lies at the heart of the church's evangelistic calling.

However, the second of these ingredients, the display of a gospel-like compassion for lost sinners within the fellowship of the church, is the area where the seeker-sensitive movement poses its most searching question: What good is lively gospel preaching when it is divorced from the setting of a gospel-driven community? If I may coin a phrase, evangelism, or gospel preaching, must be accompanied and served by a contextual evangelism in which the church behaves as a gospel-driven community. A gospel-driven community is one that prizes the preaching of the biblical evangel, earnestly desires that the lost be reached with the gospel, and orders its life by a clear sense of its calling to gather and disciple others in Christ's name. Whether it is called "pre-evangelism" or "contextual evangelism," the evangelism of gospel preaching requires a gospel setting that lives up to the historic confession about the church in the Apostles' Creed: "I believe a holy catholic church, the communion of the saints, the forgiveness of sins." The church of Jesus Christ is a community of forgiven sinners who seek to live together in a spirit of mutual service and self-denying love. The doctrine of the church includes not only an emphasis upon the official ministry of Word and sacrament but also an acknowledgment of the ministry and communion of believers, all of whom are nourished and strengthened by the gospel Word and sacrament.

The means of grace, preaching and sacrament, are always administered within the broader context of the entire ministry of Christ's church, which is the divinely appointed instrument for drawing men and women into the fellowship of Christ and his people. The fellowship with Christ to which the means of grace summons their recipients properly occurs only through fellowship within Christ's church. When the church does not honor the gospel Word it ministers, it becomes an impediment to the work of evangelism, the preaching of the biblical gospel.

Should the Church Have a Mission or Be Missional?

The last challenge that evangelical and Reformed churches face today is the emergent church movement, which insists that we need a new, postmodern doctrine of the church. According to proponents of the emergent church movement, we need to discard the older Reformation doctrine of the church, which emphasized what the church is in terms of its primary attributes (unity, holiness, catholicity, apostolicity) and marks (preaching, sacraments, discipline). What we need is a missional church, namely, a community of believers whose being, or identity, lies in its participation in what God is doing to heal the brokenness of human life in a fallen world. When believers participate in the mission of God, which aims to redeem human life from the ravages of sin and even renew the whole creation, they do not have a mission to perform—they are the mission. According to emergent church proponents, we need a radically new doctrine of the church, one that is not defined in terms of the maintenance of an institution but in terms of the missional identity of God's people. Whenever and wherever God's people share in his missionary program for the renewal of life in the midst of sinful brokenness, we witness sacramental signs of God's gracious presence in the world. The missionary works of believers in furthering God's redemptive program in the world are the true means of grace that serve the coming of God's kingdom.

Even though the emergent church's language of *being* missional rather than *having* a mission seems attractive upon first hearing, it is misleading in at least three important respects.

First, it is impossible for the church as an institution to carry out the mission that Christ has given to it without the church *being* the kind of institution that the traditional attributes and marks of the church describe. The church's nature, or identity, undergirds its mission, and without the church being church it is impossible to imagine it being able to perform its Christ-given task. Though it may sound rhetorically impressive to say that the church is its mission, rather than that the church has a mission, the simple fact is that the church could not carry out the biblical mandate given to it unless it is the kind of institution that Christ makes it to be.

For example, one of the four attributes of the church is the attribute of apostolicity. The church's apostolicity means, among other things, that it builds its life and ministry upon the foundation of the teaching of the New Testament apostles or apostolate. The church Christ has promised to build—and there is no other deserving of the name—is founded upon the testimony of the twelve apostles whom Christ appointed and commissioned to be his eye and ear witnesses (Matt. 16:13–20; John 20:21–23; Eph. 2:20; 1 John 1:1–4). Only those churches that retain the pattern of sound words, that guard the good deposit of apostolic teaching entrusted to them, can legitimately claim to be the "pillar and ground of the truth" in the world (1 Tim. 3:15; 2 Tim. 1:13–14; 4:1–5; 2 Thess. 2:15). The church's identity and existence as an apostolic community is absolutely indispensable to its performance of the mission given to it by Christ himself. Likewise, unless the church is a faithful steward of the mysteries of the gospel, it cannot make disciples of the nations through the preaching and teaching of Christ's Word (1 Cor. 4:1–2). Unless the church resolutely preserves the gospel of Jesus Christ that has been entrusted to it, it can scarcely be expected to publish that gospel to the ends of the earth. It simply makes no sense to say, as some in the emergent church conversation maintain, that the church no longer needs to be defined in terms of the traditional attributes and marks of the true church.[3]

Second, the emergent church movement fails to distinguish properly between the specific mission that Christ gave to the

---

3. For a recent, popular defense of the biblical doctrine of the institutional church in the face of the call for a churchless Christianity, see Kevin De Young and Ted Kluck, *Why We Love the Church: In Praise of Institutions and Organized Religion* (Chicago: Moody, 2009).

church and the broader tasks that belong to all who are citizens of Christ's kingdom. While it may be true that Christian believers are called to be salt and light in the world, to be a leavening influence in all of their vocations and activities, this calling should not be confused with the more limited and focused assignment that Christ has given to the church as an institution. To make this point, some in the Reformed tradition have distinguished between the church as institute and the church as organism. This distinction intends to preserve the uniqueness of the church's calling to minister the Word and sacraments in the power of Christ's Spirit as the divinely preferred means of gathering and nourishing believers in the Christian faith. No other institution has this particular calling or mission, and no other institution is entrusted with the means, the preaching of the gospel and the administration of the sacraments, to accomplish this mission. However, there are many tasks to which Christian believers, as citizens of Christ's kingdom, are called that lie outside the purview of the church's competence. Though believers may be equipped to some extent for these callings through the church's ministry of Word and sacraments, the witness of believers to the kingship of Jesus Christ in every area of life lies beyond the scope of the church's specific assignment.

And third, the emergent church fails to acknowledge the unique, primary role played by the means of grace in the church's carrying out of its mission. When everything believers do becomes an integral part of the missional identity of the church, the specific mandate given to the church—to make disciples of the nations and to do so by the means of grace that Christ has appointed for this purpose—no longer retains its proper place and principal importance. When everything believers do becomes instrumental to the communication of God's grace in Christ, nothing in particular can be said to perform this task in a unique and unparalleled way. Sharing a cup of cold water in Christ's name becomes as much an act of preaching as the exposition of the Word of God on the Lord's Day by an ordained minister of the Word and sacraments. Setting an unjust world right becomes as strategic a means to further Christ's kingdom program as the administration of baptism or the Lord's Supper. In its most radical expression, the emergent church movement spells the demise of the institutional church with its traditional means of grace, preaching and sacraments.

For these reasons, the emergent church movement's insistence that we need to substitute a missional view of the church for the older, Reformational view is not persuasive. While it may be true to say that the church has a missional identity, the mission of the church ought not to be enlarged to include everything believers do in fulfillment of their calling in the world.

Conclusion

Though the historic Reformed confessions were written in the sixteenth and seventeenth centuries, they continue to witness to fundamental truths regarding the church's message and method. Until Christ comes at the end of the age, he will build his church by the work of his Spirit through the Word and sacraments (Matt. 28:16–20). In the face of the many challenges to the doctrine of the church that confront evangelical and Reformed churches today, it is critically important that the historic doctrine of the means of grace be tested by the measure of scriptural teaching. I remain persuaded that the confessions' teaching will prove to measure up to the standard of Scripture.

But at the same time, it is no less important that evangelical and Reformed churches also examine their practice to see whether it lives up to their confession. To meet the challenges of the present day, it is not enough to make a good confession. It is also essential to put this confession into practice, energetically carrying out the evangelistic calling of the church: proclaiming the biblical evangel to the lost, administering the sacraments of baptism and the Lord's Supper, and thereby making disciples of all the nations.

Bibliography

Adam, Karl. *The Spirit of Catholicism*. Garden City, NY: Image Books, 1954.

Bainton, Roland H. *Here I Stand: A Life of Martin Luther*. 1950. Reprint, New York: Abingdon Press, 1978.

Barna, George. *Revolution*. Carol Stream, IL: Tyndale House Publishers, 2005.

Barth, Karl. *The Doctrine of Reconciliation*. Vol. 4, parts 1 and 4 of *Church Dogmatics*. Translated by G. W. Bromiley. Edinburgh: T. & T. Clark, 1969.

———. *The Doctrine of the Word of God*. Vol. 1, part 1 of *Church Dogmatics*. Edinburgh: T. & T. Clark, 1936.

Bavinck, Herman. *Saved by Grace*. Edited by J. Mark Beach. Translated by Nelson D. Kloosterman. Grand Rapids: Reformation Heritage Books, 2008.

Beckwith, Roger T. "The Age of Admission to the Lord's Supper." *Westminster Theological Journal* 38, no. 2 (Winter 1976): 123–51.

Berkhof, Louis. *Systematic Theology*. 4th ed. Grand Rapids: Eerdmans, 1941.

Berkouwer, G. C. *Karl Barth en de Kinderdoop*. Kampen: J. H. Kok, 1947.

———. *The Person of Christ*. Translated by J. Vriend. Grand Rapids: Eerdmans, 1954.

———. *The Sacraments*. Translated by Hugo Bekker. Grand Rapids: Eerdmans, 1969.

———. *The Work of Christ*. Translated by C. Lambregste. Grand Rapids: Eerdmans, 1965.

Beveridge, W. *A Short History of the Westminster Assembly*. Edinburgh: T. & T. Clark, 1904.

Bierma, Lyle. "Olevianus and the Authorship of the Heidelberg Catechism: Another Look." *The Sixteenth Century Journal* 13, no. 4 (1982): 17–27.

———. "*Vester Grundt* and the Origins of the Heidelberg Catechism." In *Later Calvinism: International Perspectives,* 289–309. Edited by W. Fred Graham. Kirksville, MO: Sixteenth Century Journal Publishers, Inc., 1994.

Bizer, Ernst. *Studien zur Geschichte des Abendmahlsstreits im 16. Jahrhundert.* Gütersloh: Verlag C. Bertelsmann, 1940.

Bolt, John, and Richard A. Muller. "Does the Church Today Need a New 'Mission Paradigm?'" *Calvin Theological Journal* 31, no. 1 (1996): 196–208.

———. "For the Sake of the Church: A Response to Van Gelder and Hart." *Calvin Theological Journal* 31, no. 2 (1996): 520–26.

The Book of Confessions. 2nd ed. Office of the General Assembly of the United Presbyterian Church in the United States of America, 1966, 1967.

Bromiley, G. W. *Sacramental Teaching and Practice in the Reformation Churches.* Grand Rapids: Eerdmans, 1957.

Burnet, George B. *The Holy Communion in the Reformed Church of Scotland.* Edinburgh: Oliver and Boyd, 1960.

Calvin, John. *Calvin: Theological Treatises.* Edited by J. K. S. Reid. Philadelphia: Westminster Press, 1954.

———. *Institutes of the Christian Religion.* Edited by John T. McNeill. Translated by Ford L. Battles. 2 vols. Philadelphia: Westminster, 1960.

———. *Selected Works of John Calvin.* Edited by Henry Beveridge. 7 vols. Reprint, Grand Rapids: Baker, 1983.

Carson, D. A. *Becoming Conversant with the Emerging Church: Understanding a Movement and Its Implications.* Grand Rapids: Zondervan, 2005.

———. *The Gagging of God: Christianity Confronts Pluralism.* Grand Rapids: Zondervan, 1996.

Catechism of the Catholic Church. Liguori, MO: United States Catholic Conference Inc., 1994.

Clowney, Edmund P. *The Church.* Downers Grove, IL: Intervarsity, 1995.

Cochrane, Arthur C. *Reformed Confessions of the 16th Century.* Philadelphia: Westminster Press, 1966.

Coppes, Leonard J. *Daddy, May I Take Communion?* Thornton, CO: Leonard J. Coppes, 1988.

Corcoran, Kevin, ed. *Church in the Present Tense: A Candid Look at What's Emerging.* Grand Rapids: Brazos Press, 2011.

Daane, James. *Preaching with Confidence: A Theological Essay on the Power of the Pulpit.* Grand Rapids: Eerdmans, 1980.

Dabney, Robert Lewis. Vol. 1 of *Discussions of Robert Lewis Dabney.* Reprint, Carlisle, PA: The Banner of Truth Trust, 1982 .

Davies, Horton. *From Cranmer to Hooker.* Vol. 1 of *Worship and Theology in England.* Combined ed. Grand Rapids: Eerdmans, 1996.

———. *The Worship of the English Puritans.* Reprint, Morgan, PA: Soli Deo Gloria Publications, 1997.

Davis, Thomas J. *The Clearest Promises of God: The Development of Calvin's Eucharistic Teaching.* New York: AMS Press, Inc. 1995.

De Jong, A. C. *The Well-Meant Gospel Offer: The Views of H. Hoeksema and K. Schilder.* Franeker: T. Wever, 1954.

De Jong, Peter Y., ed. *Crisis in the Reformed Churches: Essays in Commemoration of the Great Synod of Dort, 1618–1619.* Grandville, MI: Reformed Fellowship, 1968.

Dever, Mark. *The Gospel and Personal Evangelism.* Wheaton, IL: Crossway, 2010.

———. *Nine Marks of a Healthy Church.* New expanded edition. Wheaton, IL: Crossway, 2004.

Dever, Mark, and Paul Alexander. *The Deliberate Church: Building Your Ministry on the Gospel.* Wheaton, IL: Crossway, 2005.

De Young, Kevin, and Greg Gilbert. *What Is the Mission of the Church? Making Sense of Social Justice, Shalom, and Great Commission.* Wheaton, IL: Crossway, 2011.

De Young, Kevin, and Ted Kluck. *Why We Love the Church: In Praise of Institutions and Organized Religion.* Chicago: Moody, 2009.

———. *Why We're Not Emergent: By Two Guys Who Should Be.* Chicago: Moody, 2008.

Doulis, Thomas, ed. *Journey to Orthodoxy: A Collection of Essays by Converts to Orthodox Christianity.* Minneapolis, MN: Light and Life, 1986.

Dowey, Edward A. "Heinrich Bullinger's Theology: Thematic, Comprehensive, Schematic." In *Calvin Studies V: Presented at a Colloquium on Calvin Studies at Davidson College and Davidson College Presbyterian Church, January 19–20, 1990,* 41–60. Edited by John H. Leith.

———. "The Word of God as Scripture and Preaching." In *Later Calvinism: International Perspectives,* 5–18. Edited by W. Fred Graham. Kirksville, MO: Sixteenth Century Publishers, Inc., 1994.

Duin, Julia. *Quitting Church: Why the Faithful Are Fleeing and What to Do about It.* Grand Rapids: Baker, 2008.

Dulles, Avery. *Models of the Church.* New York: Image Books, 1974.

Ecumenical and Reformed Creeds and Confessions. Classroom edition. Orange City, IA: Mid-America Reformed Seminary, 1991.

Elwell, Walter A., ed. *Evangelical Dictionary of Theology.* Grand Rapids: Baker, 1984.

Elwood, Christopher. *The Body Broken: The Calvinist Doctrine of the Eucharist and the Symbolization of Power in Sixteenth-Century France.* New York: Oxford University Press, 1999.

Engelsma, David J. *Hyper-Calvinism and the Call of the Gospel.* Rev. ed. Grand Rapids: Reformed Free Publishing Assoc., 1994.

Feenstra, J. G. *De Dordtsche Leerregels.* 2nd ed. Kampen: Kok, 1950.

Finney, Charles G. *Charles G. Finney: An Autobiography.* Old Tappan, NJ: Revell, n.d.

Frame, John. "In Defense of Something Close to Biblicism: Reflections on *Sola Scriptura* and History in Theological Method." *Westminster Theological Journal* 59, no. 2 (Fall 1997): 269–91.

———. "Reply to Richard Muller and David Wells." *Westminster Theological Journal* 59, no. 2 (Fall 1997): 311–18.

Gassmann, Benno. *Ecclesia Reformata: Die Kirche in den reformierten Bekenntnisschriften.* Freiburg: Herder, 1968.

Gerrish, Brian A. *Grace and Gratitude: The Eucharistic Theology of John Calvin.* Minneapolis, MN: Fortress, 1993.

———. *The Old Protestantism and the New: Essays on the Reformation Heritage.* Edinburgh: T. & T. Clark, 1982.

Gootjes, Nicolaas H. *The Belgic Confession: Its History and Sources.* Grand Rapids: Baker Academic, 2007.

———. "Can Parents Be Sure? Background and Meaning of Canons of Dort I, 17." *Lux Mundi* 15, no. 4 (December 1996): 2–6.

Graham, W. Fred, ed. *Later Calvinism: International Perspectives.* Kirksville, MO: Sixteenth Century Publishers, Inc., 1994.

Grenz, Stanley J., and John R. Francke. *Beyond Foundationalism: Shaping Theology in a Postmodern Context.* Louisville, KY: Westminster John Knox Press, 2000.

Guder, Darrell L., ed. *Missional Church: A Vision for the Sending of the Church in North America.* Grand Rapids: Eerdmans, 1998.

Guinness, Os. *Dining with the Devil: The Megachurch Movement Flirts with Modernity.* Grand Rapids: Baker, 1993.

Hageman, Howard G. *Pulpit and Table: Some Chapters in the History of Worship in the Reformed Churches.* Richmond, VA: John Knox Press, 1962.

Hesselink, I. John, ed. *Calvin's First Catechism.* Louisville, KY: Westminster John Knox Press, 1997.

Hodge, A. A. *The Confession of Faith. A Handbook of Christian Doctrine Expounding the Westminster Confession.* Reprint, London: The Banner of Truth Trust, 1958.

Hodge, Charles. "Doctrine of the Reformed Church on the Lord's Supper." In *Essays and Reviews*, 341–92. New York: Robert Carter & Brothers, 1879.

——. "Romish Baptism." *The Biblical Repertory and Princeton Review* 17 (1845): 444–71.

Hoekendijk, J. C. *The Church Inside Out*. Philadelphia: The Westminster Press, 1966.

Hoeksema, Herman. *Believers and Their Seed*. Grand Rapids: Reformed Free Publishing Assoc., 1971.

Horton, Michael J. "At Least Weekly: The Reformed Doctrine of the Lord's Supper and of Its Frequent Celebration." *Mid-America Journal of Theology* 11 (2000): 147–69.

——. *The Gospel Commission: Recovering God's Strategy for Making Disciples*. Grand Rapids: Baker, 2011.

Hyde, Daniel R. "Lost Keys: The Absolution in Reformed Liturgy." *Calvin Theological Journal* 46, no. 1 (2011): 140–66.

——. *Welcome to a Reformed Church: A Guide for Pilgrims*. Orlando, FL: Reformation Trust, 2010.

——. *With Heart and Mouth: An Exposition of the Belgic Confession*. Grandville, MI: Reformed Fellowship, 2008.

Jacobs, Paul. *Reformierte Bekenntnisschriften und Kirchenordnungen in deutscher Übersetzung*. Neukirchen, 1949.

Keidel, Christian L. "Is the Lord's Supper for Children?" *Westminster Theological Journal* 37, no. 3 (Spring 1975): 301–41.

Keller, Tim. *Center Church: Doing Balanced, Gospel-Centered Ministry in Your City*. Grand Rapids: Zondervan, 2012.

——. *The Prodigal God: Recovering the Heart of the Christian Faith*. New York: Riverhead Books, 2008.

Kimball, Dan. *The Emerging Church: Vintage Christianity for New Generations*. Grand Rapids: Zondervan, 2003.

Klooster, Fred H. *The Heidelberg Catechism: Origin and History.* Grand Rapids: Calvin Theological Seminary, 1987/1988.

——. "The Priority of Ursinus in the Composition of the Heidelberg Catechism." In *Controversy and Conciliation: The Reformation and the Palatinate, 1559–1583,* 73–100. Edited by Kidran Y. Hadidian. Allison Park, PA: Pickwick Publications, 1986.

Kuyper, Abraham. *The Work of the Holy Spirit.* Translated by Henri De Vries. Reprint, Grand Rapids: Eerdmans, 1979.

Langdon, A. A. *Communion for Children? The Current Debate.* Oxford: Latimer Studies, 1988.

Leith, John H., ed. *Creeds of the Churches.* Garden City, NY: Doubleday, 1963.

Lindsay, D. Michael. "A Gated Community in the Evangelical World." *USA Today,* February 18, 2008.

MacArthur, John. *Ashamed of the Gospel: When the Church Becomes Like the World.* Wheaton, IL: Crossway, 1993.

Mathes, Glenda. *Little One Lost: Living with Early Infant Loss.* Grandville, MI: Reformed Fellowship, 2012.

Mathison, Keith A. *Given for You: Reclaiming Calvin's Doctrine of the Lord's Supper.* Phillipsburg, NJ: P&R, 2002.

McClaren, Brian. *A Generous Orthodoxy.* Grand Rapids: Zondervan, 2004.

McGavran, Donald. *Understanding Church Growth.* Grand Rapids: Eerdmans, 1970.

Meijering, M. *De Dordtsche Leerregels.* Groningen: Jan Haan, 1924.

Miller, C. John. *Evangelism and Your Church.* Phillipsburg, NJ: Presbyterian & Reformed, 1980.

Müller, E. F. K. *Die Bekenntnisschriften der reformierten Kirche.* Leipzig, 1903.

Muller, Richard. *Dictionary of Latin and Greek Theological Terms. Grand Rapids: Baker, 1985.*

——. "Historiography in the Service of Theology and Worship: Toward Dialogue with John Frame." *Westminster Theological Journal* 59, no. 2 (Fall 1997): 301–10.

Murray, Iain H. *Revival and Revivalism: The Making and Marring of American Evangelicalism 1750–1858*. Carlisle, PA: The Banner of Truth Trust, 1994.

———. *Spurgeon v. Hyper-Calvinism: The Battle for Gospel Preaching*. Carlisle, PA: The Banner of Truth Trust, 1995.

Murray, John. "The Free Offer of the Gospel." In *Collected Writings of John Murray*. Vol. 4, *Studies in Theology*, 113–32. Carlisle, PA: The Banner of Truth Trust, 1982.

Nevin, John Williamson. *History and Genius of the Heidelberg Catechism*. Chambersburg, 1847.

New Catholic Encyclopedia. Vol. 12. Washington, D.C.: The Catholic University of America, 1967.

"'New' Orthodox Attract Evangelicals." *Christianity Today* 36, no. 6 (May 18, 1992): 50, 53.

Niesel, Wilhelm. *Bekenntnisschriften und Kirchenordnungen der nach Gottes Wort reformierten Kirche*. A. G. Zollikon-Zürich, 1938.

———. *Calvin's Lehre von Abendmahl*. Munich, 1935.

Noll, Mark A. *Confessions and Catechisms of the Reformation*. Grand Rapids: Baker, 1991.

Old, Hughes Oliphant. *The Shaping of the Reformed Baptismal Rite in the Sixteenth Century*. Grand Rapids: Eerdmans, 1992.

Pelikan, Jaroslav. *The Emergence of the Catholic Tradition (100–600)*. Vol. 1 of *The Christian Tradition, A History of the Development of Doctrine*. Chicago: University of Chicago Press, 1971.

Postman, Neil. *Amusing Ourselves to Death: Public Discourse in the Age of Show Business*. New York: Penguin, 1985.

Praamsma, Louis. "The Background of the Arminian Controversy (1586–1618)." In *Crisis in the Reformed Churches: Essays in Commemoration of the Great Synod of Dort, 1618–1619*, 22–38. Edited by Peter Y. De Jong. Grandville, MI: Reformed Fellowship, 1968.

Pritchard, G. A. *Willow Creek Seeker Services: Evaluating a New Way of Doing Church*. Grand Rapids: Baker, 1996.

Reisinger, Ernest C. *Today's Evangelism: Its Message and Methods*. Phillipsburg, NJ: Craig Press, 1982.

Reymond, Robert L. *A New Systematic Theology of the Christian Faith*. Nashville: Thomas Nelson, 1998.

Rohls, Jan. *Reformed Confessions: Theology from Zurich to Barmen*. Louisville, KY: Westminster John Knox Press, 1997.

Schaff, Philip. *The Creeds of Christendom*. 3 vols. Reprint, Grand Rapids: Baker, 1985.

Schuler, Robert H. *Self Esteem: The New Reformation*. Waco, TX: Word, 1982.

Sinnema, Donald W. "The Issue of Reprobation at the Synod of Dort in Light of the History of This Doctrine." PhD diss., University of St. Michael's College, 1985.

Stackhouse Jr., John G., ed. *Evangelical Ecclesiology: Reality or Illusion?* Grand Rapids: Baker Academic, 2003.

Strobel, Lee. *Inside the Mind of Unchurched Harry: How to Reach Friends and Family Who Avoid God and the Church*. Grand Rapids: Zondervan, 1993.

Tippett, Alan R. *Church Growth and the Word of God*. Grand Rapids: Eerdmans, 1970.

Thompson, Bard. "Historical Background of the Catechism." In *Essays on the Heidelberg Catechism*, 8–30. Edited by Bard Thompson et al. Philadelphia: United Church Press, 1963.

Thornwell, James Henley. "The Validity of the Baptism of Rome." In vol. 3 of *The Collected Writings of James Henley Thornwell*, 283–412. Reprint, Carlisle, PA: The Banner of Truth Trust, 1986.

Thurian, Max, and Geoffrey Wainwright, eds. *Baptism and Eucharist: Ecumenical Convergence in Celebration*. Grand Rapids: Eerdmans, 1984.

Torrance, Thomas F. "Calvin and the Knowledge of God." *The Christian Century* 81, no. 22 (May 27, 1964): 696–99.

——. *The School of Faith: The Catechisms of the Reformed Church*. London: James Clarke, 1959.

Trueman, Carl. *The Creedal Imperative*. Wheaton, IL: Crossway, 2012.

Van Gelder, Craig, and Dirk Hart. "The Church Needs to Understand Its Missionary Nature: A Response to John Bolt and Richard Muller." *Calvin Theological Journal* 31, no. 2 (1996): 504–19.

Venema, Cornelis P. "The Belgic Confession." *Tabletalk* (April 2006): 10–13.

———. *But for the Grace of God.* 2nd ed. Grandville, MI: Reformed Fellowship, 2011.

———. *Children at the Lord's Table?: Assessing the Case for Paedocommunion.* Grand Rapids: Reformation Heritage Books, 2009.

———. "The Election and Salvation of the Children of Believers Who Die in Infancy: A Study of Article I/17 of the Canons of Dort. *Mid-America Journal of Theology* 17 (2006): 57–100.

———. "The Lord's Supper and the Popish Mass: Does Q. & A. 80 of the Heidelberg Catechism Speak the Truth?" *The Outlook* 55, no. 5 (May 2005): 17–22.

———. "The Lord's Supper and the 'Popish Mass': An Historical and Theological Analysis of Question and Answer 80 of the Heidelberg Catechism," *Mid-America Journal of Theology* 24 (2013): 31–72.

Wagner, C. Peter. *Your Church Can Grow: Seven Vital Signs of a Healthy Church.* Glendale, CA: G/L Publications, 1976.

Walker, G. S. M. "The Lord's Supper in the Theology and Practice of Calvin." In *John Calvin: A Collection of Distinguished Essays,* 131–48. Edited by G. E. Duffield. Grand Rapids: Eerdmans, 1966.

Wallace, Peter J. "History and Sacrament: John Williamson Nevin and Charles Hodge on the Lord's Supper." *Mid-America Journal of Theology* 11 (2000): 171–201.

Wallace, Ronald S. *Calvin's Doctrine of the Word and Sacrament.* Grand Rapids: Eerdmans, 1957.

Warfield, Benjamin B. *Perfectionism.* Edited by Samuel G. Craig. 2 vols. New York: Oxford, 1931.

———. *The Westminster Assembly and Its Work.* New York: Oxford University Press, 1931.

Waters, Guy, and Ligon Duncan, eds. *Children and the Lord's Supper.* Ross-shire, Scotland: Christian Focus, 2011.

Weber, Timothy. "Looking for Home: Evangelical Orthodoxy and the Search for the Original Church." In *New Perspectives on Historical Theology: Essays in Memory of John Meyendorff*, 95–121. Edited by Bradley Nassif. Grand Rapids: Eerdmans, 1996.

Welker, Michael. *What Happens in Holy Communion?* Translated by John F. Hoffmeyer. Grand Rapids: Eerdmans, 2000.

Wells, David F. "On Being Framed." *Westminster Theological Journal* 59, no. 2 (Fall 1997): 293–300.

Willis, E. David. *Calvin's Catholic Christology*. Leiden: E. J. Brill, 1966.

Wright, Christopher J. H. *The Mission of God: Unlocking the Bible's Grand Narrative*. Downers Grove, IL: IVP Academic, 2006.

Yaconelli, Mike, ed. *Stories of Emergence: Moving from Absolute to Authentic*. Grand Rapids: Zondervan, 2003.

Zwingli, Ulrich. "On the Lord's Supper." In *Zwingli and Bullinger*, 176–238. Vol. 24 of *The Library of Christian Classics*. Edited by John Baille et al. Philadelphia: The Westminster Press, 1953.

Note to the Reader

The publisher invites you to respond to us about this book by writing Reformed Fellowship, Inc., at *president@ reformedfellowship.net*

Founded in 1951, Reformed Fellowship, Inc., is a religious and strictly nonprofit organization composed of a group of Christian believers who hold to the biblical Reformed faith. Our purpose is to advocate and propagate this faith, to nurture those who seek to live in obedience to it, to give sharpened expression to it, to stimulate the doctrinal sensitivities of those who profess it, to promote the spiritual welfare and purity of the Reformed churches, and to encourage Christian action.

Members of Reformed Fellowship express their adherence to the Calvinistic creeds as formulated in the Belgic Confession, the Heidelberg Catechism, the Canons of Dort, and the Westminster Confession and Catechisms.

To fulfill our mission, we publish a bimonthly journal, *The Outlook,* and we publish books and Bible study guides. Our website is *www.reformedfellowship.net*